American
nationalism

by the same author

THE IDEA OF NATIONALISM
New York: Macmillan, 1944; 6th printing, 1956—Spanish translation, Mexico, 1949; German translation, Heidelberg, 1950; Italian translation, Florence, 1956

PROPHETS AND PEOPLES. STUDIES IN
NINETEENTH CENTURY NATIONALISM
New York: Macmillan, 1946; 3rd printing, 1953—Italian translation, Turin, 1949; German translation, Berne, 1949; Japanese translation, Tokyo, 1954

THE TWENTIETH CENTURY. A MID-WAY
ACCOUNT OF THE WESTERN WORLD
New York: Macmillan, 1949; 3rd printing, 1953; London: Victor Gollancz, 1950—German translation, Zürich, 1950

PAN-SLAVISM, ITS HISTORY AND IDEOLOGY
University of Notre Dame Press, 1953—German translation, Vienna, 1956

GERMAN HISTORY: SOME NEW GERMAN VIEWS
London: Allen & Unwin, 1954; Boston: Beacon Press, 1954

THE MIND OF MODERN RUSSIA: POLITICAL
AND SOCIAL THOUGHT IN RUSSIA'S GREAT AGE
Rutgers University Press, 1955; 2nd printing, 1957

MAKING OF THE MODERN FRENCH MIND
Princeton: D. Van Nostrand, 1955

NATIONALISM, ITS MEANING AND HISTORY
Princeton: D. Van Nostrand, 1955

NATIONALISM AND LIBERTY.
THE SWISS EXAMPLE
London: Allen & Unwin, 1956; New York: Macmillan, 1956

HANS KOHN

American
nationalism

an interpretative essay

THE MACMILLAN COMPANY · NEW YORK · 1957

to Vera and Immanuel

"So it seems that the supreme authority is about to escape from Western and Central Europe, to pass to the New World. In the northern part of that other hemisphere off-shoots of the European race have founded a vigorous society full of sap, whose influence grows with a rapidity that has never yet been seen anywhere."

MICHEL CHEVALIER
Rapports du Jury Internationel: Exposition Universelle de 1867 à Paris, Tome 1, p. lxiv.

"America, and especially Saxon America, with its immense virgin territories, with its republic, with its equilibrium between stability and progress, with its harmony between liberty and democracy, is the continent of the future,—the immense continent stretched by God between the Atlantic and Pacific, where mankind may plant, essay, and resolve all social problems. Europe has to decide whether she will confound herself with Asia, placing upon her lands old altars, and upon the altars old idols, and upon the idols immovable theocracies, and upon the theocracies despotic empires, or whether she will go by labor, by liberty, and by the republic, to collaborate with America in the grand work of universal civilization."

EMILIO CASTELAR
Speech in the Spanish Cortes, June 22, 1871, quoted by Charles Sumner, *Prophetic Voices Concerning America* (1874).

preface

This book makes no attempt to present a history of American nationalism, either in a narrative form or in a discussion of all its aspects. The task of writing such a history will be undertaken in due course by one of our leading students of American intellectual and social history. The present book is only an essay, and a first essay, to discuss some of the chief problems inherent in the very complex phenomenon of American nationalism as they appear to a student of comparative nationalism, and to try to interpret these problems in the light of national movements in other parts of the world, especially in Europe.

Such an essay has, to the best of my knowledge, not been published before. The reason for it is not far to seek. Only in most recent years have the national destinies of the United States and of the rest of the world become so patently and so intimately intermingled as to make the reflective self-awareness of American nationalism by Americans and a more reasoned appreciation of the American people and its peculiar character by others, urgently desirable. In that sense the book hopes to make in its own way a contribution to international understanding.

I have selected five problems which appeared to me as most characteristic for American nationalism: the origins of American nationalism; its relationship to the mother country; its federal structure; its multi-ethnic character; and finally, its position within the community of nations. These problems are of course interdependent and the nature of each one throws light upon the others. Their thematic order is to a certain extent at the same time a chronological order: these five problems have occupied the center of national attention one after the other. In each of them the character of the origin of American nationalism has lived on; in spite of the ever continuing and perhaps ever accelerated deep-reaching changes in

American society, the same fundamental forces and ideas are at work in all the stages of its national development.

One more word of explanation is needed: the word "American" as used in the title and in the context of this book may rightly jar upon Latin American ears. As I have pointed out in the book itself, the United States of America is the only nation without a name of its own. In the book and in the title, the word "American" is used to mean the United States of America. In Latin America the same word is frequently used to mean only the Latin American countries. The mighty, and in the last decades, wonderfully growing life there offers a spectacle of greatest variety and complexity; in all the wealth of its expression it is fundamentally different in roots and background from Anglo-American nationalism. In spite of the geographic partnership in the Western Hemisphere, American nationalism, in the sense in which the word is being used here, is closer to the nationalism of England and other Western European countries than to the nationalism of the Latin American countries.

The plan of this book originated in an invitation by my friend Ray A. Billington, Professor of American History at Northwestern University, and by the Harris Lecture Committee there under Professor Frederic E. Faverty, to deliver the Norman Wait Harris Foundation Lectures at the Evanston campus in April, 1956, and to select this subject. Thanks to the Graduate School of Public Administration and the Department of Government of Harvard University, I received the opportunity of working the brief sketches which I prepared for my lectures into a book. Research in selected topics in the field by students in my seminars at the City College of New York and at Harvard helped me in the gathering of material. Discussions in the Foreign Policy Research Institute of the University of Pennsylvania clarified some of the issues with which the last sections of Chapter Five deal. Above all, I feel grateful to Mrs. Edward C. Park, Jr., and to Miss Elaine Day for their most intelligent and efficient cooperation in preparing these essays for publication.

HANS KOHN

City College of New York
September, 1956

contents

chapter one

The roots and origins of the republic

"Let them continue to enjoy the liberty our fathers gave them! Gave them, did I say? They are co-heirs of liberty with ourselves; and their portion of the inheritance has been much better looked after than ours."

JONATHAN SHIPLEY, BISHOP OF ST. ASAPH
A Speech Intended to Have Been Spoken on the Bill for Altering the Charters of the Colonies of Massachusetts Bay, 1774.

"Here English law and English thought
'Gainst the self-will of England fought."

JAMES RUSSELL LOWELL
Ode Read at Concord, April 19, 1875.

Nationalism in the United States differs in many ways from the usual pattern of national movements. Its very beginning singles it out. According to Alexis de Tocqueville in his classic work *Democracy in America* the development of the United States offers the only opportunity to witness in the broad daylight of history the birth and growth of a national society. The influence exercised on the future condition of states by their origin is for that reason more clearly discernible in the case of America than in that of other nations. Their roots lose themselves in the darkness of a semi-mythical past. Natural and subconscious forces have generally contributed to the process of a nation's coming into being more than free human decisions.[1] Not so with the Anglo-Americans. They established themselves as a nation without the support of any of those elements that are generally supposed to constitute a separate nation. They were not helped by common descent. For though the Anglo-Americans were overwhelmingly of British stock, this factor should not have, according to widely accepted theories of nationality, encouraged their separation from people of the same stock. Yet even at the end of the eighteenth century, the Anglo-Americans represented peoples of varied descent, and continue to do so to an ever growing degree. Well known are the words of a "farmer in Pennsylvania," the Frenchman Michel Guillaume Saint-Jean de Crèvecoeur, who after having lived in North America from 1759 to 1790 wrote of "that strange mixture of blood, which you will find in no other country. I could point out to you a man, whose grandfather was an Englishman, whose wife was Dutch, whose son married a French woman, and whose present four sons have now four wives of different nations." The melting pot had begun to function even before the United States were constituted as a nation.[2]

Important elements in the formation of a nation, above all before the nineteenth century, were a common religion and a historically defined territory. Anglo-America had neither. There was no common religion in the thirteen colonies. In fact Anglo-America showed even then a unique liberty and diversity in religious life, different therein from all other countries of Western civilization; its

3

frontierland in this respect, too, carrying the religious tolerance
of the Age of Enlightenment nearer to fulfillment than any other
land. No one religion could be identified with Anglo-America, no
one religion inspired its desire for independence. New England
puritanism with its moral fervor and its revolutionary anti-mo-
narchical tradition had its share in it; but Virginia, the home of the
leading statesmen of the period, was Anglican; and George Washington and Thomas Jefferson shared the vague and hardly Christian
deism of their upper-class contemporaries in England. It may be said
that Calvinism helped to establish the Netherlandish nation and
Catholicism to form the nations of Spain, Poland or Ireland. In the
United States specific religions have done less to impregnate the
national character than perhaps anywhere else. Here, on the contrary, the American national character has impregnated the various
manifestations of religious life. Already Tocqueville emphasized that
Anglo-American civilization was the result of two distinct elements,
which in other places have been in frequent hostility, but which in
America—and to a lesser degree, in England—have been admirably
incorporated and combined with each other: the spirit of Religion
and the spirit of Liberty.[3]

In the United States all religions represented have become, to a
large extent, "Americanized." This has been as true of the various
Protestant sects as of Roman Catholicism and of Judaism. The American idea has shaped their attitudes so that they differ fundamentally
from those which prevail among people professing the same faith in
other countries, not only in Europe but also in Latin America. Dogma
and theological speculation have been on the whole de-emphasized;
social activity and practical works have been stressed and expanded.
"The American individualism," to quote a keen French observer of
the end of the nineteenth century, "has prevailed in the churches as
elsewhere. It accommodates the doctrine and the cult to its own
needs. Christianity and Judaism are bathed in the United States in
an entirely different atmosphere which transforms them; it corresponds more to a moral hygiene than to a spiritual idea." [4] The fact
that religion did not primarily determine American life, but rather
that American life influenced the forms of religion, did not diminish
the vitality of religion in an atmosphere of liberty and diversity. Religion in the United States is a living force as perhaps nowhere else in
the West. There has been throughout American history much crea-

tive religious unrest and stirring quest. The United States is the only Western country where in modern times new and vigorous religions were successfully founded that have even exercised an appeal abroad.

Although the differences between the various religions, based in some cases upon a venerable history of many centuries, have persisted, the unity of the American idea has provided a common framework within which the religious and spiritual life of the country in all its diversity could freely develop and to which it adapted itself. Judaism and Catholicism have fully shared in this process. "The intellectual leader of American Catholicism during the late nineteenth century was John Lancaster Spalding, Bishop of Peoria, and the twentieth century Catholicism has not produced his counterpart." Born in Kentucky, Bishop Spalding was a member of a family of early Catholic settlers of English stock. Characteristic of him was his humanistic progressive thought, so different from the theologic reasoning predominant in the Catholic church elsewhere in the period. "He was notable for his association with non-Catholics in promoting social welfare, in his denying the need for conflict between science and religion, and for his advocacy of women's rights. . . . He found no real conflict between his loyalty to the Church and his zeal for the social betterment and cultural progress of the whole nation. His field was not theology, but humanistic culture and social problems. . . . He was a 'progressive' bishop with John Ireland, James Gibbons and John J. Keane, and could be said to have held many of the ideas of Ireland, Keane and Hecker which French theologians elaborated into the imaginary heresy of 'Americanism' so vigorously attacked by European conservatives at the turn of the century." [5] One of the most famous American converts to Catholicism joined the church [as he wrote] "not in seeking to save my soul, to please God or to have the true religion, but to obtain the means of gaining the earthly happiness of mankind." [6]

A common religion was one of the main elements determining the rise and character of nations in the Old World. Another was their rootedness in a common territory. Dormant nationalities were reawakened to national life in the nineteenth century by the revived consciousness of their attachment to a historical soil which their ancestors had tilled for many generations and in which they had been buried since time immemorial. No such feeling of rootedness has ever existed in the vast and open spaces of North America. The mobility of frontier life has been characteristic of the nation from its very beginning. This mobility has been not only a social mobility, abolishing classes and castes, contrary to the Old World habits and concepts of the period, but a geographic mobility and detachment, running counter to the accepted tenets of nationalism. It remained so even after the disappearance of the agrarian frontier. Ever new frontiers have been beckoning. In the time of the Great Depression and during and after World War II civilians and former soldiers have shifted their homes, and people have preferred to live out their old age in new and only recently opened lands. The sixty years since the "closing" of the frontier have witnessed greater dynamic changes in locomotion and in the conquest of new frontiers, undreamt before, than the preceding age of the "open" frontier. The American people have been steadily on the move. Some German nationalists have therefore contemptuously called the Americans a nomadic people. Whereas outside America nascent nations of modern times frequently have tried to find their identity by emphasizing their roots in common descent and ancestral soil, none of these "natural" forces beyond the realm of man's mind and creative will have gained hold over American nationalism.

Nor did there exist in Anglo-American life any cultural or spiritual elements, generally accepted as a foundation of separate nationhood, which would differentiate the inhabitants of the thirteen colonies from other peoples. Language, law and literature tied the Anglo-Americans to the motherland. People in Europe in the age of nationalism proclaimed their independence by referring to their old and different traditions of civilization. No such appeal could be put forward by the Anglo-Americans. Though life in America has filled the English language with its flexibility and vitality, no American language in the full sense of the word developed. English and American law are different today but their common origin and fundamental concepts are undeniable. Half a century after the independence of the Anglo-Americans, an American literature was beginning to emerge. In an address to the Phi Beta Kappa Society of Bowdoin College on September 3, 1834, "On the Present State of Polite Learning in England and America," Alexander Hill Everett, then editor of *The North American Review,* averred that "the two countries must always in a literary view be regarded as one great community held together by the indissoluble bond of the same common language. . . . We glory, as Americans, in the literary glory of the land of our fathers. The names of Shakespeare, Milton, Locke, Bacon and Burke are as dear and sacred to us as they can be to any native son of the fast-anchored isle." At the time when the patriotic publicist observed these obvious facts, as keen an analyst from abroad as Tocqueville was strangely unaware of the many gifted American writers then coming to the fore. Thus he could regard the Anglo-Americans in spite of the ocean which separated them as ultimately only that portion of the English people which performed the labor of the pioneer —opening up the forests in the New World—, whereas in the old country the rest of the nation, at least partly free from the chores and cares of everyday life, could devote themselves to the refinement of the human spirit.

The English settlers in North America in their opposition to the mother country did not act out of the motives which generally moved people in the Age of Nationalism—that means, after the rise of Napoleon—to fight for their nationhood against "foreign" rulers. The American war for independence ought not to be compared—as it is so frequently—with any of the later European wars of national liberation or with twentieth century movements for colonial independence. The Anglo-Americans fought England not because they felt themselves un-English but because they were English. In their struggle they did not fight for rights not possessed before; they were upholding English constitutional rights, based upon the English revolutions of the seventeenth century, against their distortion by the arbitrary actions of the English government of the day. Benjamin Franklin was right when he wrote that the Americans were truly loyal. "But they were equally fond of what they esteemed their rights, and if they resisted when those were attacked, it was a resistance in favor of a British constitution, which every Englishman might share in enjoying who should come to live among them: it was resisting arbitrary impositions that were contrary to common right and to their fundamental constitutions, and to constant ancient usage. It was indeed a resistance in favor of the liberties of England." [7]

The Anglo-Americans in the American revolution wished to show, as the Provost of the College of Philadelphia expressed it in May, 1766, after the repeal of the Stamp Act, "that we were worthy of having descended from the illustrious stock of Britain." The settlers in North America were in their vast majority British by descent, by cultural tradition, by political outlook. They were not natives, but immigrants mainly from Britain who had come to America and there subdued or expelled the natives. The war of the thirteen colonies against Britain was not a war of natives against alien rulers but a British civil war for the interpretation, the maintenance, the broadening of the British constitution, a struggle between Whigs and Tories, both in the thirteen colonies and in Great Britain. The American Whigs regarded their liberties as an inheritance; they wished to conserve, as James Otis expressed it, "the British constitution, the most free one on earth." [8] When the war ended with the victory of the revolutionaries in the thirteen colonies—a victory for republican freedom ironically enough only achieved with the help of the absolutist monarchies of France and Spain—a new nation was born. The tie which united it—and separated it at the same time from other nations—was not founded on the common attributes of nationhood —language, cultural tradition, historical territory or common descent —but on an idea which singled out the new nation among the nations of the earth.

What was this idea? It has found its expression in the Constitution and in the Bill of Rights, documents which have shown an astonishing persistency and vitality. The Constitution of the young nation is the oldest existing constitution on earth today. Except for a few amendments it has not, in spite of the imperfections which the progress of time has revealed, been fundamentally changed in the course of 170 years, a period during which all other nations, most of them much older and much more consolidated than the Anglo-American nation, have frequently and fundamentally changed their constitutions. For the American Constitution is unlike any other: it represents the lifeblood of the American nation, its supreme symbol and manifestation. It is so intimately welded with the national existence itself that the two have become inseparable. Yet in its wording it is a bare and austere document, dry and matter of fact. It avoids any flourish of the kind characteristic of the constitutions of the French Republic. It does not solemnly proclaim the sovereignty of the nation nor invoke high moral or religious principles. It draws its lasting strength not from what it says but from what it is: the embodiment of the idea by which the United States was constituted—a nation without even a name to which emotions could cling, like England, France, Italia or Hellas, and yet from its beginning appealing to the imagination of men as the first nation to identify itself and to have been identified by others with an idea. To become an American has always meant to identify oneself with the idea.

What is this idea? It is the English tradition of liberty as it developed from older roots in the two revolutions of the seventeenth century. John Locke is the representative philosopher of this tradition.[9] This tradition could develop in a more unhampered way in North America, where the Restoration had not brought back King, Church and Aristocracy. Among the Puritans of New England the bold concepts of Milton and Cromwell, rejected or attenuated in eighteenth century England, lived on. "In political theory, in political practice," Carl Becker wrote, "the American revolution drew its inspiration from the [English] parliamentary struggle of the seventeenth century. The philosophy of the Declaration [of Independence] was . . . not new, but good old English doctrine newly formulated to meet a present emergency." But in one decisive respect the North Americans went beyond the English idea of liberty, and by this very step it was widely felt at the time, in Europe even more than in America, that the American revolution was "a kind of providential confirmation of ideas long accepted but hitherto demonstrated only in books." [10]

For what had been until then in England and in Anglo-America the historical birthright of Englishmen became in America, under the influence of eighteenth century ideas, the natural right of man, a universal message, the birthright of mankind. English historical tradition and political and legal practice fused in eighteenth century North America, and here alone, with the ahistorical rational philosophy of the Age of Enlightenment, with the law of nature which had so far been written only among the stars and which the Anglo-Americans for the first time brought down to earth to incorporate into the life and laws of society, a daring experiment watched, expectantly or distrustfully, by the whole of Western mankind. At a New Year's Eve dinner, at the threshold of the twentieth century, Benjamin Harrison in an address called "Hail, Columbia" defined the American conception of individual rights: "At first we talked of English rights but it was not long until we began to talk of human rights. What kings and parliaments had given, they could take away. And so our fathers were driven to claim a divine endowment, and to

allow it to all men, since God had made all of one blood. To write
the argument otherwise was to divest it of its major premise. The
grand conclusion—no king or parliament can rightfully take God's
gift of liberty from any man—was thus riveted to the eternal throne
itself. We made our convenience an exception in the case of the
black man; but God erased it with a sponge dipped in the white
man's blood. . . . Hail to Columbia, the home of the free." [11] That
this universalization of the optimistic and humanistic outlook of the
Enlightenment did not degenerate in Anglo-America into a dangerous Utopia, as it did in the French and Russian revolutions, that the
new republic, the first of its kind, did not lead to frustration and
disillusionment as happened in the first and second French Republics and in Mazzini's Roman Republic of 1848, is due to the fact that
the American idea of liberty with all its universal message was firmly
rooted in the English historical tradition. Without this root, the
Anglo-American experiment might have destroyed itself in utopian-
ism and radicalism; but without transcending its foundation, it never
would have blossomed forth into a new national idea, founding a
new nation.

The English colonies in North America—not, however, the Spanish, Portuguese or French possessions in Latin America—seemed
predestined, by nature and by the philosophy of the age, for a great
experiment. Geography was favorable: like the early Utopias, America was an island separated by seas from the rest of the world and
difficult of access. The Puritans could find here the Promised Land
for the unfolding of the true law of God, for the reenactment of Old
Testament history. The eighteenth century disciples of Rousseau saw
here the stage set for the unfolding of the laws of nature, undespoiled
by the corruptive influences of aristocratic courts, big cities and
over-civilized sophistication, a sanctuary for the true philosopher
and the virtuous man. But America seemed to respond as much to a
faith in the future through progress in science as to the longings for
a return to the state of innocence. The first believers in progress
through science and technology could see in North America, to use
the words of Henry Adams, "the most favorable field on the globe
for the spread of a society so large, uniform and isolated, as to answer the purposes of science." Thus the hopes of reformed religion,
of natural philosophy and of rational science, all pointed across the
ocean to the new shores. Shackled by traditions and privileges, by

intellectual and economic vested interests, Old Europe could not live up to the exalted hopes of the age: as a result of the discrepancy between the reality and the ideal it found itself in a deep moral crisis and began to believe in its own decay. As early as 1726 Bishop George Berkeley predicted in his well known "Verses on the Prospect of Planting Arts and Learning in America" the great future of Anglo-America, both as an imperial power and as a center of spiritual renovation for old and crumbling Europe:

> The Muse, disgusted at an age and clime,
> Barren of every glorious theme,
> In distant lands now waits a better time,
> Producing subjects worthy fame: . . .
>
> There shall be sung another golden age,
> The rise of empire and of arts,
> The good and great inspiring epic rage,
> The wisest heads and noblest hearts.
>
> Not such as Europe breeds in her decay:
> Such as she bred when fresh and young,
> When heavenly flame did animate her clay,
> By future poets shall be sung.
>
> Westward the course of empire takes its way;
> The four first acts already past,
> A fifth shall close the drama with the day;
> Time's noblest offspring is the last.[12]

Fifty years later this European voice from the North was joined by a voice from the South; they both were representative of a widespread feeling in all European countries. Abbé Gagliani of Naples, who was born two years after Bishop Berkeley wrote his poem and who spent several years as secretary of the Neapolitan Embassy in Paris, wrote from Naples on May 18, 1776, to Mme. d'Épinay: "The epoch has come of the total fall of Europe, and of transmigration to America. Everything here turns into rottenness—religion, laws, arts, sciences,—and everything hastens to renew itself in America. This is not a jest; nor is it an idea drawn from the [present] English quarrels; I have said it, announced it, preached it for more than twenty years, and I have constantly seen my prophecies come to pass.

Therefore, do not buy your house in the Chaussée d'Antin; you must buy it in Philadelphia." And in another letter of July 25, 1778, he was willing to bet in favor of America to reign over Europe in the future, because, as he wrote, genius had been traveling in all historical times from the east to the west.

In fact, did the rise of the Anglo-American nation not surpass the expectations of Rousseau and his disciples? The citizen of Geneva had been convinced, as were the ancient Greeks, that civic freedom could exist only in small agrarian communities like the Swiss rural cantons but was unthinkable in the case of a vast country which could be held together only by a centralized authority and imposed hierarchy. But now the Europeans witnessed with astonishment across the ocean a "rising empire, extended over an immense continent, without bishops, without nobles, and without kings," and yet this new nation fought valiantly for its rights and was capable of establishing a stable government, that, in the words of *The Federalist*, attracted "to its support those passions which have the strongest influence upon the human heart." Other Europeans less influenced by Rousseau's visionary virtuous republicanism admired in the English colonies in North America the happy blend—unknown anywhere else—of English liberty and of unlimited economic opportunity. Adam Smith urged in 1776 that the Anglo-Americans be admitted to parliamentary representation in the British parliament in proportion to taxation. As the result of their rapid progress in population, Smith predicted that by the end of the nineteenth century the colonies would be more strongly represented in the parliament than Britain and that "the seat of the empire would then naturally move itself to that part of the empire which contributed most to the general defense and support of the whole." [13] Adam Smith was not the only one who foresaw that in the future British empire the American colonies, because of their potential wealth, would play the predominant role. An American, Daniel Leonard, believed that the time would come when an English king would cross the Atlantic Ocean to take residence in North America, which would become the center of the empire and rule Britain by an American parliament. [14]

No wonder under these circumstances that the poetry and oratory freely dispensed in America in the second half of the eighteenth century shared these general assumptions of the future glory of America and in daring anticipations extended them not only to population and economy but to culture and science as well. John Trumbull, as a youth of twenty, in the conclusion of his commencement address at Yale in 1770 beheld America, "the first in letters as the first in arts," as the heir to Europe. Against the "fading gleam of Europe's setting ray," Trumbull greeted America as an imperial realm rising in radiant state, "the queen of empires and the nurse of arms." [15] Such expectations were not confined to adolescent poetry. They were the general rule. Even John Adams, then 78 years old, wrote to Thomas Jefferson on November 13, 1813: "Many hundred years must roll away before we shall be corrupted. Our pure, virtuous, public spirited, federative republic will last forever, govern the globe and introduce the perfection of man."

In its very origin as a nation the United States was the embodiment of an idea. As Professor Richard Hofstadter has put it felicitously, "It has been our fate as a nation, not to have ideologies but to be one." The ideology was a supra-national ideology, the philosophy of the eighteenth century. But it was based upon, and limited by, the English tradition which continued to be the single most important factor in the development of American life. Only by accepting and maintaining the English idea of constitutional liberty—and by thus remaining Anglo-American—could the English colonies in North America continue and solidify their political existence; only by transcending the English heritage and broadening it beyond the confines of historical-territorial limitation could they establish their distinctive political existence. In doing this, they lived up to the expectations of the age. A new chapter in the history of the West was inaugurated. The identification of the political rights of the Americans founded upon the British constitution, and of their natural rights founded upon the philosophy of the age, was self-evident to the Americans who grew to manhood in the 1760's and 1770's.[16] It was not so with the continental Europeans. They much underestimated the English root and saw only the glorious fulfillment of the promises of the Enlightenment. Even Tocqueville, so much more realistic than the men of the Enlightenment, has analyzed the American conditions against the continental or French background, without noticing how much of that which he regarded as uniquely American or democratic was in reality English and rooted in the traditions of self-government.[17]

It was Thomas Paine, the Enlightened enthusiast, fresh from Europe, who interpreted the birth of the American nation exclusively in the light of the abstract ideology of the later part of the eighteenth century. A few Englishmen and Americans followed his lead. But the large majority, bent upon the fusion of traditional and modern rights, upon the gradual growth of daring innovations out of intact roots, repudiated him. On the European continent revolution had to struggle against obsolete and aggressive privileges. Not so in Anglo-America. Looking back, the historian can say that the revolution of the thirteen colonies was not due to "oppression." Under British imperial rule the colonies were politically and socially freer and less burdened by taxation and obsolete hierarchies than any part of mankind at that time, including England. The British settlers in America did not have to liberate themselves. As far as it was possible then, they came nearer to Rousseau's metaphysical assumption of being born free than any other portion of mankind. It was this very feeling of strength, freedom and economic well-being which made the separation of the colonies from the motherland, in spite of all the affinities, inevitable. The federative solution of equal and kindred partners, later developed in the British Commonwealth, was unavailable in the eighteenth century. The example set by the Anglo-Americans made this later development possible and generally set the model for changes in Britain and throughout the vast territories settled by the British. Again, this desire for separation among peoples of close affinity has been in no way unique in the Age of Nationalism. A similar movement was a chief factor in the history of the Scandinavian peoples throughout the nineteenth and twentieth centuries, in spite of their close Nordic community of descent, language, cultural past and political attitudes. And today the cooperation of the United States, Canada and Britain is closer than that among the Scandinavian nations.

In the eighteenth century the Anglo-American settlers keenly felt this difference in attitudes and interests from the mother country. Eighteenth century England was, after the tremendous experiments of the seventeenth century, smug and stable. But it was not only the paternal past, it was also the paternal old-fashioned slowness against which the young colonies revolted. In North America the frontier conditions favored a dynamic and aggressive development. In its three main aspects—land, immigration, relations with the natives—

the colonies wished to be unhampered by supervision from the home government which they felt protected unduly the rights of the natives against the settlers. When the Anglo-American settlers spoke of liberty, they meant also the liberty to expand at the expense of the natives. The overflowing energy and initiative which had led Western Europeans, and among them Englishmen, since the fifteenth century, to brave hardship and to seek adventure in unmapped and unknown parts of the world, irresistibly drove the settlers into the fight with the receding wilderness and its inhabitants. But it was not only this dynamism which distinguished the Anglo-Americans from that portion of the nation which had stayed in the homeland. The social structure of the colonies had from the beginning been different from that of the mother country. The United States represented a social revolution accomplished without any revolutionary upheaval: it was the first middle class society in which a feudal aristocracy was as little known as a landless peasantry or a proletariat.[18]

What Karl Marx regarded as the central issue of modern European history, the struggle of the bourgeoisie against the aristocracy and of the proletariat against the bourgeoisie, has hardly had a counterpart in American reality. This astounding absence of classes and of class warfare in the heartland of modern capitalism had been noticed also in 1890 (the period of many labor troubles) by a French observer and was explained by him as part of the American system of individualism. "Il n'y a pas en Amérique de conflit ou d'antagonisme permanent entre les classes et les masses. La nation forme un tout continu où ne se distinguent et ne s'opposent que le parti qui a triomphé et le parti qui a eu le dessous, l'homme qui a mis de son côté la fortune et celui qu'elle a trahi. Les gens admirés et qui pourraient faire loi sont des parvenus qu'on admire *comme individus* pour leur énergie et leur savoir-faire et qu'on n'admirerait plus, s'ils se mettaient en troupeau et s'effaçaient dans le sang. Ils ne valent outre leur valeur et ne conservent leur crédit qu'isolés. Leur action deviendrait nulle le jour où elle essaierait de devenir collective." [19] Abraham Lincoln expressed this confidence in individual advance: "Twenty-five years ago I was a hired laborer. The hired laborer of yesterday labors on his own account today, and will hire others to labor for him tomorrow. Advancement—improvement in condition—is the order of things in a society of equals." [20] The great modern American parties did not represent class or—as we shall see—sectional interests, but in the typical English way represented the spirit of liberal compromise among conflicting economic and geographic interests.

American society approximated a classless society as closely as any society ever did. One result of this situation was the early demand for a classless system of education such as at that time nowhere existed. Isaac Parker, Chief Justice of Massachusetts and first Royall Professor of Law at Harvard, stressed in an address delivered in 1816 at Harvard College the unique importance of education in a country where all men must become "intelligent asserters of civil rights and liberties, . . . where political honors and trusts are indiscriminately open to the attainment of all classes and all professions, where the rulers are amenable to the people for a due execution of their trust, and where the citizens are the guardians of the constitution." In the preceding year, *Port Folio* adduced "special reasons why American merchants should be well educated, well informed, and, we might add, well bred, beyond the merchants of any other country. We have amongst us in the United States no titled orders or well-born classes of citizens, . . . no descriptions of persons exclusively privileged by law or usage to do the highest honors of society and of the country, either in a public or private capacity. To these distinctions the merchant may be called, and may therefore reasonably aspire, as well as these of any other denomination of his fellow citizens." [21]

A middle class society was based not only upon rural freeholders: it was a trading society, and in his address, "The Young American," Emerson accordingly praised the fundamental importance of trade for the social mobility and politico-cultural ideas of the United States middle class: "As quickly as men go to foreign parts in ships or caravans, a new order of things springs up. . . . Their information, their ways, their correspondence, have made them quite other men than left their native shore. They are nobles now by another patent than the king's. . . . Trade is a new agent in the world, and one of great function; it is a very intellectual force. This displaces physical strength, and installs computation, combination, information, science, in its room. . . . The philosopher and lover of man have much harm to say of trade; but the historian will see that trade was the principle of Liberty; that trade planted America and destroyed Feudalism; that it makes peace and keeps peace, and it will abolish slavery. We complain of its oppression of the poor, and of its building up a new aristocracy on the ruins of the aristocracy destroyed. But the aristocracy of trade has no permanence, is not entailed, was the result of toil and talent, the result of merit of some kind, and is continually falling, like the waves of the sea, before new claims of the same sort." [22] With the transformation of the agricultural and commercial society of the first century of the United States into a highly industrialized society, the American industrial worker did not suffer from a sense of permanent or enduring inferiority, nor did he or his leaders operate in an atmosphere of bitter and inescapable class antagonism. Successful trade union leaders behaved like "bourgeois" and did it openly and unashamedly; they were very well paid according to middle class standards and their level of living did not substantially differ from that of business management. The frequent reproach of "betrayal of class" raised in Europe against labor leaders adopting "bourgeois" standards of living was unknown in the United States.

The ideological-cultural pattern of American society shaped economic conflicts and social controversies with all their sharpness and even violence in a way different from that prevailing on the European continent. "Political values and ideologies," Professor Beer wrote with regard to England, "profoundly condition the aspirations which may emerge from economic development, determining in no small degree how people group themselves, what they demand as groups, and how they demand it. The culture of a society may provide . . . a consensus on basic social and political values which endures through sharp conflicts of class and party which may provide the means for their resolution. . . . Beyond its function of conditioning those aspirations which emerge from objective development of the economy or of other aspects of the society, the cultural context also has a certain capacity for itself initiating social and political change. . . . Such ideal factors of integration, precisely because they are widely diffused throughout the system, may not strike the eye as sharply as do the differences of contending groups, yet they are indispensable to stable and effective government." [23] What has been true of Britain, has to an even greater degree characterized American life.

When some European immigrants—and under the influence of European literature some American scholars—tried to apply the principles of class struggle to American life, they could not do justice to American reality. "The magical alchemy of American life," as Louis Hartz calls it, transformed passive European peasants into dynamic liberal farmers and bitter immigrant proletarians into incipient entrepreneurs. Calvin Colton, a Massachusetts clergyman and journalist who had spent several years in Britain (and who in 1850, in a lecture at the Smithsonian Institution, advocated a transcontinental railroad to the Pacific on the ground that it would reunite the human race which had been dispersed at the time of the building of the Tower of Babel), pointing to Europe said that here, in contrast, "every American laborer can stand up proudly, and say, I am the American capitalist." Edward Everett emphasized that "in this country" the "wheel of fortune is in constant revolution, and the poor, in one generation, furnish the rich of the next." Long before the consolidation of "progressive" American capitalism in the New Deal, Friedrich Engels could not fail to notice the absence of any sentiment of class warfare among the American proletariat. "It is quite natural," he wrote to Sorge on December 31, 1892, "that in such a young country, which has never known feudalism and has grown up on a bourgeois basis from the first, bourgeois prejudices should be strongly rooted in the working class. Out of opposition to the mother country, which is still clothed in feudal disguise, the American worker imagines that the bourgeois regime as traditionally inherited is something progressive, superior by nature, and for all, a non plus ultra." [24] Yet the fathers of scientific socialism had to fit the facts of American life into their scheme of history. Marx wrote to Sorge on June 30, 1881, that in America "the capitalist economy and the corresponding enslavement of the working class have developed more rapidly and shamelessly than in any other country," and Engels was convinced that "even in America the condition of the working class must sink progressively lower and lower." [25]

From the beginning of its national existence the United States—therein again representing a unique case—was a middle class nation in the tradition of Locke. Property and rank were based not primarily, as they were in eighteenth century continental Europe, on birth and inheritance, but on labor, on individual initiative, thrift and character. Louis Hartz called the American nation the disciples and descendants of Locke in his victory over Filmer. Modern Britain too has its origin in Locke, and not in Filmer, though there were a few adherents of Filmer in later England and in the United States too. Neither the United States nor Britain knew a de Maistre or a Bonald, nor the "millenarian passions" and apocalyptic fears which so often stirred extreme socialists and conservatives on the European continent. The Lockian assumptions, from the end of the seventeenth century on, have determined both English and American thought. In the United States, however, no feudal past impeded their full development. But England like the United States believes in limitation of authority, in a system of checks and balances, of compromise and moderation. This attitude has endowed both nations with remarkable stability and cohesion. In view of the recent origin, the geographic vastness and diversity and the extreme heterogeneity of its population, this stability has been even more remarkable in the case of the United States than in that of England. This unique stability under such difficult circumstances is added testimony to the vitality and vigor of the American idea.

American liberty, rooted in English liberty, has been able to withstand the temptation of abstract millenarianism. Conservative Americans and Englishmen have been worried about possible excesses of liberty, and throughout the history of the United States voices have been raised against the dangers of corruption and demagogy, allegedly inherent in mass democracy.[26] After Shays' insurrection in 1787 Fisher Ames wrote: "Anarchy and government are both before us, and in our choice. If we fall, we fall by our folly, not our faith. And we shall evince to the astonished world, of how small influence to produce national happiness, are the fairest gifts of heaven, a healthy climate, a fruitful soil, and inestimable laws, when they are conferred upon a frivolous, perverse and ungrateful generation." But the nation did not fall. The loss of liberty, the rise of anarchy and despotism as a result of corruption and immorality, of demagogues and mass pressures, have been predicted by critics of American political life throughout its history. All these predictions have turned out to be unfounded. In the United States as in the mother country the growing mass democracy has remained faithful to the tradition of liberty, to the limitation of governmental authority, by whomsoever exercised, and to the protection of the rights of individuals and of minorities.

The threats to liberty and the potentialities for the development of liberty have always been greater in the United States than in modern Britain. A land of apparently unlimited opportunities, which from the beginning enjoyed a degree of individual liberty and social mobility unknown elsewhere, the United States has been for two centuries the frontier land of modern Western civilization—originally in the sense of being its geographic rim but soon even more as being its field of experimentation and fulfillment. As a result America seemed more and more to draw away from Europe, to drift in an opposite direction. The United States and western Europe turned their backs to each other across the North Atlantic. But they were not in opposition, even though they often thought of themselves as very different and opposite; they were part of the same tradition, a common tradition which expressed itself in varied and often outwardly contrasting forms in the various countries, forms which at the frontier grew even more different from those continuing in the older societies. But in the eighteenth century Britain and the North American colonies formed a union not only politically: in government and in law, in religion and in literature, they drew their life-strength from the very sources that nourished the whole texture of their culture and society. At the same time the interchange of ideas between France and the English-speaking lands was more intense than in any other period of history. This interdependence was never one-sided: Americans not only received from western Europe goods and ideas and examples; they also gave inspiration to the general Western longings for the realization of political and religious freedom, of humanitarian reforms, and of economic opportunities. Both trends of English thought—Burke and Bentham alike—were conscious of the community existing between the two shores of the North Atlantic. This was true in America, too, of conservatives, like Alexander Hamilton, and of liberals. During the eighteenth century "American progressives and their English counterparts were in intimate contact and continually reinvigorated each other. Their exchange of correspondence, their common understanding, and warm sympathy, account for the similarity in the organization and sentiments of their radical associations on both sides of the Atlantic. The debt that each owed to the other is immeasurable." This community continued in the nineteenth century in all the humanitarian efforts for the emancipation of women, for the establishment of a lasting peace, and for the amelioration of the condition of the poor. "The community of interest that was created in the last third of the eighteenth century among liberals everywhere in the North Atlantic

civilization," to quote Professor Michael Kraus, "has been an enduring factor in the life of Western society to our own time." [27] Deep-
seated differences between the United States and western Europe
have existed and continued to exist, but equally deep if not deeper
differences exist between England and France or Switzerland and
Germany. The affinity between England and the United States in the
tradition of rational liberty is greater than that between any two
countries in western Europe. In that sense, the United States has
been from its beginning, and is today, the frontier land of both the
English tradition of liberty and modern Western civilization.

In any evaluation of American nationalism, it is equally important
to recall the fundamental unity of the tradition of liberty in the
United States and in Britain and western Europe, and to understand
the unique contribution of America, as the West's frontier, to this
common tradition. In this contribution the American frontier movement, in the narrower sense of the word as it is generally understood
in United States history, has played its role. The frontier movement
itself was not uniquely American. It was part of a great modern
European movement which—prompted by the search for economic
opportunity as well as by the lure of the unknown and the call of
the primitive—drew Western man away from home from the age of
the discoveries to the beginning of the twentieth century. Yet
though this pioneering spirit was a common attitude in modern
Western society, nowhere did it reach the same intensity or exercise
as decisive an influence as among the Anglo-Americans. James Bryce
rightly insisted that the western frontier intensified American distinctiveness. "The West may be called the most distinctly American
part of America," he wrote in *The American Commonwealth*, "because the points in which it differs from the East are the points in
which America as a whole differs from Europe." [28] Professor Billington in his thoughtful reconsideration of Frederick Jackson Turner's
famous thesis concerning the importance of the frontier in American
history and in American nationalism has arrived at the conclusion
that "no one force did more to Americanize the nation's people and
institutions than the repeated rebirth of civilization around the western edge of settlement during the three centuries required to occupy
the continent." [29]

The expanding Western empire and the interpretations of its
function in American life helped the United States in its newly

awakened nationalism to turn away from, and against, England and Europe. The influence of the ever moving frontier tended to lessen the consciousness of common roots and origins binding the two shores of the North Atlantic. In their westward expansion the Anglo-Americans created for themselves an American empire which they regarded as a link in the historical chain of empires built by Western energy since the fifteenth century. That century marked the divide between two conceptions of empire: on the one hand, the unbounded and, in principle, world-wide Asian empires such as those conquered by Islam or by the Mongols; on the other hand, the much more—and consciously—limited empire building of Western nations. Like the other modern Western nations, the new American empire was limited in its goals. It knew itself to be one among competing empires and accepted this position. Therein it differed from the Asian empires—and also from the Russian empire insofar as it regarded itself as the universal monarchy of the Third Rome —which in theory were universal and exclusive. But it resembled them—and the Russian empire—in one important respect. It was no longer, like the empires of Portugal, Spain, France, Holland and England, based on maritime expansion, sea power and considerations of trade. It was a land empire of agrarian settlers. The Americans regarded this form of empire not only as fundamentally different from the imperial pattern with which they were most familiar, but also as superior to it; by its independence from world commerce and by its geographic compactness the American empire promised greater safety and stability than any other empire of the period.

It is generally recognized that the American frontier was a unifying element in American nationalism because it peopled the vast lands with Americans originating from the various states and sections of the nation; it melted them in this process into something new, and filled all Americans with pride in the common venture of empire building. But of equal importance was the fact that this westward movement contributed much to the illusion that the United States was something fundamentally different and remote from Europe. The myths and patterns of thought to which this development gave rise continued to exercise their influence on the American mind long after the agrarian base on which the empire was originally founded had given way to the mightiest industrialism and commercialism so far known to mankind, and after the United States had become a maritime power of the first order controlling far flung bases.[30] The United States turned its back upon the Atlantic and set its face toward the Pacific. It not only became isolationist and, on a continental scale, insular—attitudes shared by the United States with the mother country—it grew anti-British and anti-European. This attitude was strengthened by the growth of a corresponding and even less justified inclination on the part of England and Europe to look upon the United States as something different and inferior. The educated European classes from London to Vienna, from Madrid to Amsterdam, saw in the nineteenth century American no longer the virtuous and noble savage nor the vanguard of human liberty and Western inventiveness, but the grasping nouveau-riche, the uncultured and unrefined barbarian. In an age of conservative monarchies and only slowly crumbling class barriers the classless sprawling young republic across the North Atlantic appeared as a cultural and political menace. The Russian historian Mikhail Pogodin expressed this feeling well when he wrote in 1837: "America, on which our contemporaries had pinned their hopes for a time, has meanwhile clearly revealed the vices of her illegitimate birth. She is no state, but rather a trading company, like the East India Company which independently owns territory. America cares solely for profit: to be sure she has grown rich, but she will hardly ever bring forth anything great of national, let alone of universal, significance." [31]

On the other hand, European liberals in the nineteenth century, especially around its middle span, again looked to the United States as they had done in the eighteenth century. The Swedish novelist Fredrika Bremer, who visited the United States in 1849, wrote in her reports, which at that time were very widely read and reflected the mood of defeat in Europe caused by the failure of the revolutions of 1848: "While one portion of the people of Europe, after a struggle for light and freedom, which in part mistook its own purpose, and not clearly knowing that which it desired, seemed (perhaps merely seemed) to sink back again under a despotism which knew better what it aimed at, obtaining for a time the power of might; in that gloomy season my soul raised itself in deep faith and love toward that distant land, where the people erected the banner of human freedom, declared the human right and ability to

govern themselves, and on this right founded a monarchy of states
—the commencement of the world's greatest governmental culture.
That which I sought for there was the new human being and his
world; the new humanity and the sight of its future on the soil of
the New World." [32] Thus by European conservatives and liberals
alike, the United States was accorded a unique position; and this
attitude in turn strengthened American consciousness of being
fundamentally different from Europe and providentially endowed
with a special mission. Did the Americans not represent, after 1815
and again after 1850, in an age of reaffirmed political, social and
ecclesiastical hierarchy, the only republic of equalitarian tendency?

Yet the United States was at the same time an orderly and conservative republic, different therein from the English Commonwealth of 1648 or the First and Second French Republics. No Cromwell or Napoleon threatened the republican order in the United
States. Understandably the Americans counted themselves happy
to have no tie with Europe and to be separated from it by the width
of an ocean which they regarded even more as a blessing than the
English did the Channel. Above all—in their rejection of former
ties and in their wish for differentiation from the system of government most kindred to their own—the Americans turned against
the British monarchy which like their own republic was rooted
in the Glorious Revolution. Fisher Ames observed in 1805 that "we
have been accustomed to consider the pretension of Englishmen to
be free, as a proof how completely they were broken to subjection, or hardened in imposture. We have insisted, that they had
no constitution, because they never made one; and that their
boasted government, which is just what time and accident have
made it, was palsied with age, and blue with the plague's sores of
corruption. We have believed that it derived its stability, not from
reason, but from prejudice; that it is supported, not because it
is favorable to liberty, but as it is dear to national pride; that
it is reverenced not for its excellence but because ignorance is
naturally the idolater of antiquity; that it is not sound and healthful but derives a morbid energy from disease, and an unaccountable
aliment from the canker that corrodes its vitals." [33]

In the following decades this dislike of England and rejection of
English influence expressed itself at all levels. In 1828 Captain
Basil Hall, R.N., traveling in North America, visited a Boston school.

The boys, unaware of the nationality of the visitor, delivered speeches about "the most grateful theme they could choose," some furious philippics against England: "Gratitude! Gratitude to England! What does America owe to her? Such gratitude as a young lion owes to its dam, which brings it forth on the desert wilds, and leaves it to perish there. No, we owe her nothing! For eighteen hundred years the world had slumbered in ignorance of liberty and of the true rights of free men. At length America arose in all her glory to give the world the long desired lesson!" [34] The Boston school boys were understandably proud of the American interpretation and realization of liberty. Their distrust of Britain was shared by such a conservative and cautious man as James Fenimore Cooper. He expressed a similar distrust of foreign, especially English, "propaganda" in the United States and his statement of 1838 would have sounded familiar from the mouths of American isolationists in 1938: "There is no question that the people of this country defer in an unusual manner to foreign opinions, more particularly to those of the nation from which they are derived. . . . An opinion is seldom given in Europe of anything American unless from impure motives. . . . No nation can properly boast of its independence while its opinion is under the control of foreigners and least of all a nation with institutions dependent upon the popular will." [35]

American animosity to Britain was exacerbated by British supercilious treatment, especially by the reports of British travelers in America. An American in London took the British to task for it. He regretted that Captain Hall "should have taken so much pains in his book to show why it is utterly impossible for the two nations ever to cherish kindly feelings towards each other. . . . But for such writers of travels as himself, Mrs. Trollope, and all of their class, the relations of Great Britain and the United States are in all respects favorable to good feeling, and we hope even yet, that the noxious growth, which has sprung up from the seeds of unkindness they have sown, will be thoroughly choked by the dominant virtues of the two nations." The American confidently anticipated a reaction in the British public mind against the detractors of America, "and a more earnest cultivation of those fraternal regards, which ought ever to subsist between the two nations. Men of the same blood, the same language, the same laws, and the same institutions,—and having the same sympathies in religion and for the rights of man, it is unnatural for them to differ, or be unkind. Let those, who have made us to differ, or ministered occasions of distrust, be duly esteemed. And henceforth and forever we say: A TRUCE—A TRUCE to this unbecoming and unprofitable warfare." [36]

The bitter opposition in America to England was fanned by immigrants from lands hostile to England, foremost from Ireland. Michael Forrest, a young Irishman who came to the States at the age of seventeen, "from fair Hibernia's healthy, verdant plain," expressed regret that he was born too late to fight in the war against the British, "to save a nation from base tyranny, and gain freedom for posterity." Much more important in molding American public opinion was Mathew Carey who at twenty-four had to leave Ireland because he called for armed insurrection against England, and who lived his subsequent fifty-five years in the United States in the shadow of the impressions obtained in his youth. He made his *Pennsylvania Herald* the mouthpiece for violent opposition to the British and went so far as to claim that the United States by ratifying Jay's commercial treaty with Britain would rescind the Declaration of Independence and would again become a colony of "the most corrupt and degenerate government of Europe." [37] Later on, under the influence of Treitschke and his bitterly anti-British nationalism, some Americans of German origin similarly deepened the antagonism between the United States and England. From these various and complex motivations the mutual irritation between Americans and British grew in the middle of the nineteenth century to a point of tension and distrust which found a characteristic expression in the diary of a minor American diplomat in London. On September 3, 1858, he wrote: "The people of England *hate* us, lie about us, rob us . . . They want another trouncing to bring them back to good manners." And in another passage on December 31, 1861, he went on about the English: "In their peculiar arrogance they coolly assume for themselves the merits of all human excellence, and have modestly set up their own notions of themselves as a standard by which to judge the world. With that imperious insolence, which they everywhere display when not afflicted by adversity, they have impudently dared to censure our political creed as immoral and our religious professions as un-Christian." One century later some irritated Englishman might be tempted to write in his diary similar judgments about American "peculiar arrogance." Fundamental similarities arouse at times the most vivid irritations.[38]

Tocqueville's remark, that it is impossible to imagine a more venomous hatred than that which the Americans feel for the English, will not astonish any student of nationalism. This vehemence of dislike was similar to that which most Norwegians felt toward the Danes, when the two kindred peoples separated in 1814 after a close political and cultural community of over four centuries. Norwegian nationalists wished to forget that community and to obliterate it in national life; they regarded it as deeply harmful to, if not destructive of, Norwegian personality and interests. Like the Americans, the Norwegians loved to contrast their constitution of 1814—then the most advanced one on the European continent— and their democracy of rural freeholders, with the absolute monarchy then continuing in Denmark, in which the court and the metropolitan city set the model for all political and cultural life. But, different from the Americans, the Norwegians, to distinguish themselves from the Danes, could and did look back to their distant past and invoked the age of the sagas and the imperial exploits of medieval Norway. They saw in them proof of Norway's distinctive individuality and unique glory. The Americans could not find in their past any similar support for their claims against Britain. They could look only to the future; they could not lay claim to having been different but rather to growing different. Their sense of distinctiveness was strengthened by their self-identification with virtue—an inheritance of eighteenth century Rousseauism—and with liberty—an inheritance of eighteenth century republicanism. As early as 1787 Royall Tyler, in his play "The Contrast," opposed the honesty of an American and the duplicity of an Englishman, a subject which remained, down to Henry James, one of the main themes of American literature, although it had in American life itself a parallel in the contrast between the honesty of the American from the midwest rural communities and the duplicity of the American from the Atlantic metropolitan centers of finance and learning.[39] Baron Jacobi in Henry Adams's novel *Democracy* (1880) bitterly complained about this American self-identification with purity and innocence: "You Americans believe yourselves to be exempted from the operation of general laws. You care not for experience. I have lived seventy-five years, and all that time in the midst of corruption. I am corrupt myself, only I do have the courage to proclaim it, and you others have not. Rome, Paris, Vienna, Petersburg, London, all are corrupt, only Washington is pure!" The American self-identification with innocence was not shared by the British or the Europeans: they could not claim to have been born in Rousseauan virgin forests. But the American self-identification with liberty was not as purely "American" as most Americans assumed; it derived from a similar self-identification of the English: after all, British and American liberty grew from common roots in its long development from the Magna Charta to the revolutions of the seventeenth century.

This English self-identification with liberty has been the hallmark of English nationalism since the Puritan revolution. Then Edmund Waller called England "the sacred refuge of mankind," whither "the oppressed shall henceforth resort," and Milton saw the people of the island, the soil of which was most congenial to the growth of liberty, disseminating the blessings of civilization and freedom all over the earth.[40] Since then the identification of English nationalism with individual liberty has become traditional. Such an identification was from the beginning even stronger in the United States. It has formed the basis of the national interpretation of American history. America's first great historian, George Bancroft, wrote that "the Americans seized as their peculiar inheritance the tradition of liberty. . . . In America it was the breath of life of the people. . . . The mechanics and merchants and laborers [of Boston], altogether scarcely so many as thirty-five hundred ablebodied men, knew that they were acting not for a province of America, but for freedom itself." [41] Bancroft, who occupies the same place in the development of American historiography and of the American national consciousness as Palacký does among the Czechs, Michelet among the French, Munch among the Norwegians, and Treitschke among the Germans, was a national historian not only because he saw national history in as favorable a light as possible but because he tried to formulate and document some of the most prominent traits of American national self-identification. He helped delineate the image which Americans formed of themselves. "The American revolution," he wrote, "of which I write the history, essaying to unfold the principles, to organize its events, and bound to keep faith with the ashes of its heroes, was most radical in its character, yet achieved with such benign tranquillity that even conservatism hesitated to censure. A civil war armed men of the same ancestry against each other, yet for the advancement of the principles of everlasting peace and universal brotherhood." [42]

Like all nationalist historians, Bancroft wished not so much to tell what had happened as to see it as it should have happened in a logical historical development, the goal of which was the justification of the nation, its deeds and glories. Nationalist historiography desires not only to describe a people's life but to help form it and to make its history appear as the fulfillment of a supposed national destiny. Such a historiography is less important for the knowledge of history itself than for the understanding of the image which a nation forms of itself and of its own nationalism. Therefore, for the sake of the true interest of the nation itself, all nationalist historiography—and the concept of national history itself—demands a constant critical reappraisal and reevaluation. Such historiography often lacks a sober understanding of the ever changing facts and relationships of national and international life and prefers to cling to illusions and wishful thinking. National history needs to be measured against universal ethical standards which transcend the sphere of even legitimate national interests. Yet shortcomings of scholarly judgment or objective ethos do not diminish the value of nationalist historiography for the student of nationalism. Treitschke's great *History of Germany in the Nineteenth Century* may be prejudiced and wrong in many of its views about Germany and the world in the first half of the nineteenth century. It is nevertheless indispensable for an understanding of German nationalism and of German national history after the middle of the nineteenth century.[43] It influenced both. In that sense, regardless of his rejection by a later and more critical scholarship, Bancroft will not cease to be America's representative national historian. "His book," wrote a later American historian, "remains our great defense of the rights of American nationality, our most fervent great apology for the War of Independence in all its untutored Americanism." [44]

Bancroft, however, was not only the son of the Enlightenment and of the American revolution. He started his work at a time when, after the Napoleonic wars, all European countries participated in a newly aroused national historicism and under its influence began to study systematically the national past in documents and archives. In 1834 the French minister of education François Guizot, who was himself a historian of renown, helped to establish the Society for the History of France.[45] The German patriot Baron vom und zum Stein promoted the publication of the *Monumenta Germaniae Historica,* the medieval sources of German history. Each published volume carried the inscription "Sanctus Amor Patriae Dat Animum" (The Sacred Love of the Fatherland Animates Us). Patriotic societies and individuals dedicated themselves to similar undertakings all over Europe. Nationalism everywhere resuscitated and reinterpreted the national heritage. The need for a historical consciousness made itself felt in the beginning age of nationalism. In 1813 John Adams, then seventy-eight years old, complained of the "total ignorance and oblivion of the revolution" among the younger generation, and wrote to his fellow revolutionist Thomas McKean: "Can you account for the apathy, the antipathy of this nation to their own history? Is there not a repugnance to the thought of looking back? While thousands of frivolous novels are read with eagerness and got by heart the history of our own native country is not only neglected, but despised and abhorred." [46] A short time after this complaint—which undoubtedly contained a large part of truth although some of its bitterness might have been due to the irritability of an old man—in the United States as all over the Western world active and sustained interest in national history was aroused. In these years Tocqueville was convinced "that in fifty years it will be more difficult to collect authentic documents concerning the social condition of the Americans at the present day than it is to find remains of the administration of France during the Middle Ages; and, if the United States were ever invaded by barbarians, it would be necessary to have recourse to the history of other nations to learn anything of the people which now inhabits them. . . . No one cares for what occurred before his time, no methodical system is pursued; no archives are formed; and no documents are brought together when it would be easy to do so. Where they exist little store is set upon them." Yet in these very years the situation which Tocqueville deplored was being remedied. *The Journals of each Provincial Congress of Massachusetts in 1774 and 1775* were then edited by William Lincoln, and *The Debates in the Several State Conventions on the Adoption of the Federal Constitution* by Jonathan Elliot. In 1837 the *American Archives,* a documentary history from the origin of the colonies to the ratification of the Constitution, began publication.[47] The preface explained that "the undertaking upon which we have embarked is emphatically a national one; national in its scope and object, its end and aim." The new historiography, the new attention paid to history in the United States as well as abroad, wished to present and to preserve testimony of a glorious national past. In the United States this (short) past coincided with the flowering of individual liberty and the proclamation of its blessings.

As with the other national historians in the Western community of the period, Bancroft's *History of the United States* was the work of a lifetime. The first volume appeared in 1834, the tenth and last in 1874. Bancroft was one of the first American students who went abroad after his graduation from Harvard to pursue historical studies in Germany. Though he remained impressed all his life by Germany and by its scholarship, his sojourn abroad, as with so many others, fanned his patriotism and made him feel more decidedly "American." Together with another American student at Göttingen young Bancroft celebrated the 4th of July, 1820, at a "banquet," toasting the President, the flag, the American eagle, the memory of Washington, the literary prospects of America, the sweet nymph Liberty, the heroes of the Revolution, the Constitution and the American government, "watered by the dews of Heaven and quickened by the genial warmth of freedom—the nurseries of enlightened patriots." When he returned to America in 1822 he bade Europe farewell in appropriate poetical lines:

> The weary pilgrim to his home returns,
> For Freedom's air, for western climes he burns;
> Where dwell the brave, the generous, the free,
> O! there is Rome;—no other Rome for me.[48]

In the celebration of another 4th of July, this time as a public orator in Northampton, Massachusetts, Bancroft declared in 1826 that "the popular voice is all powerful with us; this is our oracle; this, we acknowledge, is the voice of God." [49] Nine years later he amplified his position on the role of the people and the peculiar nature of America: "The absence of the prejudices of the Old World leaves us here the opportunity of consulting independent truth; and man is left to apply the instinct of freedom to every social relation and public interest. We have approached so near to nature, that we can hear her gentlest whispers; we have made Humanity our law-giver and our oracle; and, therefore, the nation receives, vivifies and applies principles, which in Europe the wisest accept with distrust. . . . The government by the people is in very truth the strongest government in the world. Discarding the implements of terror, it dares to rule by moral force, and has its citadel in the heart." [50]

But it was not only national historiography which helped to form American self-understanding in the early nineteenth century. Bancroft's vision was centered on the United States. He did not sufficiently see the Anglo-American development in the late eighteenth century as part, and as the most advanced part, of a general movement of modern Western civilization. [51] His older contemporary and fellow New Englander, Alexander Hill Everett, was by career and inclination better equipped to see the United States as a nation among nations. As a young man he accompanied John Quincy Adams on his diplomatic mission to Russia and later represented the United States in the Netherlands and in Spain. He was minister to Madrid during the critical years of the recognition of the independence of the former Spanish colonies in America and much concerned with the question whether Spain would be able to keep Cuba and Puerto Rico under her control. After Caleb Cushing had concluded the first commercial treaty with China, Everett was appointed first United States commissioner to the far eastern empire, where he died soon after his arrival. Of his writings, two books, one on Europe and the other on the western hemisphere, were widely popular during his lifetime. [52] In them he saw the United States as an integral part of the Western world. The title page of his book *America* bore the inscription *Matre Pulchra Filia Pulchrior.* "As respects the United States," he wrote, "their history sufficiently proves, if theory were wanting, that it is not in their power to separate themselves entirely from the great political system of Christendom, with which they are naturally connected by community of origin." [53] Culturally the United States was the heir of Western Europe, politically it was the offspring of Britain and its constitutional development. "In the United States, we have brought, as we suppose, the forms of government to still greater perfection," Everett stated with a sense of proportion, "have cleared away many abuses, avoided many errors, and introduced great improvements in the details of administration; but we are still proud and happy to look to Great Britain as the source from which we have drawn all our political institutions, with the alterations necessary to accommodate them to our situation and habits; and some of the most valuable—as the habeas corpus act and trial by jury—without any alteration at all. The American Constitution, as was justly remarked by the illustrious Fox, is that of England improved by the results of the experience of a thousand years." [54]

From his experiences as minister to Spain he concluded that "the natural progress of events" would render the political relations between Britain and the United States more and more amicable while at the same time the younger country would become the major partner. Britain and the United States, Everett wrote, "have now without any sacrifice of pride or principle on either side, without concession and indeed without concert, been brought by the mere force of circumstance into a situation of virtual alliance and amity, so deeply and broadly founded in the interests of both and the established political system of Christendom that it cannot well fail to supersede all the old motives of contention and to endure as long perhaps as the national existence of either. . . . Such is the rapid growth of our continent in population, wealth and political power that . . . the adherence of Great Britain to our system will then be to us of no utility, while the same causes will render the connection in an economical point of view to her constantly more and more valuable. Add to this that while our continent is yearly developing new resources of every kind, it is altogether probable that the British empire will be gradually brought within smaller dimensions by successive falling off of its distant appendages and will ultimately be reduced to its primitive possessions on the northwestern coast of Europe. The United States having thus become the most populous and powerful nation of English origin, will naturally take the place of the British islands, as the commercial and political center of the English settlements in every part of the globe." [55]

From his experience in Russia Everett regarded the rapid progress in power and civilization of the eastern empire as the greatest threat to the security and survival of the West. "A glance at the map of the world," he wrote, "is sufficient to show, independently of any other argument, how completely the west of Europe is crushed, beneath the giant mass of this political Colossus. . . . The continental states that figured as leading powers in the former system, such as France, Austria, and latterly Prussia, have lost by the introduction of this new and overwhelming rival, not only their rank but virtually their independence. This feature of the new system has not yet assumed its perfect form; but the natural termination of the progress of events which is now going on, will be the union of the whole continent into one military monarchy." Everett saw "the Western and civilized nations . . . exhausted and impoverished by their late protracted struggles, torn by parties, disunited among themselves, or acting together like cold and heartless allies, and apparently almost insensible of the common bond of interest that unites them all." They seemed not to realize the danger from Russia. Yet, according to Everett, as far back as the time of Peter the Great "a sagacious observer might . . . have perceived, that a new military power had made its appearance, which was capable of counterbalancing the combined force of all the rest of Europe, and which by the internal development of its resources, was constantly adding to its strength and importance. . . . Having completed their internal organization and secured their territory in all its points, the Russian monarchs began to turn their eyes towards the West, and there is hardly a subsequent political crisis of any importance, in which their influence has not been perceptible, and it has gradually and steadily increased with every succeeding year." Everett returned to this theme again and again. "I have stated, that the moral influence of Russian power is already extending itself fast enough through the neighboring countries; and that at no distant period it may very probably obtain an actual military dominion over the rest of Europe. . . . In such a power it is impossible not to recognize the future master of Europe; and if the ascendancy of Russia does not bring with it a return of barbarism, it will evidently not be because institutions of that empire are modelled at present on a wise and liberal plan, (although they are perhaps as good as the state of the people would admit,) but because the principle of civilization and improvement will be powerfully sustained by aid from abroad, that is from America." [56]

As an American patriot, Everett was as convinced as Bancroft of the future greatness of the United States which "at the close of the century will not apprehend European powers but will be courted

by them all as a powerful, useful friend and ally." In an address
delivered in 1834 he held up the American Constitution as a model:
"New forms of government that had hitherto been regarded as the
visions of philosophical dreamers, too beautiful to be ever realized
on the terrestrial sphere, are going on in quiet operation in full view
of an astonished and admiring world." To the Spanish revolutionaries of 1820 he dedicated "a political poem in defense of liberal
principles," in which he called upon them to look to America as an
example:

> To Europe's history, why each thought confine?
> Mark where afar in blameless lustre shine
> Columbia's stars along the Hesperian sky,
> And guide the march of struggling liberty.
>
> By her forewarned, Iberia, learn the skill
> To mix with prudent care your generous zeal;
> Like her, to well tried worth your cause entrust,
> And willing to be free, forget not to be just.
>
> So shall your realm rest in vigorous health,
> Revive once more to glory, joy, and wealth.

And in a commemoration speech on the battle of Bunker Hill, in a
Miltonian peroration, Everett called upon his hearers not to limit
their regards to a single country, not even to their own, but as
friends of liberty and of human happiness to realize that "wherever
there are men living, laboring, suffering, enjoying,—there are our
brothers. Look then still further abroad, honored friends and patriots! Behold in distant countries,—in other quarters of the globe,
the influence of your example and achievements in stimulating
the progress of social improvement. Behold the mighty spirit of
Reform striding like a giant through the civilized world and tram-
pling down established abuses at every step! . . . Behold him
working out his miracles in France, knocking off the shackles of
neighboring nations in Spanish America, pursuing his course, sometimes triumphant, sometimes temporarily trodden under foot, betrayed by false friends, overwhelmed by superior force, but still
in the main, forward and onward over Spain, Portugal, Italy, Germany, Greece!" [57]

But like so many American patriots, Everett was over-confident about the future: "The blessings we enjoy and which we never prize sufficiently till we have had the opportunity of ascertaining their value by contrast, are secured to us by two principal causes, one geographical, and the other political. The first is our distance from other nations of superior power, and the second, our internal union. Of these propitious circumstances, which may well be regarded as the peculiar favors of providence bestowed upon our country, the one gives us complete security from foreign violence without the ruinous resource of standing armies, hardly less dangerous when necessary than the evils they are intended to remedy; and the other establishes our domestic politics upon the basis of perpetual peace." [58] Everett's optimism proved unfounded. Forty years later the internal union which was to form the basis of perpetual peace was rent in a bitter fratricidal war, the wounds of which a century has not healed completely. Today, the other principal cause to which Everett attributed the blessings bestowed upon the United States—the geographic remoteness from other powerful nations—has been annulled by the development of modern technology. Whereas the Civil War is largely a matter of the past and the federal union has proved its strength, the abolition of distance will remain a permanent factor and will emphasize the role of the United States as a nation among nations in a shrinking world, a role which Everett clearly foresaw. At the time when he wrote, historical and psychological reasons prevented most Americans and most Western Europeans from recognizing the fundamental unity of American nationalism with the historical development of English nationalism and with the hopes animating Western mankind in the second half of the eighteenth century. American nationalism in its origins was closely connected with both and developed their potentialities to a degree unknown in the Old World. For that reason—and not only or primarily for reasons of geography or economy—the United States could assume in the middle of the twentieth century that leadership of the North Atlantic Community which some had foreseen for it in the eighteenth century. But before this stage could be reached, the United States had to face difficult tests inherent in its own new nationalism, which was based on unity and diversity, on individual liberty and federal organization, on "E Pluribus Unum." As a republic of many republics, as a nation of many nations, it anticipated problems which the Western world as a whole may have to face in the course of the twentieth century, and for which the United States, in bitter struggle and burning imperfection, was the first to seek, and to attempt, solutions.

chapter two

Matre pulchra filia pulchrior

"O Lovelier Daughter of a Lovely Mother"
HORACE
"Odes," I, 16, 1.

"While we have been advancing with portentous rapidity, America is passing us by as if in a canter. There can hardly be a doubt, as between America and England, of the belief that the daughter at no very distant time will, whether fairer or less fair, be unquestionably yet stronger than the mother. . . . It is America who at a given time, and probably will wrest from us that commercial primacy. We have no title: I have no inclination to murmur at the prospect. If she acquires it, she will make the acquisition by the right of the strongest; but in this instance the strongest means the best. She will probably become what we are now—head servant in the great household of the world, the employer of all employed, because her service will be the most and ablest."

WILLIAM GLADSTONE, 1878.

The political and ideological framework of the nascent nation was established by the end of the eighteenth century. This in itself was an astonishing achievement, for the United States, in its own consciousness and in that of the Western world, was a new type of nation, apparently without past or precedent, but endowed with a great future. So far only the outward structure of the Republic existed; the generations of the first decades of the nineteenth century were faced with the task of filling this structure with living substance. It is characteristic of the spirit of the New World that its people thought above all of the promotion of the general welfare as the best way of strengthening and vitalizing the newly formed nation. The American mind turned to the then new and daring proposition which it has never abandoned: that common prosperity, by giving every individual a growing stake in the national society and making his economic interests a cementing link in the new national loyalty and self-awareness, was the safest foundation for the Union, and, in fact, for every modern nation. From the beginning, the United States put an emphasis, unknown then in Europe, on internal improvements, industrial development and material factors; through them the various states and sections should come to feel their interdependence and their participation in a progressing common venture and welfare. American nationalism regarded the protection of American industry not only as an equivalent to the military protection of the national frontiers but also as a means of harmonizing various and conflicting sectional and economic interests. The development of national resources, the building of canals and railroads, would "open new vistas by giving a new and wholesome direction to the public mind. . . . Each single improvement appeared but a link in a golden chain of benefits and blessings, calculated to bind together indissolubly the states composing this vast Republic." [1] Starting from these presuppositions, America became the first nation to develop the theory and to enforce the practice of modern economic nationalism, though this theory ran counter to the accepted liberal tenets of the very period to which the United States owed its birth. Alexander Hamil-

41

ton, Henry Clay, and Mathew Carey were the fathers of this nationalist protectionism, which rightly became known as the "American system." Friedrich List, one of the first economic nationalists of Europe, learned the new theory while he lived in the United States and then devoted his life to its propagation in his native Germany.

The Americans were easily led to believe that their national genius and destiny expressed themselves above all in economic progress, for they saw it unfold before their eyes from the beginning; there was no difficulty involved in the recognition of their political and economic achievements, either by themselves or by European observers. Different, however, was the situation in the cultural and intellectual fields. There, America, ahead of Europe in other respects, seemed sadly backward. Whereas in the nineteenth century the Western European nations, apparently secure in their cultural traditions and literary and artistic achievements which went back to the twelfth or thirteenth centuries, were in search of new political and social solutions, the Americans, apparently secure in their political and social institutions, were in quest of an indigenous culture, and were anxious and doubtful about it. Throughout American history the problem of American cultural identity has remained a neuralgic point, both for American self-understanding and for American-European relations. The anxieties and controversies involved in the quest for an American culture as distinct from that of the mother land and the ensuing tensions in transatlantic communication and intercourse, have shown a remarkable consistency over the last one hundred and fifty years. Gertrude Stein expressed the uniqueness of the American quest when she remarked that "there is one thing one has to remember about America: it had a certain difficulty in proving itself American which no other nation has ever had." Both Americans and Europeans often doubted whether cultural life in the United States equaled its political vitality and economic strength. Were American claims to superiority in these respects not more than balanced by cultural inferiority? Moreover: was this cultural inferiority due only to the youth of the nation, to its immersion in the process of nation-building over a vast continent, or was it inherent in the very character of the American political and social structure? The separation of the United States from the English mother land was based not only upon the universalization of the historic English concept of liberty, but also

upon a feeling of social equality unknown in the aristocratic England—and unthinkable in the strictly stratified Europe—of the early
nineteenth century.

The Americans of that period were of course proudly aware of
this distinctive social equality. In 1816 the *Port Folio* stressed that
no visitor from Europe need "present stars" to prove his worth in
the United States. "He who behaves himself well will be well-
received. . . . He will be estimated at what he is worth." In 1820
The North American Review contrasted Europe's lack of social
equality with her achievements in other fields: to the American
writer this lack seemed only poorly balanced "by pictures and statues,
by fleets and armies, nay, by fine poetry and prose;—though all
these are excellent in their way." Hezekiah Niles, an extreme nationalist, went further in his proud assertion of American civilized
superiority. In 1815 he wrote an open letter to the English radical
writer William Cobbett, and printed it in the *Weekly Register*
which he had founded in 1811 and which by 1819 reached the, for
that time, very high circulation of more than ten thousand sub-
scribers. "There are no such men in the world," Niles boasted, "as
our independent farmers, who constitute the large majority of our
people. Many of them have libraries, like your English lords, and
what is more, they even understand the books they have." America
could never be conquered, Niles went on, "while every citizen feels
himself a part of the government, and the blacksmith argues politics with his neighbor, the congressman. . . . Our Western men
are not only the best marksmen in the world, but the most generous,
high-minded and patriotic people that live." [2]

But in the eyes of European nineteenth century observers, and
of some Americans, this then unique feeling of social equality, which
Tocqueville called democracy and which since the Second World
War has become characteristic of all modern Western societies as
Tocqueville had foreseen, hardly seemed to predispose America
to a life of cultured intensity. Liberty and the grandeur of nature
might produce and nourish civic virtues, as the eighteenth century
believed, but was it equally true—as many American patriotic enthusiasts maintained at the end of that century—that liberty, equality, and vast open spaces were also the best soil for the growth of
a new and better civilization? Did not democracy make the common man the sovereign arbiter of art and culture? Had he a real

understanding of intellectual values and of their importance to the life of a nation? In spite of the great emphasis on, and the faith in, the usefulness and necessity of education, did not the average American—the frontier settler and the businessman, the farmer and the urban worker—distrust or insufficiently esteem the contemplative life of the thinker and the disinterested scholarly pursuit of culture? Did not the average American assume such an attitude because the intellectual and artistic professions were apparently products of an aristocratic society, ornaments of the life of a leisure class, the sign of over-civilization and decadence? Eighteenth century Americans inherited Rousseau's suspicion of the intellectual and at the same time the emphasis on the practical man, the inventor and technologist, which characterized the beginning of the industrial revolution in England. The New World with its virgin nature, its pioneer needs, and its economic potentialities, intensified these attitudes. Many democratic egalitarians resented intellectual elites as much as social. Individual economic success was considered more typically American than was individual cultural preeminence in less practical and less tangible fields.

Such an attitude was undoubtedly helpful in promoting economic wealth and social mobility, but could a nation of this mentality be expected to achieve deeds of human importance in the cultural and spiritual field? Most European conservatives, after the shock of the French Revolution had turned them away from eighteenth century hopes and ideals, answered this question in the negative. The Russian historian Mikhail Pogodin expressed this negation perhaps in its sharpest form,[3] and many Western Europeans and even some Americans voiced similar opinions. In the nineteenth century intellectuals and artists more and more replaced eighteenth century optimism regarding human nature and social progress with a growing emphasis on the darker aspects of human life—its complex morality, its tragic depths, its irrational passions, its perhaps inherent disillusions and frustrations. Thus the question arose whether the very foundations of American life, laid in the eighteenth century, were not sharply opposed to a true artistic vision and to a full understanding of man. The optimistic outlook of the average American, which fundamentally continued the eighteenth century intellectual climate, might have been conducive to greater regard for the dignity and potentialities of the individual and thus to the development of a successful free society, but did it not lead to artistic philistinism and cultural sterility? One of the early great American artists, Edgar Allan Poe, answered the question in the affirmative. "The founders of the Republic," he wrote, "started with the queerest idea conceivable, viz., that all men are born free and equal—this in the very teeth of the laws of gradation as visibly impressed upon all things both in the moral and the physical universe." In a similar vein, in a letter to James Russell Lowell, Poe interpreted human nature and history in a way which ran counter to, and deeply offended, the dominant American belief in progress: "I have no faith in human perfectability. I think that human exertion will have no appreciable effect upon humanity. Man is only now more active—not more happy—nor more wise, than he was 6,000 years ago." [4]

Poe even used sharp satires to express his judgment of America's most cherished ideas. In his tale, "Some Words with a Mummy," the resurrected Egyptian count told the narrator that in ancient Egypt "Thirteen Egyptian colonies determined all at once to be free, and so to set a magnificent example to the rest of mankind. They assembled their wise men, and concocted the most ingenious constitution it is possible to conceive. For a while they managed remarkably well; only their habit of bragging was prodigious. The thing ended, however, in the consolidation of the thirteen states with some fifteen or twenty others, in the most odious and insupportable despotism that ever was heard of on the face of the Earth. —I asked what was the name of the usurping tyrant.—As well as the Count could recollect, it was *MOB*." [5] These anti-democratic views endeared Poe to his French admirer and translator Charles Baudelaire, who believed that "The United States was for Poe only a vast prison through which he ran hither and thither, with a feverish agitation of a being created to breathe in a more amoral world." Baudelaire called the United States "a gas-lit barbaric country," and referring to the dictatorship of public opinion in democracies he concluded that "from the impious love of liberty has been born a new tyranny, the tyranny of beasts, a zoocracy, which in its insensible ferocity resembles the idol of Juggernaut." But it would be unjust not to add that Baudelaire judged contemporary France as severely and one-sidedly as he did the United States, and that he found Belgium even more hateful than either of the two countries.

The middle class in general with its *morale de comptoir* horrified him. He found modern society infatuated with itself and unaware of its decay. He called France "ce villain pays" which "n'est pas artiste, naturellement artiste," and which "éprouve même pour tout dire une horreur congénitale de la poésie." In 1860 Baudelaire wrote to his mother, "Je ne me rassasierai jamais d'insulter la France," a sentiment which could have been expressed by Poe toward the United States.[6]

Most Americans, however, had no share in reflections of this kind: to them, democratic liberties, middle class society, the grandeur of American nature, its virgin soil, appeared the best soil for the growth of an indigenous and purer and possibly superior culture. In their desire for a cultural nationalism, these Americans were inspired by their political antagonism to the mother country. Therein they apparently resembled other rising nations in the Age of Nationalism; recent American cultural historians have compared their aspirations with those of the Norwegians, the Germans and the Russians at the beginning of the nineteenth century. This list could of course be continued to include Czechs and Magyars and many other "awakening" nationalities. All of them had to establish their cultural identity and their national literatures in the struggle against "older" and at that time more highly developed cultures which their educated classes had shared with other peoples: Danish in the case of the Norwegians, French in the case of the Germans, French and German in the case of the Russians. Yet all these peoples could find support for their aspirations in a distinctive language and in a long and, at least in their own interpretation, glorious past which preceded their close cultural association with another people. Some awakening nations presented, as far as modern civilization was concerned, a *tabula rasa* before their contact with a more dynamic modern and "alien" civilization. In Russia, the famous "Lettre Philosophique" by Peter Chaadayev aroused his contemporaries by proclaiming the cultural barrenness of the Russian past before Western influences penetrated into and were absorbed by the Russian educated classes.[7] The situation was entirely different in the United States. The Indians might have presented cultural virgin soil or a *tabula rasa,* but the Anglo-American settlers at the end of the eighteenth century were co-heirs and full partners of English culture. Though they were not productive in *belles lettres,* their theological and political oratory was on the highest level. The best works of English literature were widely read on the American frontier. The first Russian university was opened in 1755, largely with German teachers. The Anglo-Americans, as soon as they reached their new homes, founded colleges after the model of their native land and staffed them with men trained in the common English civil and religious tradition.

This unique cultural position of the new nation explains why on the one hand American cultural nationalism sometimes went to great lengths—especially in its declarations and declamations—to differentiate itself from the English mother land, and why on the other hand it never reached the extremes found elsewhere, and showed—especially in practice—the utmost moderation. Common sense and the fundamental universalism and tolerance of the eighteenth century heritage prevailed. Slowly and naturally a distinctive American culture arose, due to the differences in environment and social habits. Yet deep into the twentieth century, in spite of all nationalist agitation, the teaching of language and literature in American colleges and universities was guided by the common heritage of the English-speaking world. At the beginning of American independence, Noah Webster called passionately upon his fellow Americans and begged them to "Unshackle your minds and act like independent beings. You have been children long enough, subject to the control and subservient to the interests of a haughty parent. You now have an interest of your own to augment and defend—you have an empire to raise and support by your exertions—and a national character to establish and extend by your wisdom and judgement." [8]

But in the nineteenth century the Americans felt secure in their independence and could well afford to act with wisdom and judgment, though in a different way from that expected by Webster. American writers liked to indulge in the favorite pastime of twisting the British lion's tail in the cultural field too, but, on the whole, the reading public seemed hardly susceptible to the emotional appeals for being on guard against the penetration of "foreign" influence. The successful termination of the war with Britain in 1815 made some Democratic writers of the period believe that it would be "an easy transition to pass from victorious warfare against the claims of British supremacy on the sea to victories equally impressive in

national letters." But there were many contrary voices raised. The
Port Folio of Philadelphia hoped that English literature would
"never be considered as an alien or an enemy by the descendants
of Britain," and though today most Americans are no longer, as
they were at the beginning of the nineteenth century, physically
descended from Britain, but only culturally and spiritually partners in a common heritage, this hope expressed in 1816 has been
realized. There are few Americans today who would not regard
Shakespeare and Milton, Locke and Burke as much an integral part
of American life as of English life. The *American Review and Literary
Journal* of New York praised the fact that the United States was
united by language and taste with an enlightened nation, England
—a center of arts which should be considered a center for America
too. On July 3, 1819, the *National Recorder* of Philadelphia called
upon Americans to remember "that we are descended from the
same parents and that we will not forego our common claims to
participate in the reputation of Shakespeare and Milton, of Johnson
and Addison. In her [England's] soil repose the remains of those
whose works form the minds of our children to liberty and virtue." [9]

Even those Americans who fully appreciated the heritage which
they shared with the mother country felt pride in the possession
of a democratic way of life, which they frequently identified with
the truly Christian way of life. This pride easily mingled with pity
or contempt for the old countries and their lack of liberty. The
Americans were deeply appreciative of the blessings which they
knew to be unique and which they believed their way of life was
bestowing upon them. This feeling of superiority and gratefulness
found expression in countless orations and articles. The Alford
Professor of Natural Religion, Moral Philosophy and Civil Poetry
at Harvard, Levi Frisbie, declared in his inauguration address in
1817 that "in this country mankind seem to be subjected to an experiment to determine their power of improvement, instituted under circumstances incomparably more favorable than ever before
existed. . . . We are full of youthful freshness. . . . We are free
from any of those institutions by which other nations are en-
thralled. . . . Food of the mind is acquired with as much ease as
that of the body. . . . The prevailing humanity of our national
character appears in that merciful code of penal laws to which there
is no parallel in other nations. . . . We are, to give our general

character, a religious and a moral people. . . . Never in all past ages did a prospect so glorious rise to the view of any nation. . . . There is no responsibility more solemn than that of those who may affect the destinies of such a people." [10]

Two years before this address was delivered, the editor of *Niles' Weekly Register*, in the feeling of elation that followed the conclusion of the war with Britain, went much further in his praise and pride. In the introduction to the ninth volume of his periodical, he jubilantly observed that "A high and honorable feeling generally prevails, and the people begin to assume, more and more, a *NATIONAL CHARACTER;* and to look at home for the only means, under divine goodness, of preserving their religion and liberty—with all the blessings that flow from their unrestricted enjoyment. The bulwark of these is the sanctity of their principles, and the virtue and valor of those who profess to love them; and need no guarantee from the bloodstained and profligate princes and powers of *Europe.* . . . A practical proof of the advantages of these things was found in the god-like humanity of the soldiers and seamen of the United States in the late war. . . . Such things are the more resplendent because of the opposite conduct of the British." [11] But such exuberance was in no way general. In the following year *Portico* soberly rejected the favorite fanciful theory that young or primitive people were endowed by heaven with a peculiar genius and nourished by dews that were never formed upon an older soil. Modern excellence, the writer declared, was due "to successful imitation or wise adoption, of previous learning or civility." In the same year, *Port Folio* went so far as to assert that the British too had a free government. "The British monarchy, if monarchy it must be called, is certainly a good government, well suited to that country. . . . If we inquire by what power it is sustained in England, we shall find it is the good sense and mild spirit of Englishmen. . . . A similar spirit, with a fair portion of common sense, induced Americans to adopt that system under which they live." Even in the midst of the "paper war" which followed the sharp criticism of Ingersoll's *Inchiquin Letters* in the [English] *Quarterly Review,* the *North American Review* kept its calm. In an article, "The United States and England," the editor reminded the people on both shores of the Atlantic that it was indeed time "that some generous writer should volunteer on their side to counteract the tendency of national prejudices to nourish implacable hatred between the two nations." [12]

American over-confidence and boastfulness often were only a re-action against similar attitudes on the part of the older countries. Americans were deeply convinced that many Britishers regarded them with hostility and disdain. Out of this wide-spread feeling a writer in the *Analectic Magazine* urged the Americans to place themselves on a level with other nations. "Nothing is wanting to this, but to shake off the remains of that miserable degrading colo-nial spirit of subservience, which, in too many portions of this country, still remains deeply rooted in the hearts of those who, from their wealth and extended connections, exercise a vital influence." The author went on to attack bitterly that spirit which crouches at the feet of foreigners and ever gives precedence to foreign opera-tions and foreign fashions. Yet the magazine was in no way an organ of cultural isolationism. The issue following this castigation of de-pendence, especially in the realm of the mind, as a state of degrada-tion, devoted its first eighteen pages to printing Wordsworth's "Ex-cursion" and warmly praised it. [13]

The educated classes in the United States were generally well informed on English and European history and literature, whereas across the Atlantic American conditions were little known even among the well informed. This situation continued throughout the nineteenth century. At its beginning, Dr. David Ramsay—a South Carolina physician, politician, and writer of intensely patriotic his-tories, a disciple and friend of the famous Philadelphia physician, philanthropist, and educator, Dr. Benjamin Rush—complained that the United States did not receive due attention in the writing and teaching of history in the Britain and Europe of his day. Such a complaint might well have been voiced one hundred years later. Ramsay wished to remedy what he regarded as a deplorable situa-tion. To that end he planned to write a universal history "to restore to his beloved country the importance to which it was entitled." After his death his *Universal History Americanized* was published; of its twelve volumes, the last three dealt with the history of the United States. Other Americans who had the opportunity to observe this European ignorance of their country followed Ramsay's lead and wrote books designed to dispel the wide-spread misconceptions about American life. Some of these books were a passionate defense, like Robert Walsh's *An Appeal from the Judgments of Great Britain Respecting the United States of America;* others were more moderate, like *American Facts,* written by George Palmer Putnam, the founder of the well-known publishing house, during his sojourn in England. Years later, Walsh became consul in Paris; in that office he was followed by Samuel Griswold Goodrich, who represented the United States in France from 1851 to 1853 and found the ignorance about the United States so appalling that he arranged for the publication of a volume, *Les États-Unis d'Amérique.*[13a]

In 1817 the *North American Review,* faced with this wide-spread ignorance of American life and institutions on the part of European observers, accused them of displaying "a gross and indiscriminate abuse of our character, rash and ridiculous opinions, mischievous or vague and puerile advice . . . it has been our lot to be so ill-treated by foreigners; the travelers who have described us have been, with very few exceptions, so ignorant and profligate, that we almost despair of an able and unprejudiced account of the United States from a European."[14] Yet in the July issue of the following year, the *North American Review* published a very fair essay on American poetry by one of the leading American poets of the day, William Cullen Bryant. Like so many New Englanders, Bryant, during the War of 1812, had seriously considered secession from the Union. Now he condemned in his essay both extreme attitudes as injurious and unjust—the attitude prevailing abroad which despised American poetry, and the attitude prevailing at home, where the "swaggering and pretensions of many have done not a little to provoke and excuse the ridicule of foreigners." Though Bryant criticized the servile copying of the style and content of English poetry, he recommended its serious study and found American pride in the glories of English literature justified, for the Americans were, as far as literature was concerned, English.

An article by Sydney Smith, a brilliant and well known English liberal divine and critic, made history by stimulating the discussion of American national literature. The article appeared in 1820 in the *Edinburgh Review* and had a long lasting effect upon American cultural self-consciousness, far beyond its real importance. "Thus far," Smith wrote, "we are friends and admirers of Jonathan. But he must not grow vain and ambitious; or allow himself to be dazzled by that galaxy of evidence by which his orators and newspaper scribblers endeavor to persuade their supporters that they are the greatest, the most refined, the most enlightened, and the most moral people on earth. . . . The Americans are a brave, industrious, and acute people; but they have hitherto given no indication of genius. . . . They are but a recent offset indeed from England; and they should make it their chief boast for many generations to come that they are sprung from the same race with Bacon, Shakespeare, and Newton. Considering the numbers, indeed, and the favorable circumstances in which they have been placed, they have yet done marvelously little to assert the honor of such descent." Nothing stung the American writers and artists of the time as much as the question which followed: "In the four quarters of the globe, who reads an American book? Or goes to an American play? Or looks at an American picture or statue?" For the next three decades the answer to the question—were there an American literature and art and how far were they American?—preoccupied America's educated circles. America's most prominent minds participated in the debate. By 1850 the issue raised by Sydney Smith was settled in one respect: people were reading American books. And a century later they would read them eagerly in the four quarters of the globe. With respect, however, to the question whether there was a distinctive American literature fundamentally different from the English literary tradition, the issue of the debate has not been settled except in the most elementary way, namely that books written by American citizens represented American literature. But did this literature express a specific American idea? Could such an idea be distilled from the complexities and diversities of American life? Finally, was not the community of language and tradition a stronger force in shaping human expression than geographic and social differences? To all these questions highly interesting and often contradictory answers were attempted in the three decades following Smith's provocative verdict. After 1850 other burning issues absorbed the national mind and decisively shaped the course of American history and thought: the reconciliation of sectional rights and needs with the acceptance of national unity; the absorption of an ever-growing stream of immigrants and their successful assimilation into the national unity; the adjustment of the nation to the new international relationship of the technological twentieth century. But in 1820 none of these great issues of national debate had yet arisen to a recognizable extent.[15]

Nor was Smith's opinion of American literature unjustified in 1820. Thirty years later, Ralph Waldo Emerson delivered a similar judgment in his *Journals*. "To write a history of Massachusetts, I confess, is not inviting to an expansive thinker . . . since, from 1790 to 1820, there was not a single book, a speech, a conversation, or a thought in the State. About 1820, the Channing, Webster, and Everett era began, and we have been bookish and poetical and cogitative since." [16] Smith could not foresee this change. It was the generation of William Ellery Channing which seriously began to question whether the right kind of political and social institutions were sufficient as a basis of national life, whether natural and material advantages, inventive skills and rising comfort were of primary importance, or whether intellectual creative power was not rather the indispensable and decisive factor in national greatness. Channing was no narrow nationalist. In 1812 he deplored the fact that the United States took part in the war "with the oppressor [Napoleon] against that nation [England] which alone has arrested his proud career of victory." In 1816 Channing founded the Massachusetts Peace Society, and in 1837 he protested, in a letter to Henry Clay, "Thoughts on the Evils of a spirit of Conquest, and on Slavery," against the annexation of Texas and the expansionist spirit of the American nationalism of the period.

In a famous lecture in 1823, Channing took up the challenge for an American national literature. "We love our country, but not blindly. In all nations we recognize but one great family and our chief wish for our native land is, that it may take the first rank among the lights and benefactors of the human race. . . . Literature is plainly among the most powerful methods of exalting the character of a nation, of forming a better race of men, in truth, it may claim first rank among the means of improvement. . . . Do we possess indeed what we may call a national literature? Have we produced eminent writers in the various departments of intellectual effort? We regret that the reply to these questions is so obvious. . . . The more we receive from other countries, the greater the need of an original literature. It were better to have no literature than form ourselves unresistingly on a foreign one. The true sovereigns of a country are those who determine its mind, its mode of thinking, its tastes, its principles; and we cannot consent to lodge this sovereignty in the hands of strangers. . . . We need a literature to

counteract, and to use wisely, the literature which we import. . . .
We need an inward power proportionate to that which is exerted
on us. . . . A foreign literature will always, in a measure, be foreign. It has sprung from the soul of another people, which, however like, is still not our own soul. Every people has much in its own
character and feelings, which can only be embodied by its own writers and which, when transfused through literature, makes it touch-
ing and true, like the voice of our earliest friend." [17]

The following year Edward Everett, a younger brother of Alexander Everett, spoke before the Phi Beta Kappa Society at Cambridge on "The Peculiar Motives to Intellectual Exertion in America." Everett was the first American to receive a Ph.D. degree at
Göttingen; before he entered politics, he taught at Harvard where
Emerson was among his students. In his address, Everett extolled
the free institutions of his country and was convinced that their
nature must give a peculiar form or direction to the new American
literature. But what were the prospects of such a literature? In Europe, monarchies and aristocracies encouraged letters and arts, but
where could such patronage be found in "our poor republican land,
our frugal treasury, and the caution with which it is dispensed?"
Therefore should not Americans form gloomy auguries of the influence of free political institutions on literature? Yet Everett was
convinced that liberty was a mighty agent for developing the mind
and for the flowering of art and letters, because liberty, and liberty
alone, could bring to bear on every point the concentrated energy
of a numerous free people. Intellectual exertion in America not only
would produce an American literature, it would settle a momentous
question: whether a free popular system could be trusted to guide
and develop men not only politically and socially but also intellectually and spiritually.[18]

A few years later, America's then most popular novelist, James
Fenimore Cooper, energetically joined the debate. By the end of
the 1820's his novels had been published in England and translated
into French and German and other continental languages. His
sojourn in Europe from 1826 to 1833 made him a conscious defender
of "American principles" and of the mission of American literature
to defend and propagate such principles. In a book which appeared
simultaneously in England and the United States, Cooper claimed
that the American reading public had better taste than the English,

emphasized the fact that Americans were more loyal to their nation than the Europeans to their states, and announced that "a new era is about to dawn on this nation. It has ceased to creep; it begins to walk erect among the powers of the earth. All these things have occurred within the life of man. Europeans may be reluctant to admit the claims of the competitor, that they knew lately a pillaged, a wronged, and enfeebled people; but Nature will have her laws obeyed, and the fulfillment of things must come. The spirit of greatness is in this nation: its needs are within their grasp; and it is as vain as it is weak to attempt to deny results that every year is rendering more plain, more important, and more irresistible." [19]

Cooper went even further in his reply to Smith. "The literature of the United States is the subject of the highest interest to the civilized world," he wrote in 1828, "for when it does begin to be felt, it will be felt with a force, a directness, and a common sense in its occupation, that has never yet been known. . . . It is, perhaps, twenty years too soon to expect that England will very complacently submit to receive opinions or fashions very directly from America. . . . I think it will be just as much the desire of England then to be in our fashion, as it was our desire twenty years ago to be in hers, and for precisely the same reason. The influence of fifty millions of people, living under one government, backed by enormous wealth, extended intelligence, a powerful literature, and unrivaled freedom, cannot be very problematical, in the eyes of any man who is capable of regarding the subject free from prejudice or passion." Ten years later, after Cooper's return to the United States, his views had changed. In *Home as Found* he lamented that "no attempt to delineate ordinary American life either on the stage or in the pages of a novel, has been rewarded with success. . . . That the American nation is a great nation, in some particulars, the greatest the world ever saw, we hold to be true . . . but we are also equally ready to concede that it is very far behind most polished nations on various essentials, and chiefly that it is lamentably in arrears to its own avowed principles." The same theme was resumed in Chapter XXV where Cooper contrasted "old" America and its worship of everything English and foreign with "young" America and its boast that the United States was the most civilized country in the world and that its literature was rapidly reaching the top rung of the ladder. In the debate between the two viewpoints, John Effingham, widely traveled like Cooper and like him without illusions about the anti-American prejudices of Europe, "especially of our venerable kinswoman, Old England," condemned American nationalist provincialism with its disposition to set up mediocrity as perfection, as America's weakest point.[20]

The end of the 1830's, when Cooper published his *Home as Found,* witnessed the climax of the debate on American national literature. In 1837 Emerson delivered his famous address, "The American Scholar," with its appeal to individual independence and self-reliance, and in the same year the *Democratic Review* started to propagate in the cultural field the boisterous and aggressive nationalism of Jacksonian democracy. Common to all these manifestations was their dedication to America and their stress upon the great American future, but the spirit animating Emerson's America was very different from the editorial policy of the *Democratic Review.* When Emerson castigated imitation, conformity, and second-hand living in America, he did it not from a nationalist but from an individual and universal point of view. The essential calling and duty of man, as Emerson saw it, was to conduct his own life and not to have it manufactured for him; a right nation would be a nation consisting of such independent individuals and non-conformists. It was Emerson's hope that America would become such a nation. He deeply distrusted wealth, material power, bigness of all kinds, which would threaten the independence of the individual. "The truest test of civilization," he wrote, "is not the census, not the size of cities, nor crops,—but the kind of man the country turns out. When I look over this constellation of cities which animate and illustrate the land, and see how little the government has to do with their daily life, how self-helped and self-directed all families are, knots of men in purely natural societies, societies of trade, of kindred blood, of habitual hospitality, house and house, man acting on man by weight of opinion, of longer or better directed industry; the refining influence of women; the invitation which experience and permanent causes open to youth and labor; when I see how much each virtuous and gifted person, whom all men consider, lives affectionately with scores of excellent people who are not known far from home, and perhaps with great reason, reckons these people his superiors in virtue and in symmetry and force of their qualities,—

I see what cubic values America has, and in these a better certificate of civilization than great cities or enormous wealth." [21]

Emerson was painfully aware that American life did not live up to his idea of America. In an address in 1844 he called upon young Americans to become worthy of the American idea. As a contemporary of Hegel and Mazzini, he too believed that in every age of the world there has been a leading nation representing the spirit of the age. But for him such a nation had to be one which was not moved by national self-interest but which excelled by generous sentiment, and whose citizens were willing to stand for the interests of general justice and humanity, at the risk of being called by the majority of their fellow citizens chimerical or unpatriotic. Such a nation, Emerson believed, could only be the United States, and especially New England. Yet to him as a critical observer America offered in 1844 a contrary and upsetting spectacle: "Out of doors all seems a market; indoors, an airtight stove of conventionalism. . . . They recommend conventional virtues, whatever will earn and preserve property . . . whatever goes to secure, adorn, enlarge these is good; whatever jeopardizes any of these is damnable." Even the opposition, Emerson complained, was not different; its speakers and writers worshiped the same values. "They attack the great capitalists, but with the aim to make a capitalist of the poor man. The opposition is against those who have money from those who wish to have money. But who announces to us in journal, or in pulpit, or in street, the secret of heroism? . . . The more need of a withdrawal from the crowd, and a resort to the fountain of right, by the brave. The timidity of our public opinion is our disease, or, shall I say, the publicness of opinion, the absence of private opinion." Thus Emerson called for heroism to counteract materialism, but he meant not a military or nationalist heroism, but the heroism of the lonely individual who dared to stand up against the opinions and prejudices of the national crowd.

In his insistence on individual independence, the American democrat Emerson did not differ fundamentally from the French liberal aristocrat Tocqueville. "In modern society," Tocqueville wrote at about the same time that Emerson made his famous address, "everything threatens to become so much alike that the peculiar characteristics of each individual will soon be entirely lost in the general aspect of the world. . . . To lay down extensive but distinct and settled limits to the action of the government; . . . to enable individual man to maintain whatever independence, strength, and original power he still possesses; to raise him by the side of society at large, and uphold him in that position: these appear to me the main objects of legislators in the ages upon which we are now entering. It would seem as if the rulers of our time sought only to use men in order to make things great; I wish that they would try a little more to make great men; . . . that they would never forget that a nation cannot long remain strong when every man belonging to it is individually weak, and that no form of combination of social polity has yet been devised to make an energetic people out of a community of pusillanimous and enfeebled citizens. . . . I have sought to point out the dangers to which the principle of equality exposes the independence of man, because I firmly believe that these dangers are the most formidable and the least foreseen of all those which the future holds in store, but I do not think that they are insurmountable." In a like way Emerson believed that only by strengthening the independence of the individual, by arousing his will to withstand the temptations of wealth and mass conformity could democracy based upon equality increase and not diminish the value of man. Sixty years later another representative American philosopher, William James, in his Gifford lectures in 1901, called for a similar independence of mind and individual heroism against the corruption of popularity and wealth. "It is true that so far as wealth gives time for ideal ends, wealth is better than poverty. But wealth does this in only a portion of the actual cases. Elsewhere the desire to gain wealth and the fear to lose it are our chief breeders of cowardice and propagators of corruption. Think of the strength which personal indifference to poverty would give us if it were devoted to unpopular causes. Our stocks might fall, our hopes of promotion vanish, our salaries stop, our club doors close in our faces; yet, while we lived, we would imperturbably bear witness to the spirit, and our example would help to set free our generation." [22]

Not in a feeling of national self-assertion but in the spirit of asserting the dignity of the independent thinking individual, Emerson delivered in 1837 before the Phi Beta Kappa Society at Harvard his famous address "The American Scholar." It has been called by Oliver Wendell Holmes "our intellectual declaration of independence."

Even more impressed was James Russell Lowell who wrote some thirty years later: "The Puritan revolt has made us ecclesiastically, and the Revolution, politically independent, but we were socially and intellectually moored to English thought, till Emerson cut the cable and gave us a chance at the dangers and glories of blue water. . . . His oration was an event without any former parallel in our literary annals, . . . it was our Yankee version of a lecture by Abelard, our Harvard parallel to the last public appearance of Schelling." [23] Yet it would be hard to detect in this declaration of independence any trace of nationalism. It was a vindication of the daring loneliness and independence of the scholar, of the responsibility of the thinking modern man to his conscience and to the highest universal standards. This declaration was American only insofar as Emerson hoped that America would represent and realize the universal human ideal of individual independence. The address was a plea for the single man, planted upon himself and there abiding, to be a whole and a unit, and not to be reckoned in the gross, in the hundred or the thousand, as a member of a nation, a section or a party. "A nation of men," Emerson expressed his faith and hope, "will for the first time exist, because each believes himself inspired [not by a national soul but] by the Divine Soul which also inspires all men." No "chosen people" idea disfigured Emerson's address, such as distinguished the thought of so many contemporary nationalists on the European continent. "Nationality," Emerson remarked in his *Journal*, "is often silly. Every nation believes that the Divine Providence has a sneaking kindness for it." Emerson's "call for a profound voice to speak to American hearts, for a song of the American spirit," an American literary historian remarked, "was not political in conception; the American spirit was significant not because it was American but because it was a self-reliant faith in the present and the future." [24]

"*Men* count, not the mass. Act for yourself; the man has never lived that can feed us ever. The important thing is a single person. The man is all. . . . Remember that society can never be so large as one man; that the private life of one man shall be a more illustrious monarchy than any kingdom in history"—this was Emerson's message. It is not astonishing that Nietzsche, the most individualistic, non-conformistic and non-nationalist nineteenth century German thinker, declared himself to be deeply impressed by Emerson, whose creed was repeated also in Ibsen's sharp and bitter denunciation of Norwegian society and of all Norwegian nationalism on behalf of the autonomous free individual. Emerson's close friends and neighbors went even further in their stress upon the individual than Emerson did. Henry David Thoreau wrote in his essay on Civil Disobedience (1849): "This American government,—what is it but a tradition, though a recent one, endeavoring to transmit itself unimpaired to posterity, but each instant losing some of its integrity? It has not the vitality and force of a single living man." During the Mexican War, Thoreau passionately protested against "his" country. "When a whole country is unjustly overrun and conquered by foreign armies, and subjected to military law, I think that it is not too soon for honest men to rebel and revolutionize. What makes this duty the more urgent is the fact that the country so overrun is not our own, but ours is the invader."

Like all true prophets, Thoreau was unduly severe with his fellow Americans. More protesting voices were raised in America against America's national wars of 1812 and 1847 than in any other nation against similar wars. Yet Thoreau found the Americans much too uncritical, and those who were critical, not sufficiently daring to translate their criticism into action. Although the Americans were the most self-reliant people of the period and the most independent of their government, Thoreau decried the fact that "The American has dwindled into an Odd Fellow,—one who may be known by the development of his organ of gregariousness, and the manifest lack of intellect and cheerful self-reliance; whose first and chief concern, on coming into the world, is to see that the alms-houses are in good repair; and, before yet he has donned the virile garb, to collect a fund for the support of the widows and orphans that may be; who, in short, ventures to live only by the aid of the Mutual Insurance Company which has promised to bury him decently." In the same spirit, Emerson, when asked in 1847 by his English friends whether there were any Americans—any with an American idea,—any thought as to the right future of that country—did not consider politicians or government but regarded "the dogma of no government and nonresistance" as the essential trait of the American dream.[25]

Another of Emerson's friends, Amos Bronson Alcott, shared Thoreau's enthusiasm for the individual. "Individuals are sacred," he wrote in 1841. "The world, the state, the church, the school, are all felons whensoever they violate the sanctity of the private heart."

What a distance separated Emerson and his friends from their contemporary, Mazzini, who proclaimed "Nationality is sacred." Though Emerson and the transcendentalists were deeply influenced by German romantic thought, by Schelling and Coleridge, they rejected their veneration of the nation and the nation-state, and selected out of German speculation only the elements compatible with American individualism. The same spirit asserted itself half a century later when the philosophy of post-Kantian German idealists, especially of Hegel, gained influence on American thought. American idealism differed then from its German model "in its reluctance to sacrifice the individual to the universal." American philosophers tried to reconcile post-Kantian rationalism with the moral will of the individual, and post-Kantian monism with the pluralism of American democracy. Among leading modern American philosophers, William James, a spiritual descendant of the Scottish school of philosophical individualism, was "avowedly and flagrantly a moral individualist, so much so, that he can be justly accused of neglecting the human significance of society." Yet John Dewey, whose background was Hegelian and for whom individualism was a product of society, was in his philosophy as libertarian and tolerant as William James. Instead of Hegel's mystical self-surrender and absolutism, Dewey taught a fundamental disrespect for authority and for historical institutions.[26]

Whereas Emerson saw the realization of the American dream in the independence of the individual man, self-thinking and self-directed, the *Democratic Review* accepted the more conventional ideal, common to most nations in the Age of Nationalism, of *national* independence from alien influence, relegating the individual to an expression of the national spirit—to the role of the servant and standard-bearer of national destiny. The *Democratic Review* was convinced that the writer's and artist's stature depended upon the stature of their nation, not upon their own individuality, and that American men of letters could attain literary greatness only by reflecting the struggles and aspirations of their nation, its natural setting and its march through history. In the introductory essay to its first issue, the *Democratic Review* proclaimed a cultural isolationism, complaining that "our mind is enslaved to the past and present literature of England. Rich and glorious as is that vast collection of intellectual treasure, it would have been far better for us had we been separated from it by the ocean of a difference of language, as we are from the country itself by our sublime Atlantic." Understandably, the *Democratic Review* saw the true heart of America beating not in Emerson's beloved New England, but in the West. "There are glorious things to be hoped for from the free young genius of the West. We of the Atlantic shore have not yet recovered from a certain paralysing influence produced on the free development and movement of our national mind by that colonial relation towards the mother country, which the Revolution destroyed only in its political point of view. The West stands more free from those impalpable moral tremors of English dependence, which we sometimes think have sadly dwarfed the growth of our intellectual stature." [27]

The American West seemed not only less touched by European influences, its air and writers seemed to represent the common man much more than those of New England did. Like similar movements elsewhere in the Age of Nationalism, American cultural nationalism stressed the need for a literature which would appeal to the people and reflect the mind not of the independent individual but of the common man. American literature was to reflect conformity with those moral Christian and democratic ideals which were believed to be the substance of American life. The *Western Monthly Review*, founded in Cincinnati in 1827, upheld the Midwest's claim to intellectual fertility and originality not only against Europe but also against the Eastern seaboard. Yet America's most popular textbooks of the period, which too were published in Cincinnati, did not propagate a nationalist or isolationist spirit. These textbooks were written by William Holmes McGuffey, who taught most of his life in Ohio colleges and whose first *Eclectic Reader* appeared in 1836 at the height of the debate on American cultural nationalism. In the lesson dealing with American-European relations his *New Fifth Eclectic Reader* insisted that the United States acknowledge with respect and gratitude its obligations to Europe in the realms of science and art, of law, literature and manners. "The people of the United States, descendants of the English stock, grateful for the treasure of knowledge derived from their English ancestors, acknowledge also, with thanks and filial regard, that among those ancestors, under the culture of Hampden and Sidney, and other assiduous friends, that seed of popular liberty first germinated, which, on our soil, has shot up to its full height, until its branches overshadow the whole land." The author did not claim for America that it had repaid the debt to Europe by placing Europe under equal obligation, but that America had made some respectable advances toward equality. American contributions, he asserted, were not primarily literary or cultural, but moral and political. "America has furnished to Europe proof of the fact, that popular institutions, founded on equality and the principle of representation, are capable of maintaining governments . . . ; that it is practicable to elevate the mass of mankind, that portion which, in Europe, is called the laboring or lower class; to raise them to self-respect, to make them competent to act a part in the great right and great duty of self-government. She holds out an example . . . to those nine-tenths of the human race, who are born without hereditary fortune or hereditary rank." Thus McGuffey balanced the cultural indebtedness of the country with its political and social promise, the full realization of which would come from the West. "A double portion will be the lot of the interior because the foreign influences, which . . . vitiated this virtue cannot reach the heart of the continent where all that lives and moves is American." The *Readers* stressed America's mission and believed that the Union should, like the sun, "shed its glorious influence backward on the states of Europe and forward on the empires of Asia." Yet they strongly denounced wars and militarism, had their serious doubts about the wisdom and justice of the war against Mexico, and embraced in general the pacifist position.[28]

On the whole, the popular textbooks of the period did not stress or overstress American cultural achievements, but rather emphasized the political contribution of the American experiment to the common patrimony of modern mankind. Samuel Griswold Goodrich, who under the pen name Peter Parley wrote and published children's books and juvenile periodicals famous and widely read in their time, conceded that "there are doubtless other nations which surpass ours in certain refinements; but if we regard the general happiness of the great mass of the people, our country is without a rival. . . . We are sometimes spoken of as deficient in those elevating emotions which spring from the memories of the mighty past. This may be true, yet we have our compensation in the inspiring hopes presented by the brilliant prospects of the future." More lyrical was the enthusiasm of Jesse Olney, another author of very successful

textbooks. He transferred the humanitarian messianic hopes which
Michelet and Mazzini expressed in the decades preceding 1848 for
France and Italy, to the United States, where at last all the races
were meeting in brotherly cooperation and their varied energies
were being molded into one mighty and peaceful nation. There "the
various nations of Europe met to combine their efforts and gifts,
and to carry out the great principles of social, civil, and religious
liberties, on a grander scale than had yet been dreamt of in the
Eastern world. Thus tracing the geographical march of mankind
[from Asia to Europe to North America] we can say emphatically
Westward the Course of Freedom Takes its Way. . . . Here, for
the first time in human history, man will be truly *man*, developed
in all his powers, and enabled to realize the prophetic dream of his
infancy, and the growing hopes of his youth. Here shall be realized
the long prophesied, long expected *Golden Age,* which shall per-
fectly reconcile Order with Liberty, Individual Interests with the
General Good, and make Justice and Fraternity the supreme principles in the intercourse, as well of nations as of men." The arts of
freedom and peace will then spread to all mankind, even to the
deserts of Asia which will blossom with the fruit of the highest
culture. "Then shall commerce, no longer restricted by blind and
selfish monopolies, weave a golden chain of sympathy and com-
munion around our globe." To a degree rarely recognized, these
passionate and hopeful effusions of patriotic American writers only
reflected similar lyrical passages of universal benevolence and of the
coming age of the true emancipation of man written by a number
of European and especially French liberal and socialist writers at
the time.[29]

In the 1840's advocates of Americanism in literature agitated for
the support of American literature qua *American* literature, irrespective of its artistic values. Rufus Wilmot Griswold published
then widely-read anthologies which went through many editions,
The Poets and Poetry of America (1842), *The Prose Writers of
America* (1847) and, characteristic of America, *The Female Poets
of America* (1848). The reviewer of Griswold's first anthology in
the *North American Review* stressed its great importance to American patriotism. Horace Greeley made his *New York Tribune* a
mouthpiece not only for American nationalism in general but also
for American cultural nationalism. The *New Yorker,* a political

literary weekly edited by Greeley, gave every possible encouragement to American literature and proclaimed very minor and long since forgotten poets greatly superior to English poets. Only British national vanity could in Greeley's opinion explain British criticism of the pieces presented in Griswold's anthologies. When necessary, in the defense of American art, Greeley changed his position by claiming that if America had no great poetry yet, it was due to the fact that Americans were *acting* one of the grandest epics in human history. British royalty was a mere anachronism compared with American republicanism; Westminster Abbey was a barbaric profusion of carvings and groinings, sadly inferior to American places of worship; and the best that remained of Phidias and Praxiteles could not surpass, if, indeed, it could equal "Proserpine" and "Psyche," statues by Hiram Powers, a Vermonter of New England stock who lived in Florence and was a well known sculptor in his day. More justified were Greeley's statements that Europe had nothing like the McCormick Reaper, and that the French scythe was a foot shorter than its American counterpart.[30]

Few writers went as far as Herman Melville in his passionate defense of extreme American cultural nationalism. In 1850 when he was starting work on *Moby Dick*, he wrote a review of Hawthorne. In it, he turned against the "Anglophiles" among the American men of letters: "You must believe in Shakespeare's unapproachability or quit the country. But what sort of a belief is this for an American, a man who is bound to carry republican progressiveness into Literature, as well as into Life? Believe me, my friends, that men not very inferior to Shakespeare are this day being born on the banks of the Ohio. And the day will come when you shall say: who reads a book by an Englishman that is a modern? . . . Let America then prize and cherish her writers; yea, let her glorify them. . . . and while she has good kith and kin of her own, to take to her bosom, let her not lavish her embraces upon the household of an alien. . . . Even were there no strong literary individualities among us, as there are some dozen at least, nevertheless, let America first praise mediocrity even, in her own children, before she praises . . . the best excellence in the children of any other land. . . . While we are rapidly preparing for that political supremacy among the nations, which prophetically awaits us at the close of the present century, in a literary point of view we are deplorably unprepared for it, and

we seem studious to remain so." Melville called for the support of
those writers "who breathe the unshackled, democratic spirit of
Christianity in all things, which now takes a practical lead in this
world, though at the same time led by ourselves—as Americans." [31]

Poe certainly could not be called a writer who breathed the democratic spirit of Christianity in all things or who intended to carry
republican progressiveness into literature. In Melville's opinion was
he then an American writer? It is difficult and dangerous to try
to confine writers and artists to any narrow framework of Americanism. The wealth, variety and contrarieties of representative writers in the United States between the conclusion of the war against
Britain in 1815 and the beginning of the Civil War were astonish-
ingly great. This period of the formation of the American mind was
one of lively fermentation. Poe took a viewpoint opposite to Melville's. He was no cultural nationalist. He cherished the idea of
publishing a magazine called "The Stylus," which according to his
Prospectus was "to support the general interests of the republic of
letters" and to insist upon "regarding the world at large as the sole
proper audience of the author." In a review of an American poet,
Poe opined that "among all the *pioneers* of American literature,
whether prose or poetical, there is not *one* whose productions have
not been much over-rated by his countrymen." This over-rating, Poe
explained, was motivated by a blending of gratitude, surprise, and
a species of hyper-patriotic triumph in the minds of the American
readers. They had been hitherto in no frame of mind "to discuss with
discrimination the true claims of the few who were *first* in convincing the mother country that her sons were not all brainless as, in the
plenitude of her arrogance she, at one period, half affected and half
wished to believe." Poe was convinced that this uncritical attitude
on the part of the American public was changing, and this change
was due to the fact that there was no longer "either reason or wit
in the query,—who reads an American book? . . . We have, at
length, arrived at that epoch when our literature may and must stand
on its own merits, or fall through its own defects." [32]

Poe was in no way alone in insisting that the highest critical standards should, in their own interests, be applied to American writing
and art. A review of an address on art in the *North American Review*
stressed the same point. "Our taste in these things is not of national

origin," the author wrote. "We have hither to learn, and must long be content to learn, from older countries. . . . We have made more progress in years than other nations have in centuries, simply by adopting the fruits of their labors." The author advised the young American artist to go to Europe not only to study but to labor there long and hard, before he thought of returning to his country. "But one thing we repeat to him, and let him not forget it; no attainments which are not sufficient to support and raise him into notice in Europe, will save him from neglect at home. . . . We would by no means be illiberal to our own artists, who give any promise of excellence; but there is no propriety in encouraging them in false taste or mediocrity. We would hold high the standard of taste; as high as it is in any place. We would not have the arts degraded even in favor of the artists. And so far are we from approving of anything, which is said to discourage the importation of old and foreign paintings, that we wish still greater facilities were afforded for it. . . . We are not prepared to see the American system, as it is called, extended to literature or the arts." [33]

Starting from a point opposite to that of Poe, one of the pioneers of musical culture in America arrived at a similar rejection of a peculiarly American poetry and art. J. S. Dwight deeply affirmed the American political idea, which Poe rejected; yet in stark difference from the official poets and orators, he knew, and suffered from, the inherent contradictions and insufficiencies of American life. In a review of Griswold's *Poets and Poetry of America,* Dwight questioned whether American social life with its utilitarian spirit and its tyranny of public opinion did not discourage poetry. "No one, but the artist himself can conceive of the immense moral courage, which it costs to be an artist, a true one, in such a state of society. . . . We do not believe that there is, or can be in any circumstance, such a thing as a peculiarly *American* poetry. An American poetry would be a poetry which would breathe the spirit of our institutions, and that, if realized, should be purely human, wide, universal, and not merely patriotic and national. It is not the love of country, but the love of man, and the recognition of the spiritual equality of all men, which is the idea of our Constitution. But our Constitution is an ideal floating far above our heads, while our life is sordid in its motives, and narrow in its practical maxims; and love of power and

invidious distinction, and slavery to custom, so prevail, as to make
us all sadly conscious of the glaring inconsistency between profession and practice." [34]

In 1848–1849, when the European continent was shaken by the
stormy waves of nationalist unrest and when nationalist aspirations
dealt a severe blow to humanitarianism and liberalism, two representative American thinkers and poets took their stand in the debate
on American culture and nationalism. In the twentieth century
much of their former splendor as artists may have paled as a result
of changing tastes but they will retain their lasting significance as
voices of that humanitarian liberalism which was one of the outstanding traits of the English-speaking countries in the nineteenth
century. "If a man should ever be born among us," James Russell
Lowell wrote, "with a great imagination, and the gift of the right
word—for it is these, and not sublime spaces, that make a poet—he
will be original rather in spite of democracy than the consequence
of it, and will owe its inspiration as much to the accumulation of
the Old World as the promise of the New." Like the old Goethe, the
American man of letters stressed that "literature tends more and
more to become a vast commonwealth with no dividing lines of
nationality." [35] In Longfellow's story *Kavanagh,* published in 1849,
a Mr. Hathaway called on the schoolmaster, Mr. Churchill, to ask
for his cooperation in founding a literary periodical that would raise
the character of American literature. Hathaway defended the view
of American cultural nationalism. "In all events," he said, "let us
have our literature national. If it is not national, it is nothing." This
national literature, Hathaway demanded, must express the unique
American landscape and character, primitive and without parallel,
shaggy and unshorn, a literature which would make the earth shake
like a herd of buffaloes thundering over the prairies. The schoolmaster was skeptical of this vision of a national literature. Quietly
he pointed out that a literature may be greater for not being national. "Nationality is a good thing to a certain extent, but uni-
versality is better." Nor did he believe that great American scenery
would necessarily shape great literature. "Literature is rather an
image of the spiritual world than of the physical, . . . A man will
not necessarily be a great poet because he lives near a great moun-
tain. Nor being a poet, will he necessarily write better poems because
he lives nearer Niagara."

American nationalist writers have long accused Longfellow of being a writer too little shaggy and unshorn, too much indebted to Old World traditions. But Whitman was ready to defend him against the "ungracious charges of his want of racy nativity and special originality," by saying "that America and the world may well be reverently thankful—can never be thankful enough—for any such singing-bird vouchsafed out of centuries." He added that he had heard Longfellow himself say that ere the New World could be worthy to produce an original literature, she must be well saturated with the originality of others. Henry James, so different from Whitman, shared his admiration for Longfellow. He found the Cambridge poet "perhaps interesting for nothing so much as for the secret of his harmony . . . and for the way in which his 'European' culture and his native kept house together." Did Longfellow owe this harmony, James added, "to his having worked up his American consciousness to that mystic point—one of those of which poets alone have the secret—at which it could feel nothing but continuity and congruity with his European? I put the question—for all it is worth—without quite seeing how it is to be answered, and in fact merely as a manner of recording an individual impression of something in its liberal existence that was like a fine (in those days, at Cambridge, Massachusetts, a delightful) ambiguity! If it seemed a piece of the Old World smoothly fitted into the new, so it might quite as well have been a piece of the new fitted, just as intimately, into the old." [36]

Longfellow's *Kavanagh* formed the starting point for Lowell's discussion of the general problem of "Nationalism in Literature." Politically, Lowell was in no way an Anglophile. In 1848 he published anonymously his lusty stocktaking of, and plea for, an American national literature, "A Fable for Critics," in which he called upon American writers,

> Forget Europe wholly, your veins throb with blood,
> To which the dull current in hers is but mud; . . .
> O my friends, thank your god if you have one, that he
> Twixt the Old World and you sets a gulf of a sea; . . .
> To your own New-World instincts contrive to be true, . . .

In the same Fable, he aptly analyzed the psychological parent-offspring relationship between England and America:

There are truths you Americans need to be told,
And it never'll refute them to swagger and scold;
John Bull, looking o'er the Atlantic in choler
At your aptness for trade, says you worship the dollar; . . .
No matter what John says, don't try to outcrow him,
'Tis enough to go quietly on and outgrow him;
Like most fathers, Bull hates to see Number One
Displacing himself in the mind of his son,
And detests the same faults in himself he'd neglected
When he sees them again in his child's glass reflected;
To love one another you're too like by half;
If he is a bull, you're a pretty stout calf,
And tear your own pasture for naught but to show
What a nice pair of horns you're beginning to grow.[37]

But in his review of *Kavanagh,* published the following year, Lowell approached the whole problem of literary and cultural nationalism in its application to the United States in a much more searching and fundamental way. "The feeling that it was absolutely necessary to our respectability that we should have a literature has been a material injury to such as we have had," he wrote. "The Stamp Act and the Boston Port Bill scarcely produced a greater excitement in America than the appalling question, Who reads an American book? . . . It is only geographically that we can call ourselves a new nation. However else our literature may avoid the payment of its liabilities, it can surely never be by a plea of infancy. Intellectually, we were full-grown at the start. . . . Mere nationality is no more nor less than so much provincialism, and will be found but a treacherous antiseptic for any poem. . . . Literature survives, not because of its nationality, but in spite of it. After the United States had achieved their independence, it was forthwith decided, that they could not properly be a nation without a literature of their own. As if we had been without one! As if Shakespeare, sprung from the race and the class which colonized New England, had not been also ours! As if we had no share in the puritan and republican Milton, we who had cherished in secret for more than a century the idea of the great puritan effort, and at last embodied it in a living commonwealth; but this ownership in common was not enough for us, and, as partition was out of the question, we must have a drama and an epos of our own. It must be national, too, we must have it all to ourselves. . . . We are still requested by critics, both native and foreign, to produce a national literature, as if it were some school exercise in composition to be handed in by a certain day. The sharp struggle of a day or a year may settle the question of a nation's political independence, but even for that, there must be a long moral preparation. Jefferson was not the prophet looking forth into the future, but the scribe sitting at the feet of the past. . . . The English mind has always been characterized by an emigrating tendency. [Its] most truly national epic was the colonizing of America. . . . Let us not tolerate in our criticism a principle which would operate as a prohibitory tariff of ideas. . . . It detracts nothing from Chaucer that we can trace in him the influence of Dante and Boccaccio; . . . nothing from Milton that he brought fire from Hebrew and Greek altars. There is no degradation in such indebtedness. Venerable rather is this apostolic succession, and inspiring to see *vitai lampada* passed thus consecrated from hand to hand.

"Nationality, then, is only a less narrow form of provincialism, a sublimer sort of clownishness and ill manners. Yet so universal a demand must have for its basis a more or less solid sub-stratum of truth. . . . It is neither more nor less than this, that authors should use their own eyes and ears, and not those of other people. . . . That art in America will be modified by circumstances, we have no doubt, though it is impossible to predict the precise form of the moulds into which it will run. New conditions of life will stimulate thought and give new forms to its expression. It may not be our destiny to produce a great literature, as, indeed, our genius seems to find its kindliest development in practicalizing simpler and more perfect forms of social organization. . . . Our spirit of adventure will take first a material and practical direction but will gradually be forced to seek outlet and scope in unoccupied territories of the intellect. In the meantime we may fairly demand of our literature that it should be national to the extent of being as free from outworn conventionalities and as thoroughly impregnated with humane and manly sentiment as is the idea on which our political fabric rests." [38]

The close interrelation between the mother country and the growing young giant across the Atlantic expressed itself not only in literary dependence and dispute. American philanthropists, reformist and religious movements consciously followed the pattern set by similar British endeavors which mostly antedated their American counterparts. For example, the British and Foreign Bible Society, founded in 1804 and one of the most remarkable enterprises radiating the British spirit in the nineteenth century, was followed by the establishment of the American Bible Society in New York in 1816. The first Bible Society in America was founded in Philadelphia as early as the end of 1808 to distribute the Scripture to every part of the continent. To this end, the British Society sent a donation in money and a supply of Bibles in Welsh, Gaelic, French and German, versions which at that time could not be obtained in the States. By May, 1816, when the American Bible Society was founded, thirty-one local societies were already in existence; they were, as in Britain, interdenominational and thus represented one of the elements in cementing national cohesion. The annual report of the American Society for 1838 stated that "We have, indeed, the secondary praise, but still the praise of treading in the footsteps of those who have set an example without a parallel—an example of the most unbounded benevolence and beneficence; and it cannot be for us any source of pain, that it has been set by those who are of one blood with the most of ourselves; and has been embodied in a form so noble and so catholic as the British and Foreign Bible Society." [39]

Continental European visitors participated too in the great debate of those decades about American national culture. At the very same time when Tocqueville traveled in the United States, an unhappy romantic German poet, Nikolaus Lenau, an artist haunted by dreams and demons, joined a group of immigrants to establish a pioneer settlement in the wilderness on the banks of the Missouri River. He came filled with enchanting images and illusionist hopes about the healing force of virgin nature and the magic power of the paradise of liberty. Naturally, within a few months, he suffered bitterest disillusionment. The hypersensitive soul which could not adapt itself to the normal hazards of life in his native land could stand even less the barrenness and rigors of the American frontier. "America is the true country of the setting of civilization, mankind's West," he lamented in a letter to a friend. "The Atlantic Ocean isolates America from all spiritual and higher life." [40] Yet in his letters the unhappy poet paid an indirect compliment to America. He complained bitterly that practically all German immigrants got acclimated so quickly to their new home that they desired to stay there and gladly forgot their German fatherland. Lenau fervently wished to escape this "danger." Thus he left America within one year, convinced that in this doomed land everything was inevitably running to seed and that "men and animals must be declining from generation to generation." He characterized American life and institutions both culturally and politically as typical examples of *Bodenlosigkeit*, lack of rootedness in the soil, or nomadism. "One should not think that the American loves his fatherland or that he has a fatherland. Every single individual lives and works in that republican association, because, and only as long as, his private fortunes are secured by it. What we call a fatherland, is here only an insurance company for one's property. The American does not know anything else but money, he doesn't seek anything else but money; he has no idea, therefore, the state is not for him a spiritual or moral institution, a fatherland, but only a material convention." Lenau's effusions influenced Ferdinand Kürnberger, a Viennese novelist and essayist, whose "portrayal of American culture," as he himself called his novel *Der Amerikamüde*, was widely read in Germany in the second half of the nineteenth century and accepted as a valid picture of American life.[41]

Though Lenau and Kürnberger greatly influenced the image which Germans formed of America, other German intellectuals of the period judged American life and culture with greater objectivity. Karl Postl, an Austrian who emigrated to the United States and wrote a number of books under the pseudonym Charles Sealsfield, had the opportunity of observing conditions in America from close range. Like most Americans, he too frequently complained about the corruption of the American political idea in actual life. But America with its republican institutions impressed him as the supreme human achievement, and during the final years of his life which he spent in Europe he remained unwaveringly loyal to his American ideal. "We have to look towards America," he wrote, "because this means to look towards the future of mankind." When he died in Switzerland, he proudly signed his last will "Charles Sealsfield, citizen of the United States," and wished these words inscribed on his tombstone. Like Sealsfield, Julius Fröbel, who after the failure of the German revolution of 1848 spent eight years in the United States, arrived at a balanced appreciation of American cultural life and its complexities. Describing his travels in the States in 1850, Fröbel spoke of attending in Washington a lecture on geology by William Barton Rogers. There he found an audience of more than one thousand persons of both sexes, seriously interested in a scientific and "dry" subject. Fröbel was deeply impressed by this fact and was convinced that no parallel could be found either among the German immigrants in America or anywhere at that time in Germany itself. He was equally impressed by his meeting with Peter Force, an archivist who collected documents important to American history from its origins to 1789. Fröbel remarked that no other nation had then any similar collection of source material at its disposal for the understanding and study of its own history. There may be less philosophizing in the United States than in Germany, Fröbel wrote, but there is more genuine desire for knowledge without the pretentious airs so frequently found in Europe.[42]

Many foreign observers of America noticed, of course, the apparent disorders, the turbulence of American life, and its open or hidden corruptions. But nobody could have castigated these shortcomings more freely than the Americans themselves. The Americans share with the British the fundamental trait of being often more smug and complacent than other peoples and yet at the same time they are more self-critical and beset by sharp and even over-sharp pangs of conscience. The English and the Americans often outphilistine other civilized people—Matthew Arnold's charge that the English underestimate esthetic values could as well be directed against the Americans—but hardly has there been in recent history any other people filled with such an earnest and persistent zeal for reform and such an acute sense of social responsibility as these two nations. Perhaps the religious and mainly Evangelical source of modern civil life in the English-speaking peoples accounts both for the frequent self-righteousness and for the deep impulse to self-questioning and moral uplift. Therefore, the bitter struggle of religion against irreligion, the burning issue of anti-clericalism, so characteristic of other Western nations since the eighteenth century, has never played a great role in England or in the United States, where religion has been on the whole liberal, broad, and practical, not an "opium" of the people, but a strong active force behind most of the reform and humanitarian movements. The British and American critics of their own peoples frequently overstated their case: they were often more conscious of a defect at home than of an evil abroad. Thoreau represented this spirit of self-criticism as did Carl Schurz, who in many ways bore witness to the assimilating power of the Anglo-American tradition. In a patriotic oration at the Centenary of the Declaration of Independence, certainly an occasion for a self-congratulatory mood, Schurz voiced this feeling of self-reproach and humiliation. Surveying the history of the one hundred years, he maintained that "with all these splendid results on record, it cannot be denied that at no period during the century now behind us the American people have been less satisfied with themselves." One decade after the successful termination of the most destructive war in American history and the re-establishment of the Union, in the midst of great economic progress, Schurz stressed that "never was there cause for keener mortification." He contrasted the virtues of the past with the shocking evidence of the demoralization and corruption of the present, the eulogies on the wisdom and purity of the Fathers with the verdict of courts that illustrated the political morals of today. In his moral earnestness, Schurz overlooked the fact that the past had not been so pure and virtuous as he imagined and the present was not so corrupt as he insisted. During the whole span of American history the complaint which he so eloquently raised in 1876 could have been uttered—and has been uttered—with more or less equal justification.[43]

At the time when the debate over an American national literature approached its end, its fervor once more gained a mighty, and perhaps its mightiest voice in Walt Whitman. His poetry claimed to be and appeared at times shaggy and unshorn, comparable to the herds of buffaloes spreading over the prairies and shaking the earth with portentous thunder. Yet what seemed simple as a declaration of nativism and democracy, was always elusive, secretive, a highly personalized art, and full of paradoxes and contradictions, which remained alien to the people and had little touch with American reality—as little as the herds of buffaloes had. Throughout his life Whitman was preoccupied with four great themes which he confounded—Himself, the Poet, the States, and Mass Democracy in the age of Science; his writing was an attempt to reveal and at the same time to hide the reality behind these themes. The man who celebrated the feeling of *en masse*, of democratic and nationalist togetherness, lived a life of isolation and non-communication outside the ties which link man to society through family, home and profession. He liked to sing of himself as the "average man," yet he was a most singular and solitary personality, hardly recognizable to the people of his land. At the age of twenty-eight, in 1847, he published in the *Brooklyn Daily Eagle* (one of the many newspapers in which he collaborated in his early manhood) an article called "Independent American Literature," in which he pleaded for a strictly native culture. He took up the same theme eight years later in the preface to the first edition of *Leaves of Grass*. Into this he poured without any restraint, his faith in himself, in the poet, in the United States. No longer young, but still unknown, he proclaimed confidently the supremacy of the objects of his faith and self-veneration. "Of all the nations, the United States, with veins full of poetical stuff, most needs poets and will doubtless have the greatest and use them the greatest. Their Presidents shall not be the common referee so much as their poets shall. Of all mankind, the great poet is the equable man." In the age of American democracy, Whitman insisted —against all the evidence of American reality—that poets would take the place of priests and would be the prophets of the new age. "There will soon be no more priests. Their work is done. They may wait a while . . . perhaps a generation or two . . . dropping off by degrees. A superior breed shall take their place . . . the gangs of kosmos and prophets en masse shall take their place. A new order shall arise and they shall be the priests of man, and every man shall be his own priest." Pontificating thusly about the poet as prophet in the age of the new man, Whitman was hardly conscious that he was paraphrasing similar sentiments expressed a decade before among European intellectuals. The Average American man and woman, in whose name Whitman thought to speak, had little use for his work. *Leaves of Grass*, which Whitman intended to be the answer to the quest for an American national poem, and on which he continued to work to the last month of his life in 1892, did not become truly popular. A work of universal importance, it never was accepted as a national classic. Its fate revealed the tragic implications of the quest for an American national literature and language. In the preface to the second edition of *Leaves of Grass* (1856) Whitman acknowledged that the "huge English flow so sweet, so undeniable, has done incalculable good here, and is to be spoken of for its own sake with generous praise and gratitude. Yet the price the States have had

to lie under for the same has not been a small price. America, grandest of lands in the theory of its politics, in popular reading, in hospitality, breadth, animal beauty, cities, ships, machines, money,
credit, collapses quick as lightning at the repeated, admonishing,
stern words, Where are any mental expressions from you, beyond
what you have copied or stolen?" In his frenzied quest for a national literature, Whitman could go to extremes of shrillness in his
demand for the true poet-prophet as leader of a new race. "Strangle
the singers who will not sing you loud and strong! Open the doors
of the West! Call for new great masters who comprehend new arts,
new perfections, new wants! Submit to the most robust bard till he
remedy your barrenness! Then you will not need to adopt the airs of
others; you will have true airs, begotted of yourself, blooded with
your own blood."

In his later years Whitman fell from his dionysiac praise of American democracy into an overacute awareness of its imperfections and
unfulfillments. At times the separation of the United States from
the rest of the world, its uniqueness, receded from his vision more
and more before the common tie of humanity. In *A Backward
Glance o'er Travel'd Roads,* which he wrote in 1888, in the "candle-
light of old age," he confessed that he had not been understood by
his generation. He now put all his hopes into the future. He looked
upon *Leaves of Grass* as his *carte de visite* to the coming generations
of the New World, as a fond dream or a daring anticipation. He no
longer claimed to be the poet representing the nation in a better and
more fitting way than any president could, but he saw himself as the
prophet of a distant and no longer only national future. The dog-
matism of his youth mellowed into the knowledge that *Leaves of
Grass* and its theory were experimental. He knew himself face to
face with a broader challenge: "I've unwittingly taken up," he
wrote, "the challenge of the modern age of science and democracy,"
an age which was not confined to the United States, and the roots
of which did not even lie in the United States. He acknowledged
that "the ferment and germination even of the United States today,
were dating back to, and in my opinion mainly founded on, the
Elizabethan age in English history, the age of Francis Bacon and
Shakespeare." In an essay, "Poetry Today in America," originally
published under the title, "Poetry of the Future" (1881), Whitman
called the States "the children of past precedence, and young as they

are, heirs of a very old estate. . . . Years ago I thought Americans ought to strike out separate, and have expressions of their own in highest literature. I think so still, and more decidedly than ever. But those convictions are strongly temper'd by some additional points. I see that this world of the West, as part of all, fuses inseparably with the East. If we are not to hospitably receive and complete the inaugurations of the old civilizations, and change their small scale to the largest, broadest scale, what on earth are we for? . . . Indeed, the peculiar glory of our land I have come to see not in their geographical republican greatness . . . but more and more in the vaster, saner, more surrounding Comradeship, uniting closer and closer not only the American states, but all nations and all humanity. That O poets! is not that a theme worth chanting, striving for? Why not fix your verses henceforth to the gauge of the round globe? the whole race?"

Yet in the last words of his *A Backward Glance o'er Travel'd Roads* the old poet returned to the extravagant and obsessive nationalism of his younger years. "I say that no land or people or circumstances ever existed so needing the race of singers and poems differing from all others, and rigidly their own, as the land and people and circumstances of our United States needs such singers and poems today, and for the future." Strangely enough, the prophet of the New World re-iterated the gospel of cultural nationalism as first devised in the Old World by Herder and accepted this Old World legacy as guide "for the imaginative genius of the West,"—he wished to be guided, as he said, by the doctrine which Herder taught to the young Goethe—that really great poetry was always the result of a national spirit. This doctrine of German romantic nationalism which looked to the past and to primitive rural folk Whitman wished to apply to the new democratic West in the age of science. Yet Whitman apparently did not notice that Goethe became the great representative poet for the very reason that he outgrew the teachings of Herder and rejected all cultural nationalism. Then and then alone Goethe made German literature classical and universal, a light of world importance. The American poet who in his young years had thought to express and vitalize American cultural nationality never grew to fulness and clarity; he knew in his last years that he had failed: for comfort he looked to the future, convinced that the imaginative genius of the West had not yet worthily risen, "that the strongest and sweetest songs yet remained to be sung." They may never be sung in the way that Whitman foresaw them. Yet with all his failings and obscurities Whitman remains the most significant poet in the America of the nineteenth century, though he does not represent it. There is a streak of genius in him—through this very streak he rises like every genius above national limitations and opens up new paths for human sensitivity and self-expression.[44]

In his cosmic-enthusiastic and fervently utopian poetry and prose —the two are often indistinguishable in Whitman—the American poet rhapsodized in a spirit typical of the democratic movements in continental Europe of 1848, about his own and his country's mission. In *Democratic Vistas*, written in 1871, Whitman found—not without justice and discernment—in John Stuart Mill's profound essay on Liberty, the essence of modern European and American life; yet he himself showed even then none of the responsible sobriety and clarity that characterized the famous essay. In *Democratic Vistas* Whitman painted a bitter picture of American democracy, of the people's crudeness, vice, caprices. "Never was there, perhaps, more hollowness at heart than at present, and here in the United States," he cried out. "The spectacle is appalling. We live in an atmosphere of hypocrisy throughout. The depravity of the business classes of our country is not less than has been supposed, but infinitely greater. The official services of America are saturated in corruption, bribery, falsehood, mal-administration. Confess that everywhere, in shop, street, church, theater, bar-room, official chair, are pervading flippancy and vulgarity, low cunning, infidelity—everywhere the youth puny, impudent, foppish, prematurely ripe—everywhere an abnormal libidinousness, . . . with a range of manners, or rather lack of manners, probably the meanest to be seen in the world." To this disheartening and overdone portrayal of blackest and bleakest American reality the poet opposed the utopia of a resplendent luminous future without parallel. This vision was not without its strong imperial and material aspects: "Long ere the second centennial arrives, there will be some forty to fifty great states, among them Canada and Cuba. The Pacific will be ours, and the Atlantic mainly ours. What a land! Where, elsewhere, one so great? The individuality of one nation must then, as always, lead the world. Can there be any doubt who the leader ought to be?" But material greatness was in no way enough. "Nothing less than the mightiest original non-

subordinated SOUL has ever really, gloriously led, or ever can lead."
Naturally this mightiest soul of all times was to be America. No
longer did the notion prevail of an America of self-contained, self-
directed individuals which Whitman had learned from, and originally shared with, Emerson. It was superseded or complemented
by the much more grandiose vision of a national power-soul, and
this soul's other name to Whitman was LITERATURE. How could such
a miracle arise out of the bleak image of American democracy which
Whitman had described? The answer was simple: The United States
and the world stood in great need of "the divine literatus, the poet
of the modern," a sacerdotal figure, a philosopher king. This leadership, Whitman proclaimed, would inaugurate the new era. "I demand a race of orbic bards, with unconditional uncompromising
sway. Come forth, sweet democratic despots of the west!"

While Whitman thus followed the wild flight of inspirational German metaphysics, he did less than justice to the actual life of American democracy, to its present reality with all its often sordid struggles and its ever alive sense of self-criticism and self-improvement,
with its subterfuges and evasions and shams, but also its broad mind
and open heart and free interplay of human energies. Whitman
was a great poet of the mysteries of life, and a man full of fascinat-
ing temptations; but he often succumbed to nationalist mysticism
and sacrificed his poetic genius to it. In his later years he was honored by a small and devoted group of followers as the bard of a new
"religion" of democracy. He exercised a deeper influence abroad
than in the United States. He was never fully accepted by his fellow
Americans. Mazzini in Italy, Treitschke in Germany, Dostoevsky in
Russia, were representative of mighty currents in the thought of their
nations, widely recognized and cherished, in a sense in which Whitman never was. His vision of the mighty soul of America, of the
grandiose role of the poet and literatus ran counter to the common
sense, the responsible realism of American democracy. When not
seized by the divine spirit of lyrical prophecy, Whitman too could
share this common sense. In his old age, when asked his opinion of
the protectionist policy of America for the Americans, he answered,
"We are all like fellows in a ship: what jeopardizes one, jeopardizes
all. . . . The attempt at what they call protection, and all that
goes to boost up and wall up and protect out . . . is wrong, and one

feeling for all, extreme reciprocity and openness and free-trade-ism is the policy for me." [45]

The *Leaves of Grass* appeared in the last years before the Civil War; it marks in many ways the climax and the fast approaching end of the great debate about American cultural nationalism. The ability of the Union to wage the long and terrible Civil War and to emerge strengthened and intact from its physical and moral torments enhanced American national self-confidence. The people knew that their independence—political, economic and cultural—was no longer at stake. Thus after 1861 the community of the English language as an inalienable part of American national culture was hardly any longer disputed. Walt Whitman, who regarded his poetry also in the light of an experimental quest for a purely American language, acknowledged in the 1855 preface to *Leaves of Grass* that "The English language befriends the grand American expression. . . . On the tough stock of the race who through all change of circumstances was never without the idea of political liberty, it has attracted the terms of daintier and gayer and subtler and more elegant tongues. It is a powerful language of resistance . . . it is the dialect of common sense." In the last decades before the Civil War, the large-scale Teutonic immigration endangered locally the dominant position of the English language and the Anglo-American cultural community. German and Scandinavian were the native languages spoken throughout the newly opened upper Mississippi valley, the future heart of the nation. After the Civil War, a large influx of English immigrants changed the situation. "It is surprising," one of the foremost historians of American immigration wrote, "that the English, who have contributed the most to American culture, have been studied the least by students of immigration. There is no English-American historical society, no separate history of the English thought."

But this fact is not so surprising. The far-reaching identity of English and American traditions makes such a study well nigh impossible. An English immigrant, even after the colonial period, melted with great ease, "naturally," into the life of the neighborhood. "It is a commonplace of American history," the same historian, himself of Scandinavian descent, pointed out, "that in the last quarter of the century an English vogue characterized all ranks of the people.

This circumstance has been variously ascribed to the happy diplomatic relations then prevailing, to the growth of a native aristocracy which looked abroad for its standards, the personal popularity of the Queen, to the increasing tourist pilgrimages to the shrines of English history and liberty. Evidences of this vogue were most conspicuous in the cities, but the admiration for things English was not restricted to such bounds. The Norwegian novelist Knut Hamsun believed he was a competent judge of artistic and cultural matters, yet in the Wisconsin village where he sojourned his opinion counted for nought if an Englishman were present. If you want to compliment an American, he wrote (in 1889), "tell him that you mistook him for an Englishman. So far did the prestige of the country of origin go that, among old and young alike, the tone of society was established by the usages that the English newcomer sanctioned." [46]

By the end of the century the difficult relationship between "mother" and "daughter" began to crystallize into mutual recognition. For the daughter's own sake, the mother's beauty was acknowledged: in language and literature, in law and political traditions, the United States came from good stock. Witnessing the growth of an offspring who had first appeared to be negligible, to ever greater power, not only materially but in the realms of the mind too, the mother recognized the need and value of a close interdependence of the older member with the younger. An Anglo-American friendship which seemed most improbable at the beginning of the nineteenth century had become a reality at the beginning of the twentieth century, a fellowship never defined or circumscribed by words or formula and yet more alive than any legal tie could ever make it. Such a relationship could endure despite recurring jealousies and suspicions, despite real or imagined conflicts of interests. It has become one of the few permanent elements in the rapidly shifting scene of the twentieth century world.

As a young man, George Henry Boker, a Philadelphia patrician, poet and patriot, foresaw this later development in a cycle of seven sonnets "To England," which he wrote in the period between the great London Exhibition of 1851 and the outbreak of the Crimean War. In one of these sonnets the two countries were compared to Lear and Cordelia. Once Cordelia went away, like an outcast, dowerless and pale, and in a foreign land spread her young banner,

till its sway became a wonder to the nations. But now with the growing threats to England's power, which Boker foresaw,

> When the rude Cossack with an outstretched hand
> Points his long spear across the narrow sea,—

England might stand one day like Lear, and Boker prayed that then

> God grant thy daughter a Cordelia be!

Years later Boker told a friend that he had a singular experience
with this sonnet: "I once heard it recited by Daniel Webster. He
led the conversation to our relations with England, and then—to
my utter amazement—turning to me and fixing his black eyes on
me, he said: 'I think you, Mr. Boker, have expressed the true sentiment concerning the subject in that admirable sonnet of yours.' And
then he began 'Lear and Cordelia' in a great resonant voice, and
went on to recite the thing letter-perfect." [47]

The Boker-Webster mood of 1851 has not been borne out in the
intervening century; neither has England been reduced to the tragic
position of King Lear nor has the daughter country shown the mod-
esty and loveliness of Cordelia. More truly prophetic was another
sonnet by Boker, which could easily have been recalled by the generation which lived through the anxious months of the spring and
summer of 1940.

> Stand, thou great bulwark of man's liberty! . . .
> . . . Britons, ye
> Who guard the sacred outpost, not in vain
> Hold your proud peril! Freemen undefiled;
> Keep watch and ward! Let battlements be piled
> Around your cliffs; fleets marshalled, till the main
> Sink under them; and if your courage wane,
> Through force or fraud, look westward to your child!

The apprehensions which Francis Parkman, the famous historian
of the West, expressed in 1852 while reviewing the works of James
Fenimore Cooper have proved to be unfounded. He feared that the
"bounteous source" of English literature pouring across the Atlantic
might stifle American self-expression, and suggested that the complete cutting off of this transatlantic supply might promote the de-

velopment of the American national mind.[48] Half a century later American literature—very soon followed by all the other arts, music, painting and sculpture, the theater and the ballet—entered a period of effervescence, of dynamic vigor and originality, of great personalities and lasting works of a striking range and diversity, at least equal to any contemporary literature and civilization. Accordingly its influence grew rapidly in the four corners of the world. American libraries, both scholarly and public, research facilities, and learned writing were assuming a foremost rank. So were American orchestras and museums. American letters and art lost their last vestiges of provincialism. The very same generation which discovered, and fully made its own, the most advanced movements in European literature and arts, discovered "Our America" and proclaimed "America's Coming of Age." Because there was an American culture of undisputable quality, the anxious questions about its possibility lost their urgency. Yet as recently as 1938 an American poet could state that whereas no Englishman ever needed to ask of a given work in his own language, But is it really English? we in America "for a hundred years have continually felt obliged to ask of this or that American work: But is it really American? Does it represent the nation? And we have never ceased to be embarrassed at our inability to produce a really satisfactory answer."[49] But no satisfactory answer can or needs be given.

The search for such an answer was attempted sporadically in the more aggressive temper of nationalism which characterized the turn of the century and the coming of the two great wars. At that time, in many continental European countries, both literary movements and youth movements arose which stressed an irrational vitalism and often a nationalism of folk and soil, strengthened by a pseudo-Nietzschean insistence on the primacy of esthetic values and rejection of the cultural traditions and moral standards of the past. It was an age of transition, of revolt, and of a new intensity in literature, especially poetry. America did not escape this general current, though the radicalization of the intellectual climate did not go so far as in continental Europe. One example of this new temper was afforded by Hamlin Garland, who spent his youth in the bleakness of a Middle-Border prairie farm. In *Crumbling Idols* he fused Midwestern populist nativism with the lyrical assertion of American democracy in the tradition of Walt Whitman. A man of moral earnestness, reforming zeal and little formal education, Garland, like all American hypernationalists and their corresponding counterparts in continental Europe, was anti-English. He proclaimed the coming of the mightiest civilization the world has known, not from drawing-room culture or from the educated classes, but from youth and the common man. Characteristically, Garland saw hope only in "young nations" like Germany and Norway, which represented the wave of the future because they were not "so deeply enslaved to the moral and cultural heritage of the past as England is." A true American literature could find its home, Garland believed, only in the Middle West, "this broad, free inland America of ours," which was not dominated by English ideas as was the Eastern seaboard.[50]

A younger, more gifted and more radical writer, Randolph Bourne, continued this line of thought. He was a pacifist and an anarchist but he could sound as fiercely nationalistic as did the writers of the *Democratic Review* in the first half of the nineteenth century. "Our cultural humility before the civilization of Europe is the chief obstacle which prevents us from producing any true indigenous culture of our own," he wrote during the First World War. "The only remedy for this deplorable situation is the cultivation of a new American nationalism. . . . This cultural chauvinism . . . can hardly be too intense or too exaggerated. . . . When shall we learn that 'culture' like the kingdom of heaven lies within us, in the heart of our national soul, not in foreign galleries and books? When shall we learn to be proud? For only pride is creative." Though the kingdom of heaven may well lie within us, within each individual soul, no Christian ever maintained that it lies in the heart of our or any other national soul. Nor is culture, with or without quotation marks, at home in the heart of national souls; it lives in great works, in galleries and books, in moral deeds and disinterested reasoning, whether "foreign" or "native." Cultural chauvinism as expressed by Garland and Bourne was rare in the United States at the beginning of the twentieth century. Yet it contained an element that was inextricably woven into the web of missionary American nationalism, so perceptible in the First World War. It had its dual and equivocal aspects. It lived in Woodrow Wilson's idealistic message and its opposition to the supposedly narrower, more self-seeking nationalisms and imperialisms of Britain and of Old Europe. This idealism proudly turned away from the woes of the past and the experiences of an

apparently decaying world and knew itself as the harbinger of a
new and brighter future. It believed itself to be closer to the true
heart of the common people, in America and everywhere. Yet in
its other aspect this nationalism lived equally in the isolationist
repudiation of Wilson's missionary idea, a repudiation carried largely
by midwestern populism, which led to America's withdrawal into
a holier-than-thou attitude in which the idealism could turn cynical
and dissolve into a self-congratulatory orgy of high living.[51]

One of the strongholds against American cultural nationalism,
against all national chauvinism, were the American colleges. In central and eastern Europe, and later in Asia, universities—students and
teachers alike—were generally the breeding ground of aggressive
and extremist nationalist movements. The American colleges, on the
other hand, remained on the whole bulwarks of liberal civilization,
of an open mind, of transatlantic cultural contacts. American scholars
were very rarely chauvinists. American historians were frequently
highly self-critical as far as America was concerned. This liberal
spirit characterized also the field of literature. "Almost every history
of American literature from the 60s to 1913 . . . not only insisted
upon measuring American writers by British standards, but also
claimed that American literature was a branch of English letters."
American educators started with the belief—to quote from a widely
used *Introduction to American Literature* published in 1898—that
American letters were "the continuation of English literature within
the limits of what has become the United States, by people English
in their speech, English to a considerable extent by inheritance, and
English in the original character of their civilization." [52] The first
important historian of American literature, Moses Coit Tyler, characteristically chose the literature of the Anglo-American colonies
before their separation from the motherland as the theme of his
great work.[53]

In the 1880's when the study of modern languages and literature
emerged as equal, and soon superior, to classical studies in the cur-
ricula of American colleges, American literature played hardly any
role. English philology occupied the central position. At the beginning of the century courses in American literature were occasionally
offered; in 1917, when the United States entered the First World
War, there were only two chairs for American literature in American universities. Since then, the study of American literature has

steadily grown into a great branch of scholarship, equal to its older sisters and following therein no nationalist trend but the magnificent development of American letters and civilization. Yet its teaching still remains in all American colleges part of the offerings of the English department.

This Anglo-American community of letters had been strengthened in the second half of the nineteenth century by the then wide-spread acceptance of the "Germanic" theory. The English historian Edward Augustus Freeman, lecturing before American audiences in 1881, taught the theory then generally shared by leading American literary and general historians, that the tradition of liberty was of Teutonic origin. The two great branches of the Germanic race which became the English people, "those who made only their first voyage from the European mainland to a European island and those who made the further voyage from that European island to the American mainland," according to this theory, brought their liberty with them from Germany and developed it in their new homes. The two peoples, now geographically and politically divided for the last hundred years, continued a parallel history after thirteen centuries of common history. "Whatever is ours is yours also. Whatever belongs to the older England in the European island belongs no less to the younger England on the American mainland. . . . Some might say that the likeness is the likeness between parent and child; I would rather call it the likeness of a man at one stage of his growth and the same man at some earlier or later stage." [54]

This Germanic theory has long been abandoned in England and in the United States. It thought to find the birthplace of liberty in the virgin forests of ancient Germany. It hardly explained why modern liberty has been so little known and so little appreciated in nineteenth century Germany. It widely underestimated the decisive share of seventeenth century England in laying the foundations of modern liberty. At that time England was no longer a Saxon land, its inhabitants were not simply descendants of those Anglo-Saxons who so many centuries ago had crossed the North Sea. Seventeenth century England represented a happy blending of racial strains and cultural influences, Roman and Celtic, Saxon and Viking, Norman and French, to mention only the most important ones. Out of this melting pot a united and distinct nation emerged, with its own independent character and with an ordered government based on individual liberty as its greatest indigenous achievement. The growth of English letters and art was not indigenous in this sense: it would have been unthinkable without classical, Italian and French influences and models; what England learned and owed in these fields it repaid by setting the example of civil liberty.

An Anglo-Saxon theory was even less applicable to the United States than to England. Men of mixed British and English stock formed the foundation on which the structure of American life has been raised, but many other races and ethnic stocks have helped to build and perfect the structure. It is held together not by blood and not by a distant past reaching back over many centuries, but by a living development, by the all-pervading vitality of the English tradition of an ordered government based on individual liberty.

The ties of language and of spiritual and political traditions are much stronger than differences of geographic environment or of race: through language and traditions, the roots of which go back to England, men of African and of East European, of Mediterranean and of Scandinavian descent became indissolubly members of one cultural and spiritual community, in every essential trait of their life different from their ethnic ancestors—active participants in the great, ever broadening and ever changing stream of Anglo-American civilization. The "Americanization" of nineteenth century immigrants consisted largely in giving them, in schools and clubs and churches, a solid grounding in English literature and, on a higher level, English history and political ideas.[55]

American culture today is not English culture but a branch from the same tree, distinct and yet inseparably connected with it as the younger Canadian and Australian cultures are. They face the same problem, although on a minor scale, due to their later emergence as nations and to their much smaller populations. Today each of them is leading a complete and independent life of its own, with its own literature and art, as the United States does, and yet each lives in close interdependence with all the other English-speaking peoples, basing its culture on common traditions. Each represents a unique amalgam of the English literary and political traditions with a specific and, in each instance, very different setting. In the case of the United States, several fundamental traits, each one complex in itself, have entered into the environmental picture, unknown in England or at least not known to a similar degree: the vitality and continuity of the Puritan tradition; the three-hundred-year-old and ever-repeated experience of the frontier; the cultural diversity and fertility of a proudly self-asserting sectionalism; and, finally, the variety of immigrant contributions melting into and richly coloring the common stream. The mother-daughter relationship which troubled so many Americans and Englishmen in the first part of the nineteenth century has long since disappeared. It has been replaced by a partnership of equals, each member securely grounded in the common tradition and each striving to adjust itself to its own peculiar setting and to the unique problems which its geography and its recent history pose.

chapter three

A republic of many republics

"That which struck me most in the [Senate] was the mode of representation. . . . This mode of representation brings forth much nationality, and much that is picturesque in the living, peculiar life of each state. The Granite State and the Palmetto State, 'Old Virginny' and new Wisconsin, Minnesota and Louisiana, each so separate and so peculiar in situation, scenery, climate, products, population, stand forth in Congress as individuals, and take part in the treatment of public questions, which are interesting to the whole human race, according to characteristics which are peculiar to themselves and common to all."

FREDRIKA BREMER
The Homes of the New World; Impressions of America (New York, 1853), vol. II, p. 129.

It took the United States a long time to consolidate as a nation. This is not astonishing. The area which it covered was a continent rather than a country. In less than seventy-five years the thirteen colonies on the Atlantic seaboard had spread into a vast empire twenty times larger in size and population than the original nucleus. A similar growth of a nation had never occurred before. Could such an overgrown empire still preserve national unity? E Pluribus Unum was the motto of the United States. But for a long time the question was not decided as to which of the two elements combined there was to be emphasized. The federal solution devised by *The Federalist* was a daring innovation, accepted only very reluctantly by many of the Americans of the period. The unity in the United States was embodied in an idea, in a political and intellectual tradition—the roots of which went back to the mother country across the ocean; the diversity expressed itself in a multiplicity of indigenous realities —great contrasts of economic interests, geographic divisions, climatic differences, sharp divergences in social conditions and ways of life. Sectional antagonism was increased by the fact that economic interests and geographic divisions on the whole coincided. This antagonism found its climax in the war between the states in the 1860's, the most sanguinary and bitter conflict fought in the whole Western world between 1815 and 1914. In this case the no longer united states had to struggle with another nascent true nationalism, distinct from the original American nationalism and yet stemming from the same roots. American nationalism won against its separatist rival; but as late as 1925 one of the leading American historians, Frederick Jackson Turner, could write: "Our sections are becoming more and more the American version of European nations . . . We have become a nation comparable to all Europe in area, with separate geographic provinces which equal great European nations. We are in this sense an empire, a federation of sections, a union of potential nations." [1]

Turner believed that sections were hostile to one another, because they were, like European nations, competing for hegemony over a continent; with the existence of a central government in the United

States this struggle for hegemony became a struggle for the control of the central government. The rapid territorial expansion added to the elements of conflict and at the same time to the hoped-for spoils of hegemony. It was, as William Grayson foresaw during the discussion in the Virginia Convention, "a contest for empire . . . whether one part of this country shall govern the other." [2] This struggle for hegemony—or for the maintenance of one's position against the rising threat of another's hegemony—would become aggravated should ideological moments add resentment and bitterness to the weight of political and economic desires and fears. Such a bitterness was hardly known in the European contests between nations in the eighteenth century. It had made itself grievously felt in the wars of religion in the sixteenth and seventeenth centuries; it reappeared, this time fanned not by theologians but by poets and historians, publicists and intellectuals, in the European wars of the Age of Nationalism. Nations then no longer represented instruments in the rivalries of kings or cabinets. The nations themselves became imbued with the spirit of a self-righteous moral or spiritual issue. Wars became bitter to a degree unknown in the eighteenth century. No such issue existed between American sections. Therefore, Turner's analogy between United States sections and European nations in spite of all rivalry does not hold good. The sections (except in the one case of the South) never rose to the rank of a nation, they never developed a national consciousness. The feeling of unity was too strong, even at the beginning. A national structure and a national idea existed in the United States, at least after 1789, the year when George Washington became its first president—a situation fundamentally different from that in Europe, where in the same year the French revolution and its consequences called forth and strengthened a virulent and self-centered nationalism—unrestrained except for the transitory period of the Holy Alliance by the recognition of any superior bond—as the decisive element on the European continent.

The chief movements endangering national unity in the United States in the nineteenth century sprang from the very two sections which had formed the core of the nascent nation—New England first, the South afterwards. Even the war of 1812 touched not only New England but also Southern sectional interests. Felix Grundy, representative from Tennessee from 1811 to 1814 and later a member of the Senate, proposed in 1812 the annexation of Canada in order to preserve the equilibrium between South and North. "When Louisiana shall be fully peopled, the Northern states will lose their powers; they will be at the discretion of others; they may be depressed at pleasure and then this Union might be endangered. I therefore feel anxious not only to add the Floridas of the South, but the Canadas to the north of this Empire." Sectional self-interest clearly marked the secessionist movement in Massachusetts in 1812. The Louisiana Purchase in 1803 threatened a shift of the balance of power to the South. A member of the Essex Junto, Senator William Plumer of New Hampshire, remarked then in Congress: "Admit this western world into the Union and you destroy, at once, the weight and importance of the eastern states, and compel them to establish a separate and independent empire." [3]

The war of 1812, provoked by the expansionism and chauvinism of the new West and almost ending in disastrous defeat, seemed to many New Englanders not only provocative but to have been fought for the economic interests of the agrarian West in order that they might ruin the commercial northeast. The nation was divided; war against Britain was declared on June 18, 1812, by a vote of seventy-nine to forty-nine in the House and nineteen to thirteen in the Senate. Massachusetts too was split, but the general sentiment was against the war. A meeting in Springfield declared: "We consider the late act of the President unjust, unnecessary, and ruinous to the best interests of this country, as a war of aggression and conquest . . . we hold in utter abhorrence an alliance with France, the destroyer of all republics." [4] The bitter denunciation of the government was also motivated by the opposition of the Federalist party, with its dwindling influence, to the Republican party in power. Some extreme Federalists like Timothy Pickering suggested that New England form a Northern Confederacy with the British provinces of Canada and Nova Scotia and establish a bond of union with Britain. Gouverneur Morris, an influential member of the Constituent Convention of 1787, a great defender of religious liberty and of the emancipation of the slaves, later United States minister to France, went so far as to "lose all loyalty to the nation" in 1812.[5] Throughout New England many clergymen opposed the war and claimed that the declaration of war had utterly disdained the laws of God and the hopes of man. Some ministers went so far as to warn that a man who volunteered his services in an unjust war, undertaken "at the command of weak or wicked rulers," or supported it in any way, "is an accomplice in the wickedness . . . and, in the sight of God and His law, a murderer." [6]

The New England states were unwilling to allow the militia to be used in the federal service. According to Section 8 of the Constitution, the Congress was entitled to call forth the militia to "repel invasion." Did such a case exist? Was a belief in a possible threat of invasion sufficient to call forth the militia for preventive action? The agitation resulted in the calling of the convention at Hartford in December, 1814; the extremists planned a separate peace with Britain and a revision of the United States Constitution. However, moderation prevailed, and the whole attempt was abandoned when on December 24, 1814, the United States concluded at Ghent a most favorable peace treaty with the British. Though victorious, the British acceded to the American demands and abandoned the Indians to the land-hungry western frontiersmen. The British, preoccupied with, to them, much greater problems, did not press their advantages; the nationalist plans of the federal government and the expansionist aspirations of the western frontier carried the day.[7] The victory achieved by a westerner, General Andrew Jackson, at New Orleans after the conclusion of the peace treaty paved his way to the presidency, which he reached fourteen years later. This apparent success strengthened nationalist exuberance throughout the United States. "The Star-Spangled Banner," later to become the national anthem, originated in the concluding stage of the war as did the term "Uncle Sam," a sobriquet applied not to the people of the United States but to its government.[8] The young nation clearly gained in self-confidence. "In 1815," Henry Adams insists, "for the first time Americans ceased to doubt the path they were to follow. Not only was the unity of the nation established, but its probable divergence from older societies was also well defined. . . . The public seemed obstinate only in believing that all was for the best, as far as the United States were concerned, in the affairs of mankind." [9]

An era of prosperity and "good feeling" followed the war. Sectional differences lost their importance. The opportunities offered by the West bridged the existing differences in a mighty national forward movement. The Northwest Ordinance of 1787, the "greatest achievement" of the Congress of the Confederation, was one of the cornerstones in the building of the American nation. None of the thirteen original states could stake out any claims for itself in the growing empire of the West. The West became a national empire, a cementing element, in which the advancing frontiersmen from the various states intermingled and, like the immigrants to the United States, lost their old loyalties and gained new ones. The fundamental principles of civil and religious liberty prevailing in the states of the Confederation were extended to the new territory in a compact, forever unalterable, between the original states and the people and states in the new territory. As soon as permanent governments had been established there, they would be admitted to a share in the federal councils on an equal footing with the original states.

Perhaps the most important article of the ordinance was the third, which reflected the spirit of the time. In its first part it ordered that "religion, morality, and knowledge being necessary to good government and the happiness of mankind, schools and the means of education shall forever be encouraged." This part of the article was faithfully followed. But the remaining part was more honored in the breach than otherwise. "The utmost good faith shall always be observed toward the Indians; their lands and property shall never be taken from them without their consent . . . but laws founded in justice and humanity shall from time to time be made for preventing wrongs being done to them, and for preserving peace and friendship with them." As in all imperial expansion, the central government tried to preserve the rights of the natives, as formerly the government in London had done. It was the settlers themselves who disregarded the letter and the spirit of the central imperial authorities. "The presence of the Indians has had a brutalizing influence on the frontier; for Americans are not softened by responsibility for a weaker race." [10] In that sense, like all other colonies where settlers face native populations, the young West could hardly make a contribution to civilization or to humanitarianism. Liberty under law, the essence of democracy, was then safer in the old East than in the new West.

The war of 1812 had been largely due to the expansionism of the settlers. It was perhaps the most unpopular and badly managed war in the history of the United States.[11] Yet Albert Gallatin, who was one of the peace commissioners in Ghent, could note that "the War has renewed and reinstated the national feelings and character which the Revolution had given, and which were daily lessened. The people have now more general objects of attachment with which their pride and political opinions are connected. They are more Americans; they feel and act more as a nation." [12] As George Dangerfield pointed out, the early months of 1819 marked the climax of the nationalist exuberance which began in 1814. In February the strongly nationalist Secretary of State, John Quincy Adams, called a new continent into being by drawing lines upon a map. In March, Chief Justice Marshall conjured a national government out of the eighth section of the first Article of the Constitution. These two events were riveted by the Chief Justice himself. "Throughout this vast Republic," he said on March 6, "from the St. Croix to the Gulf of Mexico, from the Atlantic to the Pacific, revenue is to be collected and expended, armies are to be marched and supported." The State Department and the Supreme Court took the same confident nationalist view of the future; "the unbridled expansionism of Andrew Jackson gave it military sanction," to use Professor Henry C. Graff's words.[13]

But this era of good feeling was not to last long. National cohesion was far from established. When Tocqueville visited the United States in 1832 he was impressed by the fact that the ordinary citizen gave greater importance to the state governments than to the federal government, and had a warmer attachment to the former than to the latter. He was convinced that in the case of a conflict between the two, the loyalty of the people would be given rather to the state than to the union. Almost in anticipation of Turner's sectional interpretation Tocqueville wrote: "I cannot believe in the duration of a government whose task is to hold together forty different peoples [!] spread over a surface equal to the half of Europe, to avoid rivalries, ambitions and struggles among them, and to unite the action of their independent ways for the accomplishment of the same plans." For the future, Tocqueville foresaw a weakening of the union. "Unless I am strangely mistaken, the Federal Government of the United States tends to become daily weaker, it draws back from one kind of business after another, it more and more restricts the field of its action. Naturally feeble, it abandons even the appearance of force. On the other side, I think I perceive that in the United States the sentiment of independence becomes more and more lively in the States, and the tone of provincial government more and more pronounced. People wish to keep the Union, but to keep it reduced to a shadow: they would like to have it strong for some purposes and weak for the rest—strong in war and almost nonexistent in peace—forgetting that such alternations of strength and weakness are impossible." [14]

Though these observations proved wrong, they show that by 1830, when southern sectionalism was rearing its head, as astute an observer as Tocqueville found everywhere a greater loyalty to the state than to the nation. Yet this conflict in the United States was not unique. The situation was similar in Switzerland: to a much greater degree the loyalty there in the 1830's belonged primarily to the state or canton, and hardly to the Swiss Confederation. In Switzerland the nation did not even exist as a political structure, such as the United States Constitution provided after 1788. The Swiss Federal Pact of 1815 resembled much more closely the Articles of Confederation of March 1, 1781, in which each state fully retained its sovereignty, freedom and independence, and every power, jurisdiction and right which was not expressly delegated to the United States, in Congress assembled. In the 1830's Switzerland—which as far as it could be considered a nation was held together like the United States by a tradition of civic liberty and by the need for collective security to protect this liberty—was in quest of its own national personality and of a strong structure to support it. [15]

In spite of all the historical and geographic differences in the two cases—in time Switzerland was four centuries older than the United States, in area it was infinitely smaller—the Swiss cantons offer a better approach to an understanding of American sectionalism than does Turner's parallel with the European nations. The American sections did not resemble European nations: otherwise the United States would not have survived all the trials and tests since the Civil War with the force of cohesion which it has shown throughout and with a conformity in loyalty which by far surpasses all the divisions of ethnic origin, economic interests and sectional allegiance. Instead of comparing the United States with Europe as a whole, as Turner and his followers did, we shall gain a better understanding if we view the United States against the background of other nations or national groups in western Europe—Switzerland, Scandinavia, Germany, Italy, the Habsburg monarchy—which in the middle of the nineteenth century sought a way to unite various sectional interests and traditions within a national whole that would allow liberty of development to all its parts without imposing the hegemony of one of them. Many European nations—and, in the vision of a Mazzini or a Napoleon III, Europe as a whole or at least western Europe—were at the middle of the nineteenth century in quest of a federative solution, a solution which had been first found by the United States and even there was being questioned and threatened. From 1846 to 1871 a number of wars and revolutions were fought all over central Europe about the possibility of federating political entities with different historical traditions and economic interests, which evinced the desire to form a stronger national unity yet preserve their personalities on a footing of equality. The federative principle involved which promised a solution has been well described by an American historian of the European scene of the period, as "a polity that emphasizes the political relation of adjustment among equals rather than the political relationships of inferiority and superiority, and methods of law rather than methods of force. . . . For Europe as a whole, federative polity declined [after the middle of the nineteenth century] almost to the point of extinction in this era, but survived among Anglo-Saxon peoples, in the United States of America, the British Empire, and in the relation of Britain to the United States." [16]

National unity in Germany and Italy was achieved not through a true federation but through the imposition of the hegemony of Prussia and of Sardinia. In the first case Bismarck preserved a semblance of federation. In the latter case extreme nationalists like Mazzini agitated for complete national fusion without regard for local traditions, and the Sardinian government followed in that respect; as a result, Italian nationhood never matured, the south remained a "colonial" area, in mind and social structure different from, and hostile to, the central government representing the north. The suggestions for a federal solution of the Habsburg monarchy, advanced by the Kremsier Reichstag in 1849, were not acted upon, to the eventual dismay of the monarchy itself and of the peoples composing it. Even the efforts of the Scandinavian peoples—so akin in their origin, languages, cultural and political traditions—to establish a union demanded by many influential intellectual leaders between 1840 and 1864 failed, fundamentally because the peoples involved were eager for, or afraid of, hegemonial positions. Outside of the English-speaking peoples, only Switzerland achieved an adjustment of political relations on a footing of equality and liberty of peoples of various strength, an achievement the more remarkable for the great linguistic, religious, economic and ideological differences among the peoples involved. The spirit of compromise and tolerance, a mixture of sober respect for law and tradition and of daring pragmatic response to the challenge of new circumstances—a temper very similar to the one prevailing among the English and North Americans—made this unique success on the European continent possible. But it too was achieved only after a war between the cantons—a war of secession, as the German name of the Swiss civil war, "Sonderbundskrieg," implies.

This war had much in common with the American civil war, though it was of much shorter duration and the number of casualties was infinitely smaller. But there, as here, agrarian economic interests were arrayed against a more progressive commercial and industrial economy; the former feared not only the overwhelming political and economic power of their opponents but also the undermining of their own traditional social structure and way of life. Both sides believed that they were fighting for liberty and for the rights guaranteed in the Federal Pact, though they interpreted them differently—the cantons on the one side in a conservative way, more consonant with the past of the confederation, the cantons on the opposite side in a way which took into account the new dynamic forces released by the development of capitalism and of technological innovations. The conflict, primarily a struggle for the control of the future of the Confederation, received its emotional overtones from an ideological tension: the conservative and agrarian cantons were Catholic, the progressive cantons were overwhelmingly Protestant. The Catholic cantons insisted that they were fighting not only for their faith but for the preservation of ancient liberties against corruption by mob influences, for order and civilization against the spirit of disorder, for the ancestral virtues of a free-holding peasantry against the greed and cupidity of modern money interests. The conservative cantons, believing that the survival of their way of life and their vital interests were threatened or at least unprotected by the majority of the confederacy, and hoping for support from the conservative powers in Europe, formed their own confederation of secession in self-protection against the majority of the cantons. The civil war in Switzerland ended, as the American civil war did, with the victory of the progressive cantons and with the establishment of an enduring national unity.[17]

The Constitution of the United States served as a model for the Swiss solution of the problem how best to accommodate the needs of national unity with the survival of the individuality, traditions and rights of the cantons. In 1833 the Swiss I. P. V. Troxler wrote: "The Constitution of the United States of America is a great work of art which the human mind created according to the eternal laws of its divine nature. It is a model and a pattern for the organization of the public life of republics in general, in which the whole and the parts shall both be free and equal. In the year 1787 the Convention at Philadelphia solved the great problem of the conciliation of national unity with the autonomy of constituent states and this autonomy with the freedom of all citizens. The New World has solved the problem for all peoples, states and countries." The Swiss constitution of 1848 followed, both in its federalism and its bicameral institutions, the example of the United States Constitution for which there was no precedent to be found in Swiss history.[18] In the same year (1848) the United States Constitution was also proposed as a model for a Scandinavian union by a Norwegian jurist Ole Munch Raeder, who visited the United States in 1848. He spoke of the "beneficial influence" of the constitution under which "a powerful, happy nation has developed in these sixty years out of a group of weak, disunited, despised little republics. This example ought to appeal to us in our present state of political impotency. . . . Now the structure rears itself more proudly than ever. Foreigners by the hundreds of thousands flock hither every year and find happy homes in America; its flag is respected on every sea; its missionaries in the cause of religion and freedom penetrate to every corner of the earth, and its genius makes contributions in every field and with never ceasing energy towards the progress of the human race. In many respects it has become a model state for Europe." [19]

Thus the United States was in the middle of the nineteenth century not the only nation still in quest of its definitive form and general acceptance; its quest was part of a general process going on in the Western world on both sides of the Atlantic. In the United States, in Switzerland, and in the British Commonwealth, thanks to the federative principle nations were formed in which citizens of several regions and polities, in spite of diverse economies and environments, backgrounds and traditions, have been able to live together in free and ordered circumstances and to develop in common a high degree of prosperity. What endowed this variety of sectional interests with a surprisingly strong national cohesion, was the combination of individual liberty and federal principle, based on the tradition set by England's Glorious Revolution of substituting discussion and concession and compromise legislation for force.[20]

Tocqueville underestimated in 1830 the strength of this federal tie. But the nation had to pass through an unprecedented trial, infinitely more terrible than the civil wars fought in Switzerland, Austria, Germany and Italy during the same period, before it could find itself. The crisis was forty years in the making; at the time of his visit Tocqueville saw clearly one of its elements: "The most formidable of all the ills which threaten the future of the Union arises from the presence of a black population upon its territory; and in contemplating the cause of the present embarrassments, or the future dangers of the United States, the observer is invariably led to this as a primary fact." [21] During those forty years the conflict grew more and more embittered, the battle lines became more clearly drawn, the opposite interests more firmly entrenched. Again the parallel with Switzerland in the two decades there before the outbreak of the civil war is striking. In both cases the gift for compromise and the sobriety of common sense—generally so characteristic of both nations—seemed to give way to a rhetorical emotionalism and to most bitter controversy.

In the United States the nationalists stressed more and more the need for the unity of the vast continent. But before the nationalist wave of imperial expansion in the 1840's the possible division of the continent had been found entirely acceptable to many Americans. It was then assumed that, owing to geographic considerations and to the right of self-determination, two or more powers of similar origins could very well coexist in the width of the North American continent. Jefferson thought in imperial terms, and in his Louisiana purchase took the first great step in creating the American empire, which so many Americans in the first decades of the Republic hoped for. But he did not think in continental terms and as a convinced agrarian he objected to a navy. In 1809, in a letter to Madison, he agreed to the possible acquisition of Cuba because it "can be defended by us without a navy, and this develops the principle which ought to limit our views. Nothing should ever be accepted which would require a navy to defend it." [22] Jefferson doubted the wisdom of an imperial expansion of the United States to the Pacific. When John Jacob Astor started a settlement on the Columbia River Jefferson wrote him on March 24, 1812, that he was looking forward to a time when the whole West would be populated by Anglo-Americans, but that he did not believe in a political union with these "free and independent Americans, unconnected with us but by the ties of blood and interest, and employing like us the rights of self-government." Jefferson reiterated his belief in an independent empire for the western part of the continent in another letter on November 9, 1813; even as late as November 7, 1848, Daniel Webster in a speech at Faneuil Hall asked "if there be any sensible man in the whole United States who will say for a moment, that when fifty or a hundred thousand persons [of Anglo-Saxon descent] shall find themselves on the shores of the Pacific Ocean, they will long consent to be under the rules of the American Congress or the British Parliament. They will raise a standard for themselves, and they ought to do it." But the imperial forces driving for continental unity were much too powerful. Webster himself had soon to deny the stand which he had taken. The nation had to be one and strong and to fill the whole imperial space. Passions were aroused against any attempt at "checking the fulfillment of our manifest destiny to overspread the continent allotted by Providence for the free development of our yearly multiplying millions," to use John Louis O'Sullivan's words defending the annexation of Texas in 1846. Yet in the same article, though he predicted California's impending separation from Mexico and its control by Anglo-America elements, he was not certain whether California would not be independent.

There were Little Americans then as there were about the same time Little Englanders in the former mother country. In discussing the occupation of the Oregon River in 1825, Senator Mahlon Dickerson of New Jersey, who sat in the Senate from 1817 to 1833 and later was Secretary of the Navy under President Jackson, declared in Congress: "We have not adopted a system of colonization and it is to be hoped we never shall. Oregon can never be one of the United States. . . . Is this territory of Oregon ever to become a state, a member of this Union? Never. The Union is already too extensive." [23] Horace Greeley opposed American expansion in 1836 and believed the Americans would be fortunate to preserve the then existing Union for a century longer. He "would have been content to see our western limits fixed at the Rocky Mountains." [24] Orestes Brownson in his fourth of July oration in 1840 before the Democracy of Worcester (Massachusetts) praised the Democratic party for being a states' rights party, for thus alone it could rise to the dignity of the American mission. The American continent was too vast to be ruled by a consolidated empire, he said. Such a monster would simply swallow its citizens. Consolidation would mean tyranny or split.[25] But the Little Americans were losing out on this side of the Atlantic very much as the Little Englanders did across the ocean. Manifest destiny, the mighty ground swell of a rapid industrial expansion, the tightening net of communications, seemed to carry the peoples irresistibly along.

The momentum of such a trend demanded a greater emphasis on national unity and on centralized strength than originally envisaged by the framers of the Constitution, which had been adopted in a primarily rural economy and at a period of almost insuperable distances. Jefferson himself, in a letter to Edward Livingston, written at Monticello on March 25, 1825, characterized the Constitution as "a compact of many independent powers, every single one of which claims an equal right to understand it and to require its observance," and he foresaw that "however strong the cord of compact may be, there is a point of tension at which it will break." [26] The point of tension was reached around 1860, though it had been mounting for at least thirty years. The Civil War—in which Jefferson, as far as one can venture a statement of this kind, would have sided with his native Virginia and with the rural society— was without doubt the greatest single event in the history of the United States. It questioned and at the same time completed the crystallization of American nationalism. Its central position in national history has always been recognized. Today, almost a century later, it still stirs deep emotions throughout the states, and the fascination which it exercises shows itself in the ever growing number of books which continue the unending discussion of all its aspects. No comparable interest attaches to the civil wars which Switzerland, Germany or Italy fought at about the same time around the problem of unity. They are recalled in suitable publications at their centenaries, but they do not become live issues, attract-

ing and agitating scholars and the general public equally over the
years. Even the war of 1775 exercised no such impact on the American mind.

The Civil War has been called by some the second American
Revolution, by others the second War for [Southern] Independence.
In a certain sense it was both, but it was so in reverse. 1775 was
fought, to use the modern term, for the principle of self-determination against a government which wished to impose imperial unity,
and the principle of self-determination won out; 1861 was fought
for the maintenance of imperial union against the principle of self-
determination which lost out. In 1775 it was a predominantly rural
economy which rose against the demands of a much more highly
commercialized and urbanized economy, and the rural society—
with which Jefferson identified himself and which he idealized—
won out; in 1861 a rural society, perhaps nearer to the Jeffersonian
ideals—though midwestern ruralism might claim more of Jefferson's
heritage—than were the growing squalid urban centers of the
North, went down in defeat before a much more highly commercialized and industrialized mass society. There was, however, one point
which the outcome in 1783 and in 1865 had in common: the thirteen
colonies did not suffer any real oppression from Britain nor did the
southern states from the northern states. Yet undoubtedly the thirteen
rebel colonies stood for a progressive principle, socially and politically, compared with the Britain of 1770. Similarly the northern
states stood for a progressive principle compared with the southern
rebel states of 1860. In both cases victory went to the progressive
side. Monarchical assertion and aristocratic oligarchy within the
rapidly progressing British empire had truly become obsolete by
1770 and a reform was overdue; slavery had become obsolete in
the United States by 1860 and a reform was overdue.

Both wars, that of 1775 and that of 1861, were civil wars between two parties within the same national realm, between a more
liberal and a more conservative interpretation of one and the same
national heritage. In both cases the liberal interpretation carried the
day, ultimately not only in the victor's camp. The battle lines were
rarely drawn clearly and the issues were complex and confused. In
1775 there were many Tories or Loyalists in the thirteen colonies
and many supporters of American Whiggism in Britain; in 1860
there were a great number of southerners who wished to remain

loyal to the Union and there were many in the North who sympathized with the southern position. O'Sullivan, the father of the theory of "manifest destiny" and one of the foremost American nationalists, even openly sided with the South and propagated its cause abroad. Thus the community was split in 1775 and in 1861 on many lines of loyalty. Both wars, because they were civil wars, left deep traces of estrangement, though the peace which followed was intended to heal. The British were perhaps in an easier position to make a generous peace with the Americans, both in 1783 and in 1814 (they showed for the first time the ability of not ungraciously renouncing imperial ties in the hope of transforming them into friendly cooperation), than were the northern states in 1865.[27] In the latter case, too much bitterness had accumulated in an unprecedentedly bloody struggle, too much inhumanity had been shown by man to his fellow man. Yet for seventy years the combatants had been fellow members of one nation, had shared in one common government. The leaders on both sides had sat together in cabinet meetings and in congressional sessions. They were trained in the same military schools and had fought together in the same battles. But though the northern victors could not find so quickly the road back to reconciliation as did the victors in the infinitely less bloody Swiss civil war, wiser counsels soon prevailed and the constitution proved capable of providing a unifying link when handled with the prudence and moderation demanded of all Anglo-American, and of all successful democratic, institutions. Nevertheless, for many decades the victorious North Americans felt a deep grievance, a sense of injury, against the British; more legitimately the defeated southerners have felt for many decades, and even feel today, resentment against the northern victors. This attitude is not surprising: the fact that the emotional impact of the southern War of Independence, the loyalty to the Lost Cause, has grown with the years, beyond the intensity of the war years themselves, follows the general pattern of modern nationalism.

For the war of 1861 can be well understood as a war for national independence with nationalism as its chief issue. Naturally it can be viewed and explained in other ways too. For almost one hundred years the causes of the war have been discussed, and all the differences of climate and geography, of economic systems and social organization, are well known. In themselves they would not have brought about separation. Feeling for separation has been voiced in other geographic and economic sections. In the Congress debate over the admission of Louisiana as a state, Josiah Quincy of Massachusetts warned that the bill if passed would virtually dissolve the Union, free the states from their moral obligation, and "as it will be the right of all, so it will be the duty of some, to prepare definitely for a separation; amicably if they can, violently if they must." [28] But it did not come about; a New England nationalism never developed even in an embryonic stage. Nor was such a development "natural" in the South. No nationalism is created by nature or given by God. The South presents as little a geographic and economic unit predestined for separate nationhood as New England does. John Hope Franklin rightly rejects the point of view of Jesse T. Carpenter that "the roots of southern unity are grounded in the law of nature." The South is by nature and in its economic structure diversified enough. A feeling of sectional and later national unity was growing slowly as an emotional attitude and a political consciousness in the years between 1820 and 1860. By 1820 the South was still the dominant part and the heartland of the Union; most of the Union's presidents and leading statesmen had come from the South. Twelve states which clung to slavery were balanced against twelve states which had by then abolished slavery. It would demand a mighty emotional impulse to incline the South to leave the Union and to unite the southerners "whose traditions spelled division and diversity" into a common effort.[29]

This impulse was provided by nationalism. Overtones of an emotional nationalism made themselves heard for some time before the Civil War. Henry W. Hilliard called the South in the Alabama legislature in 1839 "my own, my native land—my home and the birthplace of my children. Her people are my people; her hopes are my hopes; her interests are my interests." And six years later a congressman from Georgia, Alexander H. Stephens, spoke in the House on January 25, 1845, of the South as "my home, my fatherland. There sleep the ashes of my sire and grandsires; there are my hopes and prospects; with her my fortunes are cast; her fate is my fate and her destiny my destiny." These are typical expressions of modern nationalism, and they were climaxed in Stephens's words in June, 1861, at Washington, Georgia, that "our enemies rely upon their numbers, we rely upon the valor of free men, battling for country, for home, and for everything dear as well as sacred. . . . Of all the virtues, none is purer, holier, loftier, or so God-like as that which prompts a man to offer himself, his life, his home, and his all as a sacrifice upon his country's altar. . . . The country must be sustained. Everyone agrees to it. Our all depends upon it. Constitutional liberty depends upon it. The perpetuation of the grand idea of self-government announced by our sires and grandsires in '76 depends upon it. The hopes of mankind and the world depend upon it." These are clearly words which could have been spoken, with minor alterations, by Irish, Polish, Greek, or Arab nationalists.

The words which Rufus Choate, a Massachusetts Whig, used about "American nationality" in a Fourth of July oration delivered in Boston in 1858, one year before Choate's death, were as applicable to southern nationalism in 1861 as to any other nationalism: "Think of [nationality]," he said, "as a state of consciousness, as a spring of feeling, as a motive to exertion, as blessing your country, and as reacting on you. Think of it as it fills your mind and quickens the heart of millions around you. Instantly, under such an influence, you ascend above the smoke and stir of this small local strife; you tread upon the high places of the earth and of history; you think and feel as an American for America; her power, her eminence, her consideration, her honor are yours; your competitors, like hers, are kings; your home, like hers, is the world; your path, like hers, is on the highway of empires; our charge, her charge, is of generations and ages. . . . Think of it [nationality] as an active virtue. Is not all history a recital of the achievement of nationality, and an exponent of its historical and imperial nature? Even under systems far less perfect than ours, and influences far less auspicious than ours, has it not lifted itself up for a time above all things meaner, vindicating itself by action, by the sublimity of a working hope?" [30]

In their nationalism the "rebels" of 1861 appealed to the same principles as the "rebels" of 1775 had done. They regarded themselves as the defenders of the inherited constitutional rights and at the same time as the protagonists of the natural rights of self-determination and self-government. They claimed that their cause was the cause of true liberty and true humanity, that they were fighting against despotism and for civilization. Lincoln himself contributed to the simplifications so characteristic of periods of wars or of great emotional stress, when he called the struggle "part of the eternal conflict between right and wrong." On both sides, but especially in the North, the war assumed a moralizing and crusading aspect, much in accord with an American tradition which was already visible in 1775 and made itself felt in World War I. But the Civil War would not have assumed its tragic dimension and its lasting fascination if it had been a conflict between right and wrong. It was, as so many great conflicts in history are, a conflict between two relative rights, which each side enhanced into an absolute right. In this paradoxical complexity slavery was not the real main issue, though it was raised—through the extremism and holier-than-thou attitude of northern moralists and through southern obstinacy and pride—into the ideological symbol around which all the issues at stake tended to crystallize. "Economic and political grievances," a recent southern historian wrote, "were, by being merged with the hatred for slavery, raised from the low level of self-interest to the higher plane where feelings of righteousness and self-sacrifice could stir the souls of men." [31] This ideological stiffening of economic and political rivalries and fears led in the North to emotional self-righteousness and in the South to over-compensation against the criticism of the North and against the general trend of the times; the South went so far as to assert that not only was slavery an institution of God but it was intended to form the basis of the best social state and the only safeguard for the permanence of a democratic and republican government. Slavery, it was claimed, abolished the feud between capital and labor, gave to the laborer security and freedom from misery in depression times and counteracted the disintegration of society into mobs.

Whereas in the 1820's southerners had pleaded that slavery was a moral and political evil, much to be deplored but incapable of being eradicated, now they maintained that no human institution was more manifestly consistent with the will of God and with the traditions of civilized history or better designed to enhance the happiness of the Negro. Senator James H. Hammond of South Carolina said in 1836 in the Congress that slavery "has rendered our southern country proverbial for its wealth, its genius, and its manners." For the South was believed to be more chivalrous, less calculating and grasping, more magnanimous and disposed to prefer civilized ease to accumulation of wealth than the North, and these virtues were regarded as closely tied in with slavery. Like

many spokesmen of backward regions in the nineteenth and twentieth centuries, of colonial countries and others finding themselves
threatened by the dynamism of modern Western society—like Russian Slavophiles and Asian nationalists—the southerners rationalized
or rather emotionalized their inferiority by cultivating a legend of
their spiritual superiority to the ways of life of a materialist, aggressive and commercial civilization.

The question of slavery had long troubled the northern mind too:
in 1838 James Fenimore Cooper in *The American Democrat* defended slavery as an institution as old as humanity. "Slavery is no
more sinful, by the Christian code, than it is sinful to wear a whole
coat, while another is in tatters, or otherwise to enjoy ease and
plenty, while our fellow creatures are suffering and in want." Cooper
believed that the African was in nearly all respects better off as an
American slave than in Africa. In his nationalism he went so far
as to assert that "there is scarcely a nation of Europe that does not
possess institutions that inflict as gross personal privations and
wrongs, as the slavery of America." He quoted as one instance the
existence of compulsory military service in most European countries, and triumphantly went on: "From all this, the slave is exempt,
as well as from the more ordinary cares of life." Though Cooper
regarded slavery as little a good as any other form of misery, he
opposed rash attempts at abolition. He was convinced that emancipation would be followed by "a war of extermination" between the
two races and warned that: "In the management of this interest it
ought to be remembered, that to the citizen of the non-slave-holding
state, slavery offers little more than a question of abstract principles,
while to the citizen of the slave-holding state it offers a question
of the highest practical importance, and one that, mismanaged,
might entirely subvert the order of his social organization." [32]

A good picture of the complexity of the problem emerges from
the reports of a Swedish traveler, Baron Axel Klinkowström, who
visited the States in 1818–1820 and repeatedly discussed the position
of the Negroes. One of his first contacts with them was in a hotel
in Baltimore where the proprietor kept over forty slaves. The newcomer still tried to practice his comfortable Swedish dining habits
and enjoy his food; but he complained that he had little chance to
eat his ten-course meal because if he so much as turned to speak to
his neighbor the waiter would snatch away his plate and bring the

next course. Later he learned the reason: he went to inspect the basement quarters and found the slaves eating a sumptuous dinner from the leavings they had so carefully salvaged from the dining room. In New York he became annoyed with the laziness and impertinence of the free Negroes, and almost struck one with his cane. His friends warned him urgently about this, and Klinkowström learned that the law gave special protection to this sensitive minority. He was amazed that a white man might be fined $100 for striking a Negro, but that one Congressman could kill another in a duel and the courts would do nothing. Klinkowström's respect and wonder were excited on one occasion when he was talking with a Negro and found him fully assimilated to Anglo-American ideas. The Swede criticized some of the sectarian ideas and customs of the Methodists, and the judicious Negro quietly commented—as J. S. Mill would have done—that a man should "investigate everything and retain the good." [33]

Melville, a New Yorker who as a youth shipped out on his first voyage to England, observed in *Redburn: His First Voyage* (1849) the treatment accorded to American Negroes in England. "Owing to the friendly reception extended to them, and the unwonted immunities they enjoy in Liverpool, the black cooks and stewards of American ships are very much attached to the place, and like to make voyages to it. Being so young and inexperienced then and unconsciously swayed in some degree by those local and social prejudices, that are the marring of most men, and from which, for the mass, there seems no possible escape; at first I was surprised that a coloured man should be treated as he is in this town; but a little reflection showed that, after all, it was but recognizing his claims to humanity and normal equality; so that, in some things we Americans leave to other countries the carrying out of the principle that stands at the head of our Declaration of Independence."

Abraham Lincoln's attitude to slavery was ambiguous too. He was not an extreme abolitionist; his primary consideration was not slavery but the maintenance, if need be by force, of the Union. On December 22, 1860, he wrote to Alexander Stephens: "Do the people of the South really entertain fears that the Republican administration would directly or indirectly interfere with their slaves or with them about their slaves? If they do, I wish to assure you, as once a friend, and still, I hope, not an enemy, that there is no cause for such fears." On March 4, 1861, Lincoln assured the South in his inaugural address that he had no intention, directly or indirectly, of interfering with slavery in the states where it existed. In his annual message to Congress on December 3, 1862, he proposed to abolish slavery by 1900 through agreement and promised payment in federal bonds to the states in proportion to the number of slaves emancipated. The leading generals in both camps did not fight on the issue of slavery. Ulysses Grant who lived in Missouri and southern Illinois just before the outbreak of the war was a minor slaveholder whose slaves were liberated in 1865, whereas Robert E. Lee had not only freed his slaves but had declared slavery "a moral and political evil." But pride drove the southerners more and more into a position which found its climax in Stephens's famous "cornerstone" speech of March 21, 1861, declaring that "the great truth that the Negro was unequal to the white man, that slavery—subordination to the superior race—is his natural and moral condition," was a cornerstone, the foundation of the edifice of the new Confederation.[34] Slavery was exalted as a sign of superior civilization and the mainstay of a superior social structure, infinitely less corrupt and much more refined, more stable and orderly, more God-fearing and hallowed by history than the disorder and the various radical movements and mob insecurity found in the North.

From there it was only one step to regard the North and the South as "two nations, made by their institutions, customs and habits of thought, as distinct as the English and the French," to quote the *Charleston Mercury*. Was perhaps the English civil war of the seventeenth century being re-enacted by the descendants of seventeenth century England; did, as the argument then ran, the "Cavaliers" of the South, advocating as they believed constitutional legitimacy and rational liberty, face again the "Puritans" of the North with their wild passions and narrow-minded persecution of all their opponents? But could this parallel still be applied? An English visitor wrote in 1861 about the South, "Cavalier and Roundhead no longer designate parties, but nations, whose separate foundations . . . were laid on Plymouth Rock and the banks of the James River." [35] Were South and North still the descendants, as they had been in the eighteenth century, of the same stock? Had not immigration in the North, the new temper there in the overgrown grimy cities, created a new race, basically different from the people in the South? Thus argued many southerners who felt themselves not only different from the North but better. As a southern clergyman said, "We have been selected to be a bulwark against the worst developments of human nature, fanaticism, democracy, license, atheism." [36] The southern pulpit regarded the South as the last great citadel of Christianity against a paganism rising throughout the modern world which, masking under the name of science and progress, was preparing mankind for a new Armageddon.

In these expressions of romantic nationalism the South remained within the framework of many nineteenth century nationalist movements on the European continent. But its nationalism corresponded also to the movements for emancipation from colonial oppression, using the arguments of the Irish in the nineteenth and of Asian leaders in the twentieth century. The South felt that the North forced it into a role of political subordination and above all of economic exploitation. It complained that its wealth was drained off to the North in order to improve conditions there and so to widen the economic gulf between the two sections. All its manufactured goods came from the North and by having to buy them the South again paid its economic tribute to the North. Like so many colonial peoples, the South found itself in the morally satisfactory position of being able to blame its shortcomings and its economic backwardness not on its own insufficiency, on its traditionalism or even its climate, but on imperial exploitation by the economically more advanced North. It sounded like the general American defense of innocence against the wiles of Britain when southern spokesmen complained that cunning Yankee traders imposed upon and swindled the plain, homespun innocent southerners.

Yet with all their differences, the southerners were, and knew themselves to be, participants in the tradition of the common American nationalism, co-heirs of the English and American past from the seventeenth to the nineteenth century. They separated from the Union not because they wished to assert themselves as un-American but because they believed themselves the better Americans, more faithful to the original idea. They didn't fight for new rights, not possessed before. They wished to uphold the Constitution as they interpreted it, resisting arbitrary changes. William L. Yancey spoke in 1858 of calling forth a new Lexington, of fighting a new Bunker's Hill. Yancey had founded earlier in the decade a League of United Southerners and in 1858 he wrote: "If we could do as our fathers did, organize Committees of Safety all over the cotton states, we shall fire the Southern heart—instruct the Southern mind—give courage to each other, and at the proper moment, by one organized, concerted action, we can precipitate the cotton States into a revolution." [37] All this sounded very much like New England in the 1770's. Nor did the southerners wish to reject the Constitution of the United States. They regarded it as the best ever devised, assuring liberty and prosperity as no other. They were deeply attached to it. They wished only to defeat what they considered its distortion by a centralizing despotism. They wished to use their rights as Americans, rights guaranteed by the Constitution. Fundamentally the Civil War was a struggle for the right interpretation of a document, the greatness of which was not disputed by either side.

Lincoln regarded the Union of the states as perpetual and emphasized in his first inaugural on March 4, 1861, that "The states have their status in the Union and they have no other legal status." This interpretation was not generally accepted and historically it was probably not correct. Another point of view had been upheld by the Kentucky legislature on November 16, 1798, when it passed a resolution written by Jefferson and asserting "that the several States composing the United States of America, are not united on the principle of unlimited submission to their general government; but that by compact under the style and title of a Constitution for the United States and of amendments thereto, . . . that to this compact each State acceded as a State, and is an integral party, its co-States forming, as to itself, the other party: . . . that as in all other cases of compact among parties having no common Judge, each party has an equal right to judge for itself, as well of infractions as of the mode and measure of redress." In this spirit the South Carolina convention of 1852 restated the position which in substance a former convention in the state had taken just twenty years earlier, in these words: "We, the people of the State of South Carolina, in Convention assembled, do declare and ordain, and it is hereby declared and ordained, that South Carolina, in the exercise of her sovereign will, it is her right, without let, hindrance, or

molestation from any power whatsoever, to secede from the said
Federal Union; and that for the sufficiency of the causes which may
impel her to such separation, she is responsible alone, under God,
to the tribunal of public opinion among the nations of the earth."
The southerners in 1862 appealed, as the Anglo-Americans had done
in 1776, to "the inherent right of every free people to change or reform their Political Institutions," to use the words of the accredited
commissioners from the Confederate government sent to the Federal government in the vain effort to achieve a peaceful separation.

Writing to an editor of the *Richmond Enquirer* on November 23,
1860, James M. Mason, then serving his fourteenth consecutive year
in the Senate, argued the right of secession as a justification for separation from the Union: "Fortunately for the occasion and its consequences, this is not an open question in Virginia. Our honored State
has ever maintained that our Federal system was a confederation of
sovereign powers, not a consolidation of States into one people, and,
as a consequence, whenever a State considered the compact broken,
and in a manner to endanger her safety, such State stood unremitted,
as in sovereign right, to determine for herself, and under no responsibility, save to the opinion of the civilized world, both the
mode and measure of redress." [38] The Confederacy regarded itself
as reenacting the American Revolution. July 4 and February 22 (the
birthday of George Washington, a southern country squire and
gentleman) were made national holidays, and on the latter day
Jefferson Davis was inaugurated as President of the Confederate
States in Richmond, Virginia, the new capital of the Confederacy.
Therefore, when the Convention of the Confederate States of
America decided on March 11, 1861, to adopt a constitution, the
Constitution of the United States was followed practically in every
detail except for some minor improvements, for the southern leaders were experienced politicians and some of them political thinkers. The only difference between the two constitutions was to be
found in the Preamble. There the very first words spoke expressly
of "We, the People of the Confederate States of America, each State
in its sovereign and independent character . . ." and left out among
the purposes not only "to promote the general welfare," but even
"to provide for the common defense [!]." On the other hand, whereas
the eighteenth century constitution had in the spirit of the Founding
Fathers omitted all reference to religion or God, the constitution

of 1861 invoked "the favor and guidance of Almighty God." And similarly the motto E Pluribus Unum was replaced in the South by Deo Vindice.

In other respects, too, the southerners were fully imbued with the common feeling of the American nationalism of the period. They too upheld America's manifest destiny. Many southerners were as expansionist as the westerners, believed as fervently in God's guidance toward glory as did the eighteenth century New Englanders. In an 1848 Thanksgiving discourse, "Program of Liberty," William A. Scott declared that "God has a great design for this continent—for our generation. As the Jews of old—as the Apostles—as the Reformers—as our fathers of 1776—so are we, as a race and as a nation, a peculiar people and called to a high and glorious destiny." [39] Andrew Jackson and Sam Houston obeyed the same imperialist impulse. Southern imperialism was oriented toward the Gulf Coast.[40] It dreamt of the annexation of Cuba and Mexico at least to the Isthmus of Panama as the basis of a mighty slave empire. One of the first southern nationalists, Langdon Cheves of South Carolina, declared at the Nashville convention on November 14, 1850: "Unite, and you shall form one of the most splendid empires on which the sun ever shone, of the most homogeneous population, all of the same blood and lineage, a soil of the most fruitful, and a climate of the most lovely. . . . O, Great God, unite us, and a tale of submission shall never be told." [41] The *Southern Standard* published at Charleston, South Carolina, insisted that: "With Cuba and St. Domingo, we could control the productions of the tropics, and, with them, the commerce of the world, and *with that*, the power of the world . . . Our true policy is to look to Brazil as the next great slave power." In 1857, William Walker of Louisiana demanded the acquisition of Nicaragua as a matter of "immediate and vital consequence to the people of the Southern States." [42]

In spite of all dissatisfaction there would have been no revolution for southern independence if the chain of circumstances had not favored it and if it had not been fanned by intellectuals and rhetoric. This has been the role of the moulders of public opinion throughout the history of nationalism. Much influence was exercised in the early stage of the still embryonic nationalism by the constitutional theories of two important South Carolinians, the statesman John C. Calhoun and the educator Thomas Cooper who became president of South Carolina College. Calhoun had been in his youth an ardent American nationalist, who supported the war of 1812 and voted for the protective tariff of 1816.[43] In his later manhood he was the first in the nullification episode to organize southern resistance in his home state, and though he was until his death in 1850 a moderating influence, bent upon preserving the Union, he declared in August, 1848, "Though the Union is dear to us, our honor and our liberty are dearer."[44] In his important political treatise *Disquisition on Government and a Discourse on the Constitution and Government of the United States* he was concerned with the protection of minorities in a democracy and maintained that "the relation, . . . in which the States stand to the [federal] system, is that of the creator to the creature; and that, in which the two governments stand to each other, is of coequals and co-ordinates."[45] Cooper was one of the first to declare that it was time for South Carolina in 1827 "to calculate the value of the Union." "This historic utterance gave rise to shocked expressions of horror, even among some Carolina hotheads, but it had been indelibly burned into the thinking of a generation." An English traveler who visited Dr. Cooper in 1835 and talked to some of his professors and friends noted in his diary: "I could not help asking in a good natured way, if they called themselves Americans yet; the gentleman who had interrupted me before said, 'If you ask if I am an American, my answer is No, sir, I am a South Carolinian.'"[46] The words which Dr. Osterweis uses to characterize Cooper's opinions, "He valued liberty more than union and calculated the worth of the latter purely in terms of its relationship to his state," recall similar words of a prominent leader of the Swiss secessionist cantons at the time of the Swiss civil war, Philipp Anton von Segesser. He, who represented for forty years his native canton Lucerne in the Swiss National Council, wrote in 1848 to a friend: "Switzerland interests me only because the canton of Lucerne, which is my fatherland, lies there. Should the canton of Lucerne no longer exist as a free and sovereign member of the Confederation, then the latter is to me of as little importance as the Great or Little Tartary."[47]

Some southerners felt the same way about the Union. Many of them, however, as late as 1860 thought it a strange and sad sight to see the great American experiment in democratic government abandoned.[48] Most of them wished to safeguard southern rights within the Union, to proceed only by legal means, above all to preserve peace. Especially the border states, first and foremost Virginia, "founder and keeper of the southern tradition," was eager to avoid a definitive split. The confusion of sentiment and intentions was equally great in the North. Moderate opinion was against coercion and favored some compromise. The radical abolitionists were dead set against any compromise but they were a minority. They expected widespread insurrections by the slaves should any war follow an attempt at coercion. Other radical abolitionists, wishing to avoid the war, were willing to let the southern slave states go so as to free the remaining United States from the blight of slavery. William Seward, who was to become Lincoln's secretary of state, in 1860 put forward the idea of compensating for any loss of southern states by the annexation of Canada and Mexico; Senator Benjamin F. Wade of Ohio took up the idea in a speech in the Senate on December 17 and prophesied a short war, in which the South might vindicate its right to independence and the North through its new expansion would face a glorious future. The *New York Times* on December 26 enthusiastically endorsed the Senator's suggestions.[49] Public response was, however, not sufficient to encourage the expansionist plans of the radicals. A large part of the North, even including conservative Republicans, was either for the reconstruction of the Union on lines acceptable to the South or for peaceful separation. On April 6, 1861, the *Springfield Weekly Republican* expressed its belief that the American people had already predetermined that if peace and conciliatory methods failed to win back the states it would be better to let them go.

But all efforts at mediation failed. In December, 1860, South Carolina seceded; in February, 1861, the Deep South states met at Montgomery, Alabama, and established the Confederate States of America. Lincoln's decision to coerce South Carolina and to stamp out rebellion forced Virginia and other border states into the Confederation. The case of Virginia was symptomatic: was she not the mother of the American states? Lowell in his ode "Under the Old Elm" in commemoration of the centenary of Washington's taking command of the American army on July 3, 1775, hailed Virginia who gave to America "this imperial man":

> She gave us this unblemished gentleman:
> Mother of States and undiminished men,

> Thou gavest a country, giving him . . .
> Virginia, fitly named from England's manly Queen.[50]

But now Virginians and other southerners had come to feel as the
thirteen colonies did in 1775, that they were suffering "under a sense
of long and continued aggression and unsupportable injustice." As
so often in nationalism, intangibles were involved, which soon made
it difficult for moderate men to speak their minds. 1861 like 1775
marked a breakdown of statesmanship, and the birth of new nations.
In his poem "Ethnogenesis" Henry Timrod hailed the first southern
congress at Montgomery:

> Has not the morning dawned with added light?
> . . . . At last we are
> A nation among nations; and the world
> Shall soon behold in many a distant port
> Another flag unfurled.[51]

At the beginning of the war the South fought with greater valor
and broader popular support than the North. It fought for national
self-determination and was carried forward by the inspiring and
exhilarating experience—at least in its earlier stages—of freeing and
establishing one's "own" national identity. But the preservation and
consolidation of American continental unity was essential for the
case of North American peace and for the progress of freedom. Was
it possible to destroy the economic interdependence of South, Northeast and West? Was the Mississippi not destined to flow through
one national territory? northern nationalists asked. The right of the
southern states to national self-determination, to be governed only
with their consent, was disregarded, because southern victory might
have threatened the peace of the North American continent for any
foreseeable future and have retarded the expansion of individual
liberty and human rights—as different from and frequently opposed
to national independence and self-determination—there and elsewhere. Its consequences might have been more grievous for the
North American continent than the disintegration of the Habsburg
empire after World War I and of the British empire after World
War II was, or will be seen to have been, for peace and the orderly
progress of human liberty in central Europe and in Asia.

The defeat of the southern states was due not only to their nu-

merical and economic inferiority but also to the fact that in 1861 the
South was only a potential nation, as the thirteen former colonies
had been in 1788—or as Czechoslovakia and Yugoslavia were in 1918
and India and Indonesia in 1948. Perhaps given time for consolidation the South might have grown into a nation, but its national independence was in its very beginning suppressed by the North which
by 1860, in spite of domestic stresses and intermingling of immigrant
strains, was already a nation. Even had the South been allowed its
independence, the conflict between a nascent southern nationalism
—which had no name around which to rally, for the Confederate
States of America radiated even less warmth than the name United
States of America with its greater stress on national unity—and the
traditional loyalties and potential nationalisms of the various states
might have prevented a consolidation. In 1861 the northerners
fought for the United States; the southerners knew that they were
fighting for their independence, for their traditions and their way
of life, but did independence mean the independence of the Confederate States as a nation or the independence of the individual
states as sovereign nations united in a protective alliance? Were
not southern hearts beating rather for South Carolina and Virginia,
for Texas and Mississippi than for the confederation? [52]

As a result of northern victory unity had been preserved in 1865
by a policy of blood and iron, a policy similar, though involving so
much more blood and iron, to that followed one year later by Bismarck in achieving German unity. But the underlying traditions
and ideas were fundamentally different. Bismarck's success was a
misfortune for Germany and Europe. In the heart of the continent,
at a time when liberal thought and institutions after the Western
model were spreading all over Europe, Bismarck turned the wheel
of history back and set Germany's face determinedly against Western liberalism. His creation apparently so secure and destined to
live did not last long. Founded in war and glorifying war as its
cornerstone, the Bismarckian empire collapsed in war only twenty
years after its founder's death. The attempt fifteen years later to re-
establish German hegemony on a more popular mass foundation
but on the old myth of military and thereby civic superiority over
Western middle class society ended in complete failure.

The success of the North in reimposing imperial unity, on the
other hand, saved and strengthened liberal thought. It averted the

militarization of the American continent. Lincoln as a personality and in his ideas was the very opposite of Bismarck. He was a civilian through and through in the Western tradition; together with Gladstone he was the greatest statesman of the liberal middle class cause in the nineteenth century; and the twentieth century so far has produced no equals to them in the vigorous pursuance of the Anglo-American tradition of liberty. The Gettysburg Address has rightly become one of its great documents and the United States has remained the frontier land and fulfillment of Western liberty. Yet in the struggle for liberty Lincoln's administration violated civil rights more consistently and more extensively than any other American administration. High-handed and oppressive justice was meted out. William B. Mumford became a hero of the Confederacy after he was hanged in New Orleans for removing, after the fall of the city, the United States flag that had been run up on the Mint Building. Even far away from the front, liberty was insecure. The freedom of the northern press quickly fell victim to drastic steps; editors were arbitrarily arrested, military authority ignored civil courts and many citizens who did not approve governmental policies went to jail without protection by habeas corpus. Lincoln's administration more often took recourse to non-constitutional and dictatorial measures than did that of Jefferson Davis.

Out of all these paradoxes and contradictions inherent in the Civil War American nationalism emerged stronger than ever, yet fraught with difficult problems. The Confederate States did not forget that they had formed a nation with an organized government, backed by the consent of the people, with a large and well defined territory, and that they lost their nationhood only as the result of a long struggle during which they fought well for their independence. Defeat and above all Reconstruction made southern nationalism a matter of the past, but of a past to which the southerners have looked back, for almost a century, with faithful love, viewing the ante-bellum period in the light of romantic legend and lamenting the chivalrous dead who had given their lives for the Lost Cause. The Confederate flag is still flying, Confederate heroes are still glorified and Confederate holidays celebrated. In recent years, with the wastefulness and inefficiency of the economy of the Old South receding into the dim past, the loyalty to the Stars and Bars has been growing. In many southern hearts the Confederate Cause, though lost, is not dead.[53]

In the North, Horace Greeley's attitude may be quoted to illustrate the paradoxes and contradictions which the Civil War presented to the American nationalist. Greeley was constrained to admit that if a number of states large enough to form a political community and maintain a national existence really wanted to leave the Union, the American nationalist ought to insist that they be permitted to leave in peace, yet he could not believe that the southerners really wished to secede. Like many nationalists in other countries, he liked to convince himself that not the people at large but only a small minority of firebrands and agitators really wanted to gain independence from the nation and to establish their own nation.[54] After the attack on Fort Sumter Greeley was whole-heartedly in favor of annihilating the rebellion, but he hoped that out of the war a true union of hearts would emerge, "a true exemplification of many in one—many stars blended in one common flag—many states combined in one homogeneous Nation." As soon as the war ended, Greeley demanded to "clasp hands across the bloody chasm." He insisted on universal amnesty and impartial suffrage for all in the South. "The nation needs peace, not vengeance," he wrote early in 1865. He wished to concentrate on the economic development of the South in order to enhance national strength and unity. "So shall North and South, at length comprehending and appreciating each other, walk hand in hand along their common pathway to an exalted and high destiny."

But his hopes were not fulfilled. Provisional governments in the southern states, maintained by military occupation, helped to impose measures which the southerners regarded as expressions of their subjection. Conciliation came only slowly. Nationalism had been inflamed by the Civil War not only in the South but also in the North, where voices were raised, overstressing and even sanctifying the principles of national unity and strong central government as against the traditions of broad federal diversity and states' rights.

Long before the United States had to undergo the experience of the international crises and tensions of the twentieth century, an American historian diagnosed the effects of great wars on free societies: Though such a society always has to face up to necessity of fighting for the preservation and extension of the liberty of the individual and the dignity of the human being, it should be conscious of the fact that wars tend to strengthen the power of the central government, a trend which even under favorable circumstances may imply a diminution of the rights of the individual and of the autonomous liberties of regional bodies. Such was the effect of the Civil War too. John Bascom wrote of it that "not only the victory itself, but the long, hard struggle which preceded it, tended strongly to give new force to national ties. The preservation of the nation had been a supreme idea for a number of years. Every local interest and feeling had given way before it. The power of the General Government had been called out to the full and been increased beyond all precedent. Great armies, large expenditures, high positions, heavy taxation had become familiar to the public. Congress and the country had ceased to hesitate at any measure which seemed to lie in the line of a successful prosecution of the war. The nation loomed large, and cast into its shadow personal and local disaster. The Constitution was used with the freedom incident to a revolutionary exigency." [55] Though the outcome may have been conducive to the general good, Lincoln had faced a deeply tragic decision; there was an element of guilt in the attitude of both sides leading up to the "irrepressible conflict" which unleashed demoniac passions, to which Lincoln himself and the ideas of liberty and charity for which he stood fell victim.

The great sacrifices which the Civil War demanded, enhanced the value of the nation to its citizens. In 1863 Edward Everett Hale wrote his deeply felt patriotic tale "The Man Without a Country." [56] The following year James Russell Lowell, after a rather self-righteous introduction, succeeded in catching the spirit of stirring anxiety and emotional stress involved in the war: "There have been many painful crises since the impatient vanity of South Carolina hurried ten prosperous Commonwealths into a crime whose assured retribution was to leave them either at the mercy of the nation they had wronged, or of the anarchy they had summoned up but could not control, when no thoughtful American opened his morning paper without dreading to find that he had no longer a country to love and honor. Whatever the result of the convulsion whose first shocks were beginning to be felt, there would still be enough square miles of earth for elbow room; but that ineffable sentiment made up of memory and hope, of instinct and tradition, which swells every man's heart and shapes his thought, though perhaps they were present to his consciousness, would be gone from it, leaving it common earth and nothing more. Men might gather rich crops from it, but that ideal harvest of priceless association would be reaped no longer; that fine virtue which sent up messages of courage and security from every sod of it would have evaporated beyond recall." [57]

Much effort was needed to keep the flagging spirit of nationalism alive in the North. Lowell himself confessed "that we had our doubts at first whether the patriotism of our people were not too narrowly provincial to embrace the proportions of national peril. We felt an only too natural distrust of immense public meetings and enthusiastic cheers." [58] Oliver Wendell Holmes in an address on the 4th of July, 1863, wondered whether "we have not degenerated from our English fathers so that we cannot do and bear for our national salvation what they have done and borne over and over again for their form of government? Could England, in her wars with Napoleon, bear an income tax of ten per cent, and must we faint under the burden of an income tax of three percent? . . . But let us say it plainly— it will not hurt our people to be taught that there are other things to be cared for besides money making and money spending; that the time has come when manhood must assert itself by brave deeds and noble thoughts . . . We have grown rich for what? To sweep the foul sidewalks with the heaviest silks that the toiling artisans of France can send us? . . . Let us not whine over our imaginary ruin, while the reversed current of circling events is carrying us farther and farther, every hour, beyond the influence of the great failing which was born of our wealth, and of the deadly sin which was our fatal inheritance!" [59]

Victory, finally achieved, dispelled all the doubts and worries deeply felt during the war. Anxiety gave way to heightened self-confidence and exuberant expectations of the future. The United States emerged from the trial of war enhanced in its own eyes as well as abroad. Lowell expressed this sentiment in his well known essay "On a Certain Condescension in Foreigners" which he wrote in 1869: "Till after our Civil War it never seemed to enter the head of any foreigner, especially of any Englishman, that an American had what could be called a country, except as a place to eat, sleep, and trade in. Then it seemed to strike them suddenly, 'By Jove, you know, fellahs don't fight like that for a shop-till!' No, I rather think not. To Americans, America is something more than a promise and an expectation. It has a past and traditions of its own. A descent from men who sacrificed everything and came hither, not to better their fortunes but to plant their idea in virgin soil, should be a good pedigree . . . Above all, we beg [our visitors] to remember that America is not to us, as to them, a mere object of external interest to be discussed and analyzed, but in us part of our very marrow. Let them not suppose that we conceive of ourselves as exiles from the graces and amenities of an older date . . . The full tide of human existence may be felt here as keenly as Johnson felt it at Charing Cross, and in a larger sense." [60] Lowell's was a voice of old Boston; similar sentiments were expressed by a recent immigrant, Edwin Lawrence Godkin, who came to the United States five years before the Civil War began. Godkin believed that the people in the northern states felt the cause of the Union with a "fanatical veneration" on account of "their remembrance of the blessings and joys under its shadow, the peace, the plenty, prosperity, security and liberty, which had been bestowed on three generations." The Civil War "was more than any other the heroic age of the American Commonwealth. The revolution of 1776 was carried to a successful issue through the perseverance of a few leading men; the war of 1861 was essentially a popular uprising which carried the leaders forward, often in spite of themselves." [61]

The triumphant self-confident nationalism after the Civil War seduced some Americans into strange overstatements. The Reverend Elisha Mulford tried to apply to the American nation the organic theory of the nation-state which he had learned from German thinkers, to whom he frequently referred: Hegel and two men less well known today but then famous in the educated world, Friedrich Julius Stahl, professor of ecclesiastical law in Berlin, and Richard Rothe, professor of theology at the universities of Bonn and Heidelberg—all three of them representatives of the conservative, authoritarian state-ideology. In his violently anti-British book *The Nation: The Foundations of Civil Order and Political Life in the United States,* which appeared in 1870, Mulford sought, "however imperfectly, to give expression to the thought of the people in the late war, and that conception of the nation which they who were so worthy held worth living and dying for." Yet the concept of a nation which he established sounded like a caricature of the free society which the United States was. His concept represented the very opposite of the English theory of government, which had prevailed in England and North America since Milton and Locke. Mulford, following his German teachers, regarded the Nation as a mystic body endowed with a spirit and majesty of its own, a body which has apparently existed and will exist forever, a body the foundations of which were laid in the very nature of man. With the American nation being thus apparently preordained by the Divine Will, the Confederacy became by necessity something sacrilegious. It had the audacity to assume the origin of society to be in voluntary legal compacts of the citizens. Therefore, Mulford assured his readers, "the Nation and the Confederacy [had] at last [to meet] in mortal conflict. Confederatism, in its attack upon the Nation, is in league with hell. . . . It denies the divine origin of humanity, and the sacred rights it bears in its divine image. . . . It gathers to itself the pride, the treachery and infidelity of men, the worship of money, the vulgarity of fashion, and the distinction of caste. . . . The Nation is as old as history. . . . It is a work of God in history. . . . Its vocation is from God, and its obligation is only to God." But in spite of his borrowing from German political theory, Mulford was not a nationalist in the German fashion. He emphasized that the Civil War was fought for the equality of all races and of all men in the American tradition; thus, Mulford declared, a nation which identifies itself exclusively with one race or which builds upon racial distinction, was not a true nation. "It has no longer a moral foundation, nor a universal end when it asserts as its ground the rise of a race and not the rise of man." [62]

Though others did not go as far in the idolization of the nation as the German inspired clergyman did, they too waxed enthusiastic about the newly won unity which they unduly extolled above all federal liberties. In 1867 Charles Sumner in an address "Are We A Nation?" thundered that "state rights, in all their denationalizing pretensions, must be trampled out forever. . . . To my mind, our government is not federal, but national." Out of the crucible of the war Sumner welcomed the birth of the nation with its "indestructible unity," with its "central pervasive power." He concluded with a paean to national unity: "All hail to the Republic, redeemed and regenerated, One and Indivisible! Nullification and Secession are already, like the extinct monsters of a former geological period, to be seen only in the museum of History. . . . There will be a new consciousness of national life, with a corresponding glow. The soul will dilate with the assured unity of the Republic, and all will feel the glory of its citizenship. Since that of Rome, nothing so commanding. Local jealousies will be lost in the attractions of a common country. Then, indeed, there will be no North, no South, no East, no West; but there will be One Nation. . . . Not the Southern Cross flaming with beauty, not even the North Star, long time guide of the mariner and refuge of the flying bondman, but the whole star-spread firmament will be our worship and delight." [63]

But these instances of a dithyrambic emphasis on national unity did not long prevail against the common sense of American life. In a much attenuated form this overemphasis on the glamour of strong unified government has been revived in recent efforts to strengthen the central executive power, an attitude in agreement with the temper of impatience, with the desire for quick solutions, with the reluctance to compromise, which characterize many trends in twentieth century civilization, though to a much lesser degree in the English-speaking countries than elsewhere. Theodore Roosevelt represented this trend when he declared in 1910 that "the American people are right in demanding that New Nationalism, without which we cannot hope to deal with new problems. The New Nationalism puts the national need before sectional or personal advantage. It is impatient of the utter confusion that results from local legislatures attempting to treat national issues as local issues. It is still more impatient of the impotence which springs from over-division of governmental powers, the impotence which makes it possible for local selfishness or for legal cunning, hired by wealthy special interests, to bring national activities to a deadlock. This New Nationalism regards the executive power as the steward of the public welfare." [64] This emphasis on executive power in Theodore Roosevelt's New Nationalism was carried on during the periods of the New Freedom and the New Deal. Yet in spite of occasional aberrations, the United States respected the sense of balance and moderation needed in a republic of many republics, which knew that it differed from other nations not only by its basis in individual liberty but also by its fundamental federalism. A free diversity on a footing of equality has remained the characteristic expression of

American unity, a unity not centered in a life-absorbing representative capital but diffused in a living manifold of many equally important cities and regions, each different, each proud of its local distinctiveness, and each living its own life.[65]

This sense of moderation was also evident in the crisis of the middle 1950's, when the time had ineluctably come to take up one of the burning issues left unresolved by the victory in the Civil War, above all by the way in which this victory had been exploited. The need for assuring full equality to the Negro population in the United States had gained a new urgency after the Second World War. The two great wars, especially the second, changed completely the position of the Negro. The incredible pace of industrialization demanded an increased manpower and brought with it a rapid rise in economic opportunities. Negroes migrated in great numbers from tradition-bound southern rural areas to northern industrial agglomerations. A thorough improvement in educational facilities on all levels followed. The Second World War brought industrialization to the South itself and with it a new mobility and fluidity of social and economic conditions. Until then the Negro in the South had been held within the bounds of a caste system, which he on the whole accepted as the lower classes had accepted similar caste status in nineteenth century Europe. In the North the Negro, as regards economic opportunities and educational and housing conditions, had been on the whole treated like first generation immigrants from southern or eastern Europe, a treatment which sharply contrasted with the fact that, outside the Indians, no single group is so indigenously American as the American Negro. It is true that he—and he alone among all the immigrant groups—came to the United States involuntarily, but he had become one hundred per cent American, with no memory of a non-American language spoken by his ancestors and with no attachment to a non-American homeland or to a non-American social way of life.

Under these circumstances, the advancement of the Negro toward economic, political, social and educational equality since the Second World War, and especially since 1952, has been steady and rapid both in the South and in the North, above all in the armed forces and in the Federal District of Columbia. In spite of the larger influx of Negro labor to the North after 1940 no race riots occurred which could compare with those which dishonored northern and midwestern cities in the years following the First World War. The disgrace of lynchings, a remnant in American life of the lawlessness and of the cult of womanly purity of frontier days, has fallen into desuetude. The Negroes in the South have acquired a new generation of leaders in young men trained in northern colleges. This leadership, often represented by ministers of the churches, rejects the old acceptance of the caste system, yet it does so with a deep sense of responsible moderation. A social revolution—one in the long chain of those social revolutions which without violent upheaval mark the course and form the essence of American history—is under way in the United States and has been given legal expression by the Supreme Court decisions of May 17, 1954, May 31, 1955, and November 7, 1955. They are the beginning of the gradual end of Jim Crow in the South.[66]

Throughout American history, from George Washington to Dwight Eisenhower, the problem of the Negro population and its status in American society has deeply disturbed the American ideals in the North as well as in the South. A holier-than-thou attitude on the part of the North would hardly do justice to historical and social reality. Finally, in the 1950's, the Negro is on the way to receiving the full status of equality guaranteed to him by the American national idea as well as by the fourteenth and fifteenth amendments to the Constitution. But in this process another and equally fundamental problem is involved; the proper functioning of the republic of many republics, one of the greatest contributions of United States nationalism to the developing Western and world community. The individual traditions and rights of the various parts of the federation demand most careful consideration. It must never be forgotten that the federal principle and states' rights impose—as do individual rights and liberties—certain limits upon efficient and even desirable national action. William Faulkner, for many years one of the few outstanding liberals and an ardent defender of Negro equality in his home state of Mississippi, has made these limitations clear in an interview which he gave in the beginning of 1956. In his outlook Faulkner is essentially an heir of the Jeffersonian tradition, with perhaps a greater emphasis upon the chivalric code of personal honor. "The Negro has a right to equality," he declared. "His equality is inevitable, an irresistible force, but as I see it you've got to take into consideration human nature, which at times has nothing to do with moral truths. . . . I don't like enforced integration any more than I like enforced segregation. If I have to choose between the United States government and Mississippi, then I'll choose Mississippi. What I'm trying to do now is not to have to make that decision. As long as there's a middle road, all right, I'll be on it. But if it came to fighting I'd fight for Mississippi against the United States . . ." [67] Thus the South, in the words of one of its intellectually most prominent representatives ninety years after the end of the Civil War, continues to live on in its memory and shadow. The fundamental issues of that great conflict are still alive. They force upon the student of history the realization of the difficulty and complexity of the problems involved in the nationalism of a free Western people who have made not centralized power but the respect for individual liberty and for federal rights the basis of its existence. A free people in the West cannot have recourse to the shortcuts and oversimplifications which appear to make authoritarianism and centralization an easier and more efficient way of government. In the long run the elasticity, the power of accommodation, and the certainty of slow and irresistible progress make free government stronger than any other, yet at the same time such a free government stands forth beset with many problems openly discussed and presented to the world in the full light of public view. One of the problems which has disturbed the republic of many republics since 1821 has been the status of the Negro. This problem gained additional weight in a multi-ethnic nation; thus it formed one of the crucial elements in the complexity of the nation of many nations, another fundamental concept of American nationalism, which renders it more difficult and vulnerable but also more hopeful and promising than other nationalisms are.

chapter four

A nation of
many nations

"Centralization is the convergence of all the rays of
power into one central point; nationalization is the
diffusion of the same life-blood through a system of
arteries, throughout a body politic, indeed, it is the
growing of the body politic as such, morally, and
thoroughly cemented, out of a mass, otherwise un-
cemented."

FRANCIS LIEBER
Manual of Political Ethics (1839)

"We are the Romans of the modern world—the
great assimilating people."

OLIVER WENDELL HOLMES
The Autocrat of the Breakfast-Table

"O mother of a mighty race
Yet lovely in thy youthful grace . . .
There's freedom at thy gates, and rest
For earth's downtrodden—opprest"

WILLIAM CULLEN BRYANT
America

Of the three foundations on which American nationality rests, the historical root in the English tradition of liberty which the settlers brought with them from across the ocean comes first in time sequence and in importance; second only, but indispensable for the formation of a separate American nation, was the immense, thinly populated continent which invited the Anglo-Americans to seek independence and imperial expansion and provided the opportunity for America's pioneering innovation, the federal solution of a republic of many republics; finally, historical roots and spatial opportunities combined in the idea of universal liberty with America's power to assimilate the millions of immigrants who poured into the country, helping to fill the open spaces and to realize the apparently unlimited potentialities of America's soil and of her inventive skill. The character of the United States as a land with open gateways, a nation of many nations, became as important for American nationalism as its identification with the idea of individual liberty and its federal character. The difficult problems posited by liberty and federalism have been there from the beginning; those created by immigration assumed a fundamental importance for American nationality only after 1846 when the Irish and the Germans started coming in great numbers. This rising swell of immigration met two different situations: in Europe it coincided with economic and political distress and with the introduction of the steamship which facilitated the crossing of the ocean; in America it came simultaneously with the vast forward movement with its beckoning opportunities, a movement filling the whole North American continent and inspired by the exuberant feeling of manifest destiny. Three decades later, with the rapid growth of industrialization and urbanization after the Civil War immigration began to reach unprecedented dimensions. These immigrants came to a country in many ways different from that of 1790: immense territories had been opened up and settled, great fortunes had been amassed, distances were overcome, the rural character of the nation was fast disappearing—as late as 1830 only two American cities had more than 100,000 inhabitants—the suffrage had everywhere become democratized, the party system had been stabilized on a national and supra-sectional basis.

The elements who came from Europe were to a large extent people of great poverty and scant if any education. Nevertheless, they were among the hardiest and most energetic segments of European society. They were willing to uproot themselves, to take risks, to face the unknown, to become masters of their own destiny. Different from the still widely apathetic masses of Europe, the immigrants had a faith in their ability and in the future. Their energy and faith fitted well into the American environment. Mixture of blood had enhanced the vitality of England, but a process which took centuries there was condensed in the United States into a few decades. "Long after the English stock emerged [from the mixture of Briton, Roman, Pict, Saxon, Dane, Norsemen and Norman], it was continually improved by the addition of foreign elements. French Huguenots, German emigrants, fugitive Jews, Dutchmen and Spaniards, all added more or less of a foreign strain to our English blood. It has been our salvation. The mixing of Welsh and Irish, Scotch and English, Celts of the Highland and Danes of Northumberland, which has gone on for centuries and is going on to-day, has produced a type which is being reproduced on a gigantic scale and with infinite modifications across the Atlantic." [1] All through the nineteenth century Britain was the citadel of refuge for the political refugees from the European continent; monarchs and revolutionaries alike—Metternich and Marx, Napoleon III and Mazzini, Charles X and Alexander Herzen—all went to England. In this respect the United States in the twentieth century took its place beside the United Kingdom. But political refugees played only a minor role in the history of American immigration; to the broad stream of non-political immigrants the United States owed the enhancement of its exuberant energies in the latter part of the nineteenth century. In the expanding American system this mighty influx of non-Americans did not diminish American nationalism. On the contrary, it strengthened it and acted from the beginning as a cementing force. For the immigrants did not feel bound to any of the traditional American sections or states. They came not in order to become northerners or southerners, easterners or westerners, citizens of Massachusetts or Virginia; they came to become Americans. Many came only to profit from American opportunities and were eager to return enriched to their homelands. Even they went back enriched not only with dollars which allowed them in many cases a living standard unknown to their fellow citizens in their Sicilian or Lebanese villages, but enriched also with American ideas, a recollection of individual liberty, social mobility, personal initiative, which frequently earned them the sobriquet of "Americans" and sometimes acted as a leaven in their native environment. But the large majority of immigrants had no desire to return. They found in the United States what they missed in their homelands: social opportunities and a new freedom, if not for themselves then for their children. Under the impact of the American environment, through the medium of American education, the children in many cases became the most fervent American patriots.

Though immigration grew into a broad stream only after the middle of the nineteenth century, it had from the beginning occupied an important position in the build-up of American nationalism. Immigration was closely linked with America's consciousness of her national character, of her distinctiveness from Old Europe. Yet the ambivalent attitude towards immigration can be found as early as the middle of the eighteenth century. Benjamin Franklin in his *Poor Richard Improved* (1752) extolled Anglo-America as a place of refuge:

> Where the sick Stranger joys to find a Home,
> Where casual Ill, maim'd Labour, freely come;
> Those worn with Age, Infirmity or Care,
> Find Rest, Relief, and Health returning fair.
> There too the Walls of rising Schools ascend,
> For Publick Spirit still is Learning's Friend,
> Where Science, Virtue, sown with liberal Hand,
> In future Patriots shall inspire the Land.

But the same Franklin privately expressed his fear of German (Dutch) immigrants to Pennsylvania, and brought against them the two main complaints later raised against immigrants from southern and eastern Europe, their underbidding American labor and standards and their acting as a disrupting and unassimilable element in Anglo-America. "This will in a few Years become a German Colony: Instead of their Learning our Language, we must learn their's, or live as in a foreign country. Already the English begin to quit particular Neighbourhoods surrounded by Dutch, being made uneasy by the Disagreeableness of dissonant Manners; and in Time, Numbers will probably quit the Province for the same Reason. Besides, the Dutch under-live, and are thereby enabled to under-work and under-sell the English; who are thereby extremely incommoded, and consequently disgusted, so that there can be no cordial Affection or Unity between the two Nations." [2]

Thomas Jefferson, who as a young man had opposed immigration, wished in 1817 to keep the doors of America open, "to consecrate a sanctuary for those whom the misrule of Europe may compel to seek happiness in other climes. This refuge once known will produce reaction on the happiness even of those who remain there, by warning their taskmasters that when the evils of Egyptian oppression become heavier than those of the abandonment of country, another Canaan is open where their subjects will be received as brothers and secured against like oppression by a participation in the right of self-government." [3] This proclamation of an open port for immigrants was in keeping with Jefferson's faith in America's national mission as mankind's vanguard in the fight for individual liberty, the embodiment of the rational and humanitarian ideals of eighteenth century Western man. The American nation was to be a universal nation—not only in the sense that the idea which it pursued was believed to be universal and valid for the whole of mankind, but also in the sense that it was a nation composed of many ethnic strains. Such a nation, held together by liberty and diversity, had to be firmly integrated around allegiance to the American idea, an idea to which everyone could be assimilated for the very reason that it was a universal idea. To facilitate the process of integration, Jefferson strongly opposed the settlement of immigrants in compact groups, and advocated their wide distribution among the older settlers for the purpose of "quicker amalgamation." Jefferson's attitude prevailed throughout American history. Several attempts were made, above all by the Germans and the Irish, to concentrate their settlements geographically, so that the immigrants could preserve their speech, culture and folkways. The bolder spirits among the German intellectuals talked of peopling one of the American states and, as was possible under the Constitution, adopting German as the official language. "Then, when the expected breakup of the Union should take place, this Teutonic Commonwealth could embark on an independent career and make such alliances as it desired with the German Confederation or the Zollverein. The first step in the fulfillment of any of these dreams was the acquisition of land. But the government of the United States, though possessed of millions of acres, proved unwilling to give a single acre for the purpose." In 1818 it rejected a request from the Irish societies of New York and Philadelphia and maintained that it would be undesirable to concentrate alien people geographically and thus to allow the formation of national minorities. "Probably no decision in the history of American immigration policy possesses more profound significance. By its terms the immigrant was to enjoy no special privileges to encourage his coming; also he was to suffer no special restrictions. His opportunities were those of the native, nothing more, nothing less." [4]

A few decades later, when immigration had begun to increase, Ralph Waldo Emerson went further than Jefferson. Emerson believed that it was "the capital advantage of our Republic that by the organic hospitality of its institutions it is drawing the health and strength of all nations into its territory and promises by perpetual intermixture to yield the most vigorous qualities and accomplishments of all." [5] In his address, "The Fortune of the Republic," Emerson declared opportunity to be the true policy marking the genius of the country. "Opportunity of civil rights, of education, of personal power, and not less of wealth; doors wide open . . . invitation to every nation, to every race and skin, . . . hospitality of fair field and equal laws to all. Let them compete, and success to the strongest, the wisest, and the best. The land is wide enough, the soil has bread for all." In this address delivered in 1878, Emerson repeated the more lyrical statement which he had made some thirty years before in "The Young American": "A heterogeneous population crowding on ships from all corners of the world to the great gates of North America, namely Boston, New York, and New Orleans, and thence proceeding inward to the prairie and mountains, and quickly contributing their private thought to the public opinion, their toll to the treasury, and their vote to the election, it cannot be doubted that the legislation of this country should become more catholic and cosmopolitan than that of any other. It seems so easy for America to inspire and express the most expansive and

humane spirit; new-born, free, healthful, strong, the land of the
laborer, of the democrat, of the philanthropist, of the believer, of
the saint, she should speak for the human race. It is the country of
the Future. From Washington, proverbially 'the city of magnificent
distances,' through all its cities, states and territories, it is a country
of beginnings, of projects, of designs, of expectations." Emerson's
belief that "America is another word for opportunity. Our whole
history appears like a last effort of the Divine Providence in behalf of the human race," was shared by many immigrants at all
times.[6] As early as 1796 a Hamburg merchant on a voyage to the
United States remarked that recent immigrants who had only arrived a few years before, had been already transformed by their
new fatherland. "Their whole behavior reveals a new way of thinking as Americans. Their former stiffness has been lost." Every wave
of incoming immigrants, he found, was trying hard to imitate their
former compatriots who had become new Americans.[7]

The Hamburg merchant who noticed this speedy integration of
the immigrants with their new homeland was only a visitor to the
States. His observations were confined to the eastern states, for the
midwest had not been opened up yet. In its vast and empty spaces
immigrants settled a few decades later in closed communities where
they preserved their language and traditions, their separate personality, for a relatively long period. That was true for instance of
the Norwegians. Naturally, many of them living in isolated outposts felt a longing for the Old Country. From his frontier parsonage
Olaus Duus wrote in the 1850's: "But America is not Norway. Here
there is always a sense of strangeness, something unlike home, and
I don't suppose we will ever feel completely at home here." [8] The
Norwegian immigrant of the mid-nineteenth century, like so many
later immigrants, felt uprooted without having yet struck new roots
in his new homeland. "The immigrant straddles two cultures," a
historian of Norwegian immigration wrote, "and if he is homeless
in both, it is due in no small measure to his linguistic difficulties." [9]
Many of the immigrants built their own schools and colleges, frequently supported by the national church, cultivating the language
and the culture of the homeland. Up to the First World War such
schools and colleges were frequent, especially in the Middle West,
and they enriched and diversified the cultural life of the United
States. But soon the children of these immigrants were drawn ir-

resistibly into American life, not only by the material advantages it offered, but for the cultural values of liberty and tolerance unknown in their old countries. As the immigrants came into contact with Americans of older vintage, a new attitude was awakened among them, "a feeling of independence and freedom, a spirit of tolerance in matters of religion, and an open mind for information, together with that conviction of their worth as men and citizens which is a cornerstone of the moral virtues." [10] One of the early Norwegian settlers, J. R. Reiersen, wrote in a letter of 1852: "I have learned to love the country to which I emigrated more sincerely than my old fatherland, of which I can never think with any heartfelt longing . . . I feel free and independent among a free people who are not chained down by any class or caste systems; and I am very proud of belonging to a mighty nation, whose institutions must in time come to dominate the entire civilized world, because they are founded on principles that sound intelligence must recognize as the only ones that are right and correct." And in 1881 John Storseth summed up this general experience: "A great commonwealth is forming here in America. People of every tongue, religion and race are getting more and more conscious of being one. All of them came here with their ideas and aspirations. And they brought with them their tribal memories from a thousand years back. It is all these memories that the different nations brought with them which, put together, have made America what it is today." [11]

More clearly verbalized was the identification of one of the most prominent German immigrant scholars in the United States who had been an active German patriot in his youth, Francis Lieber. A disciple of Father Jahn, he was originally invited to teach gymnastics in Boston. Soon, however, he became one of the leading political scientists in his adopted land. In this capacity he stressed the English foundation of American nationality and liberty. He disapproved George Bancroft's glorification of the American revolution as the culmination in the historical struggle for liberty: to him the English revolutions of the seventeenth century appeared as the high point in that monumental development. He believed that the Americans essentially formed part of the "Anglican race." "We belong to that race," he wrote, "whose obvious task it is . . . to rear and spread civil liberty over vast regions. . . . We belong to that tribe which alone has the word 'Self-Government'." "Nations must go to America and England," he wrote, "to learn liberty, as we go to Italy to study music and to have the vast world of fine arts opened to us, or as we go to France to study science, or to Germany that we may learn how to instruct and spread education." [12] The American branch of the Anglican race, Lieber believed, was blessed above that in its homeland, because it was placed "with a full inheritance of freedom on the freshest soil in the noblest site between Europe and Asia." Lieber disapproved of schools in which German was the language of instruction and of the desire of Irishmen and Germans to remain Irish or German at the time when they became Americans. As early as 1870 he urged the importance of regulating immigration to the United States.[13]

By that time immigration had become so important that in order to protect immigrants arriving in the various ports of the United States, President U. S. Grant favored national legislation in a special message to Congress on May 14, 1872: "The immigrant is not a citizen of any State or Territory upon his arrival, but comes here to become a citizen of a great Republic, free to change his residence at will, to enjoy the blessings of a protecting Government, where all are equal before the law, and to add to the national wealth by his industry. On his arrival he does not know States or corporations, but confides implicitly in the protecting arm of the great, free country of which he has heard so much before leaving his native land. . . . I do not advise national legislation in affairs that should be regulated by the states; but I see no subject more national in its character than provision for the safety and welfare of the thousands who leave foreign lands to become citizens of this Republic." [14]

From the beginning however, the rapidly growing immigration to the United States met resistance, originally on religious grounds, later on ethnic and social grounds. The first form which the anti-immigration sentiment took was a heritage of the deeply ingrained Protestant prejudice against, and fear of, Catholicism. In 1775 Anglo-America was an almost purely Protestant country. Here Thomas Jefferson and the first amendment to the Constitution set an example of tolerance beyond anything then known in the Western world. The United States, founded in the Age of Enlightenment, was the foremost realization of its spirit. The efforts of Roger Williams and of Locke, the struggles of the French skeptics and deists, were here consummated. The non-religious character of the American government became one of its fundamental characteristics. Under Jefferson's influence the legislature of Virginia enacted on December 17, 1785, a law, "that no man shall be compelled to frequent or support any religious worship, place or ministry whatsoever, nor shall he be enforced, restrained, molested or burdened in his body or goods, nor shall he otherwise suffer on account of his religious opinions or beliefs; but that all men should be free to profess, and by argument to maintain, their opinions in matters of religion, and that the same shall in no wise diminish, enlarge or affect their civil capacities." In 1796 a treaty was signed between the United States and Tripoli, in which one article opened with the words, "As the government of the United States is not in any sense founded on the Christian religion"; and this treaty was ratified by the Senate without objection. In public proclamations neither George Washington nor Jefferson nor James Madison was given to the expression of Christian or even of religious sentiment.[15]

This eighteenth century tolerant spirit gave way when, with improved ocean transportation and worsening economic conditions in Europe, immigration began to grow rapidly in the second quarter of the nineteenth century. Several reasons combined to create misgivings about the increased flow of immigrants and to give rise to exaggerated fears. The number of paupers among the immigrants was disproportionately large when compared with the settled population of the states. Did not some of the immigrants bring with them lower standards of morality and education than those which prevailed in the United States? The Irish and German immigrants after 1840 were mostly Catholics. In 1807 there had been only seventy thousand Catholics in all the states with one bishop and seventy priests. Now the Catholic church in America grew at a rapid pace. Moreover, the hierarchical organization of the Catholic church seemed out of line with the American tradition, and the exercise of papal authority "over the people of a free country" was felt to be "repugnant to our republican institutions." The nativist movement, as it was called, wished to preserve the free and Protestant character of the United States.

The Protestants expressed fears of a Popish design, which was allegedly supported by the conservative monarchs of Europe, to

gain control of the United States and especially of its new heartland, the Mississippi Valley. These fears were at that time in no
way unique to the United States; they recall similar fears voiced
by Swiss Protestants when the Jesuits in the 1840's were suspected
of gaining control of education in the Catholic cantons. These fears
were fanned in the United States by the uncompromising attitude
then adopted by the Catholic church. Its spiritual leader in America, Archbishop John Hughes of New York, proclaimed in 1850
that "the object we hope to accomplish in time, is to convert all
Pagan nations, and all Protestant nations, even England with her
proud parliament and imperial sovereign. It is a commission of God
to his church and not a human project." [16] Later this attitude of the
Catholic hierarchy in the United States changed with the progressive Americanization of the church and gave way to a growing
spirit of cooperation and tolerance unknown in most other parts
of the Catholic world.

Soon the movement directed against immigration broadened its
originally purely religious basis by appealing to the fear of competition and by trying to enlist support among working men hostile
to immigrant labor. The *Native American* complained on November
29, 1844, that "our laboring men, native and naturalized, are met
at every turn and at every avenue of employment, with recently
imported workmen from the low wages countries of the Old World.
They fill our large cities, reduce the wages of labor, and they increase the hardship of the old settler." The *Native American* was a
newly established Philadelphia paper which pleaded for the extension of the period needed for naturalization, for the reservation
of elective offices to native born citizens, and for the rejection of
foreign interference in all American institutions. Another element
in the anti-immigration movement was added when, as a result of
the liberal and nationalist movements in the Europe of the 1840's,
many immigrants, especially some Irish, showed an active interest
in the struggles of the mother country. Their activities aroused apprehension of interference with American isolationism and involvement of the United States in Europe. A working man's organization called the Order of United Americans, a benevolent and
patriotic society, was formed in New York in 1844. It restricted its
membership to American born laborers and pledged itself to fight
"for upholding our national liberties, and for freeing them wholly

from all foreign and deleterious influences whatever." Similar organizations sprang up in other parts of the country, and in 1854 they fused into the American or Know-Nothing party, which for a few years seemed destined to play a major role in American policy until it disintegrated as quickly as it had, for a brief moment of history, swept the country.

The Know-Nothing movement was perhaps strongest in Massachusetts where the Irish immigration threatened to gain control of the large cities. In 1855, 68,100 of the 260,742 inhabitants of greater Boston were born in Ireland. In 1854 the Know-Nothings elected their candidate to the governorship by an unprecedented majority and gained complete control of the legislature. They ruled the state until 1857. Although they made numerous mistakes—because the new legislators represented the rank and file and were not recruited among the experienced politicians and lawyers—"their administration was progressive and fruitful." They reorganized the school system and abolished imprisonment for debt, established the first insurance commission, took the first steps to eliminate danger from railroad crossings, extended the power of juries, strengthened the temperance, homestead and women's rights movements, made vaccination compulsory, and assumed a firm anti-slavery position. Their achievements as a reform party were outstanding. On the other hand, "their anti-foreign accomplishments were quite insignificant. To begin with, they disclaimed any intention of excluding immigrants, but stressed the necessity of making them 'be as we are.' Ostensibly the party had acquired power to restrict the influence of immigrants in politics. Yet, though it had absolute control of the government, it failed to pass a single measure to that effect." [17] This failure of the anti-immigration policy in Massachusetts was repeated on the national stage.

Though the American party gained in 1854 a strong foothold in the Congress, it was unable to carry even the mildest of its various proposals to limit naturalization or immigrants' rights. In this as in so many later cases—and the most recent was the agitation aroused by Senator Joseph McCarthy—the liberal ideas of the Constitution proved much stronger than even the most powerful mass movements guided by emotionalism. What Professor Billington states about Know-Nothingism has been as applicable to all the later nativist movements. They had nothing permanent to offer.

Their principles were inimical to those on which the American nation had been founded; their demands were of a sort that could never be realized in a country constituted as was the United States.[18] Yet the American party seemed destined to success: it polled about one-fourth of the popular vote in the congressional election of 1856. Carl Schurz, a German immigrant himself who had risen to the important role of statesman in his new homeland, in a speech on "True Americanism" in Boston on April 18, 1859, after the victory of the American party in Massachusetts, defined the very principles of the American tradition against which the Know-Nothing movement foundered, as did all similar movements of intolerance and illiberalism whatever their momentary attractions for the masses: "By recognizing perfect freedom of inquiry, [religious freedom] will engender among men of different belief that mutual respect of true convictions which makes inquiry earnest and discussion fair. It will recognize as supremely inviolable, what Roger Williams, one of the most luminous stars of the American sky, called the sanctity of conscience. Read your history, and add the thousands and thousands of Romanists and their offspring together, who, from the first establishment of the colonies, gradually came to this country, and the sum will amount to many millions; compare that number with the number of Romanists who are now here, and you will find that millions are missing. Where are they? You did not kill them; you did not drive them away; they did not perish as the victims of persecution. But where are they? The peaceable working of the great principles which called this Republic into existence, gradually and silently absorbed them. True Americanism, toleration, the equality of rights, has absorbed their prejudices, and will peaceably absorb everything that is not consistent with the victorious spirit of our institutions." [19]

Carl Schurz recognized the assimilating and transforming power of the American national idea, a phenomenon approached to a certain extent in some Latin American states but quantitatively and qualitatively unique in the case of the United States. Folk movements with their typical narrowness and xenophoby, their fears for their own ways of life and their dislike of differences, have not been unknown in the United States. In fact, they are in their flow and ebb an apparently permanent feature of American folk mores. Similar movements can be found among the common people everywhere, even in countries where no significant immigration has taken place. The history of nineteenth century Norwegian nationalism bears witness to the antipathy of the peasants who according to nationalist intellectuals represented the "true" native Norwegian stock and folkways, against the educated burghers in the cities who were accused of having succumbed to Danish cultural influence. Yet here it was a case of peoples sharing the same Lutheran faith and closely akin in origin and language. In hospitable and cosmopolitan Paris, so different from the xenophobic and tradition-bound French provincial towns, foreigners who have gone there inspired by an admiring love for French culture have often been regarded by the "natives" as *métèques*, undesirable aliens. This xenophoby, characteristic of the common man everywhere, has its hold on America too. Yet no other nation has had to face the problem of immigration and assimilation of the most diverse strains on a scale even approaching that with which the United States had to deal and which it has solved on the whole with astonishing success and tolerance.[20]

American life, both among the "natives" on the frontier and among the immigrants in the big cities, has often been disturbed by violence, mob passion and uncompromising group assertion. Yet at the height of the Know-Nothing movement, an American Protestant divine of German origin, Philip Schaff, rightly declared to his German audiences that "even in the midst of the storms of political agitation," the American people "listens ever and anon to the voice of reason and sober reflection." In England and America, he pointed out, constitutional liberalism formed the safest barrier against extremism, which "continually breaks on the free institutions of the country and the sound sense of order in the people." This constitutional attitude and common sense quickly influenced and transformed the immigrants. The "happy intermingling" of races and creeds in America was one of the reasons which the German Lutheran theologian adduced to explain why he returned from his visit to Europe "with an elevated sense of the vast importance of America for the destiny of mankind." In the United States, he wrote, "all is in a ferment as yet, in the first formation state; but looks to the grandest future. A process of amalgamation is now going on there, like that among the Germanic, Romanic, and Celtic races at the migration of the nations, and that in England after the

Norman invasion; but on a far broader foundation, on a much larger scale, and under much more favorable conditions. In the United States all nations, all churches and sects, all the good and evil powers of the old world, meet without blows or bloodshed; and while Europe began with paganism and barbarism, America begins with the results of Europe's two thousand years' course of civilization, and has vigor, energy, enterprise, and ambition enough to put out this enormous capital at the most profitable interest for the general good of mankind." [21]

At about the same time that the German immigrant praised the process of amalgamation going on in the United States, the native American writer Herman Melville wrote in *Redburn: His First Voyage* (1849): "There is something in the contemplation of the mode in which America has been settled, that, in a noble breast, should forever extinguish the prejudices of national dislikes. Settled by the people of all nations, all nations may claim her for their own. You cannot spill a drop of American blood without spilling the blood of the whole world. Be he Englishman, Frenchman, German, Dane, or Scot; the European who scoffs at an American calls his own brother *Raca*, and stands in danger of the judgment. We are not a narrow tribe of men with a bigoted Hebrew nationality— whose blood has been debased in the attempt to ennoble it, by maintaining an exclusive succession among ourselves. No; our blood is as the flood of the Amazon, made up of a thousand noble currents all pouring into one. We are not a nation, so much as a world; for unless we may claim all the world for our sire, like Melchisedec, we are without father or mother. For who were our father and our mother? Or can we point to any Romulus and Remus for our founders? Our ancestry is lost in the universal paternity; and Caesar and Alfred, St. Paul and Luther, and Homer and Shakespeare are as much ours as Washington, who is as much the world's as our own. We are the heirs of all time, and with all nations we divide our inheritance. On this Western Hemisphere all tribes and people are forming into one federal whole; and there is a future which shall see the estranged children of Adam restored as to the old hearthstone in Eden." [22]

Some European observers—the latest of them André Siegfried [23] —have emphasized and exaggerated the antipathy felt by "native" Americans toward immigrants, or at least toward some categories of immigrants, and have attributed it to the desire or need for basing the American nation on a unity of race or faith such as is supposed to exist in the formation of European nations; thereby, they apparently believe, the American nation would be endowed with a greater cohesion and strength. Yet the American idea of liberty—with its recognition of diversity in origins and religious background—has proved a stronger national cement and a more secure basis for ordered liberty and economic prosperity than bonds of common blood or religion or the uniformity of a closed society. In spite of the lesser homogeneity of the population, there is greater national cohesion in the United States—and less danger of disruptive factionalism—than in France, Germany or Italy. In America diverse people are held together by their common faith in individual liberty and equality; these carry in America a different meaning from that observable on the European continent; they create therefore an entirely different ambience which continental European observers often fail fully to understand. A French author, who studied the United States in 1890, has drawn a brilliant picture of the different attitudes in France and in the United States toward liberty and equality. "With us [the French], liberty and equality, conquered only at a late hour against the government and the privileged classes, believe themselves always exposed to a counteroffensive of the dispossessed adversaries. They call up memories which put the individual on his guard against the state. In America, liberty forms part of the very foundations of the state. Liberty was born at the same time as the state. Or rather individual liberty has anteceded the birth of the state. It is not a 'natural right' of the individual recovered after a long historical struggle; it is rather a common heritage, common to the individual and to the nation, a collective possession rather than a private one but one of which the individual by a tacit accord has kept the guardianship . . . Though equality came later, it is none the less the natural attribute and the rightful flowering of a society entirely formed of newcomers, of homines novi. Liberty, equality: these two great goods call forth in the heart of the Americans not an arrogant defiance which isolates them in their personality but a rapture which makes them proud of their country and its institutions. In the United States, it is individual freedom which can boast of ancestors and of annals, not the government. That is the opposite of what one finds in a great part of Europe." [24]

The immigrants often in the first generation, certainly in the second, have learned to share the happiness and pride of the native American in their liberty and equality, in the institutions and opportunities of the new homeland. In view of the multitudes who poured into America and their so different backgrounds, one can say that the melting pot worked well. It was not a racial melting pot: the immigrants were not assimilated to the original Anglo-American stock; for that they were much too numerous; though cases of intermarriage have been frequent, ethnic and religious groups have tended to preserve, at least for some time, their separate personalities. But these immigrants were assimilated in a much deeper sense, in the sense of a spiritual transformation. They became Americans in the full sense of the word, a sense which does not include race or ethnic origin but is based upon loyalty to an idea; this idea expresses itself through an infinite multiplicity of voluntary associations of all kinds, due to individual and group initiative even in fields like religion, to a degree unknown on the European continent; yet through its underlying ideological unity this variety produces a cultural and social homogeneity and a common pride in a common future.

This emphasis on the future instead of on the past, besides the insistence on the individual, helps to create this new nation out of many nations, to strengthen the Unum in the Pluribus. European and Asian nationalists have been accustomed to look to the past and to try to revive its real or imagined splendors. Ancestral heroic deeds and cultural achievements have thrown their spell over the living generation which felt itself justified and heightened by the glories of the achievements of individuals and generations long dead. Territories settled or conquered in the past, frontiers drawn long ago and changed since, have in the age of nationalism in many cases appealed for reenactment into a new living reality and have by this confusion of the past and the present caused unbelievable suffering and disaster. Real or more often imagined humiliations and wrongs suffered in the past have haunted and disfigured the emotional life of many peoples. Americans on the other hand are not accustomed to look back upon the past. They are a new nation established on virgin soil. Born in a movement of independence from the British motherland, the Americans often even went out of their way not to look on the common British past as their matrix. Thomas Jefferson spoke for the American people when he wrote on August 1, 1816: "I like the dreams of the future better than the history of the past." The thought that Americans should recur to the annals of their ancestors for inspiration and guidance, struck Jefferson as a Gothic idea, "which this country will not endure." [25]

This futurist outlook in the United States was not founded only in the optimism of the Enlightenment. As a nation of many peoples and many faiths, the United States could not allow its various component parts to look too much to the past, which divided them and often set one against the other. It could unite them in liberty and tolerance only if the immigrants looked not back toward the innumerable defeats and victories, scars and triumphs of their ancestral history, but forward to a common future based upon individual activity within the framework of the common constitution and the common American ideas. As early as 1827 Goethe, who like most men of his eighteenth century generation looked hopefully toward America, praised it happily for its concentration on the future. His well known verse expresses the same distrust of Gothic ideas as Jefferson did:

> Amerika, du hast es besser
> Als unser Kontinent, das alte,
> Hast keine verfallene Schlösser
> Und keine Basalte.
> Dich stört nicht im Innern,
> Zu lebendiger Zeit,
> Unnützes Erinnern
> Und vergeblicher Streit.
>
> Benutzt die Gegenwart mit Glück!
> Und wenn nun eure Kinder dichten,
> Bewahre sie ein gut Geschick
> Vor Ritter-, Räuber- und Gespenstergeschichten.[26]

Goethe's wishes for the new country were accepted by the general trend of American life rather than realized by the best of American literature which was only beginning to form when he wrote. Though there has been a distinctly democratic and humanitarian trend in American literature that turned toward the future in the sense which Goethe foresaw, the greatest representatives of which were Ralph Waldo Emerson, Walt Whitman and Mark Twain, another school of American writing was definitely "Gothic," often rejecting optimism and democracy, frequently seeking in the silent dark houses of New

England or in the crumbling plantation mansions of the South the fascination of the past. Edgar Allan Poe and Herman Melville were haunted by the malevolence and horror of existence, and Hawthorne and William Faulkner are at times obsessed with the ancestral curse coming down to the Americans from the recesses of their history. In that respect much of America's greatest literature ran counter to the main trend of the American common mind, as so much of western European literature in the nineteenth century did too. The main trend of American life, and to a lesser degree of Western nineteenth century life in general, was definitely, as Goethe had foreseen, anti-Gothic, humanist and optimistic. The eighteenth century had longed to take refuge in the bosom of nature as it had supposedly existed undefiled in primitive times; the nineteenth century looked confidently forward to a future of progressive improvement built by the industry and inventiveness of self-reliant man.

This community of the future, a future already realized in the present and yet ever expanding beyond all realization, was the strongest bond uniting the Americans of all generations and of all strains. In the November 1839 issue of his *The United States Magazine and Democratic Review,* John Louis O'Sullivan wrote an article "The Great Nation of Futurity." In it he overstated his case with the flamboyant nationalism characteristic of the Democratic expansionists of the 1840's. Yet there is an important nucleus of truth in his stressing the uniqueness of America. "The American people having derived their origin from many other nations, and the declaration of national independence being entirely based on the great principle of human equality . . . demonstrate at once our disconnected position as regards any other nation; that we have, in reality, but little connection with the past history of any of them and still less with all antiquity, its glories, or its crimes . . . Our national birth was the beginning of a new history, the formation and progress of an untried political system, which separates us from the past and connects us with the future only; so far as regards the entire development of the rights of man, in moral, political and national life, we may confidently assume that our country is destined to be the great nation of futurity."

Starting with the typical disregard for history characteristic of progressive America, O'Sullivan rose to a dithyrambic glorification of the American future. "We have no interest in the scenes of antiquity, only as lessons of avoidance of nearly all their examples. The expansive future is our arena. We are entering on its untrodden space with the truth of God in our minds, beneficent objects in our hearts, and with a clear conscience unsullied by the past. We are the nation of human progress, and who will, what can, set limits to our onward march? Providence is with us, and no earthly powers can. We point to the everlasting truths on the first page of our national declaration, and we proclaim to the millions of other lands that the gates of hell— the powers of aristocracy and monarchy—shall not prevail against it. The far reaching, the boundless future will be the era of American greatness. In its magnificent domain of space and time, the nation of many nations is destined to manifest to mankind the excellence of divine principles . . . a Union of many republics, comprising hundreds of happy millions, calling no man master . . . For this blessed mission to the nations of the world, which are shut out from the life-giving light of truth, has America been chosen . . ." Thus O'Sullivan expressed the defiant exuberance of Jacksonian democracy.

Among American poets none voiced his country's futurity more insistently than Walt Whitman, this most puzzling and complex of American poets, rhetorical like, and a distant disciple of, Rousseau but a singer of a nature infinitely more dynamic. Whitman entirely lacked the quietism and puritanism of the citizen of Geneva. Probably no other poet came as near as Whitman to realizing the image which Tocqueville had drawn of the future poet of democracy. "Aristocracy naturally leads the human mind to the contemplation of the past, and fixes it there," Tocqueville wrote. "Democracy gives men a sort of instinctive distaste for what is ancient." The poet in democratic society, Tocqueville believed, is not so much interested in particular men or in the description of nature. His imagination fixes on man. The life of the individual in the United States may be crowded with paltry interests and thus may be essentially anti-poetic, but all that belongs to the existence of the human race as a whole, especially to its future, becomes an abundant source of democratic poetry. This poetry will center upon man. "I need not reverse earth and sky to discover a wondrous object woven of contrasts," Tocqueville wrote, "of infinite greatness and littleness, of intense gloom and amazing brightness—capable at once of exciting

pity, admiration, terror, contempt. I have only to look at myself.
. . . The destiny of mankind, man himself, will become the chief
theme of poetry among democratic nations." [27]

Whitman was not disturbed or frightened as the more aristocratic
minds were by the turbulent spirit of American democracy with its
various and conflicting strains. He found it better than the "apathy
wherewith the populace of Russia and Austria and the miserable
German states—those well-ordered governments—endure the black-
hearted rapacity of their rulers. And it is from such materials—from
the democracy with its manly heart and its lion strength, spurning
the ligatures wherewith drivelers would bind it—that we are to expect the great FUTURE of this western world, a scope involving
such unparalleled human happiness and rational freedom, to such
unnumbered myriads, that the heart of a true man leaps with a
mighty joy only to think of it." With a similar confidence Carl
Schurz proclaimed that "out of this republic we shall make an empire in relation to which, speaking Moorishly, Rome was a pre-
school affair. In this nation, the sum, the amalgam of all civilized
nations, there is a Titanic strength which will draw humanity forward like a giant locomotive. Old Europe is going to feel its
power." [28]

It goes without saying that this unique process of forming a nation
of many nations, united by a common idea with its roots in the
tradition of English liberty and in the common heritage of English
speaking peoples on both sides of the North Atlantic, met many difficulties. The number of immigrants was rising rapidly. There had
been 8,000 in 1824, 78,000 in 1844, and 427,000 in 1854.

In the ten years from 1891 to 1900, nearly 4,000,000 people were
recorded as immigrants, and in the year 1906 alone 1,100,000, of
whom 880,000 landed in New York City. In 1900, 10,500,000 Americans were foreign-born and 26,000,000 were second generation
Americans, both of whose parents or, in one-fifth of the cases, one
of them, was born abroad; this total of 36,000,000 seemed very large
if put against a total white population of 67,000,000. The single largest group among the new Americans was formed by Germans. Carl
Schurz, himself a recent immigrant whose heart continued to feel
a warm attachment for his native land, found to his satisfaction the
Germans well on their way to assimilation. From St. Louis he wrote
on July 8, 1867, to his wife about the German colony in Augusta,

Missouri: "The old people have preserved the tradition of the German spirit and German training, but they are unable to bequeath this tradition to their children. It is an observation which I have made almost everywhere, that here in America, perhaps with the exception of individual cases in the great cities, the children of educated Germans contrast strikingly with their elders. The German spirit fades away. If the training remains wholly German and all contact with Americanism is avoided, a stupid Pennsylvania Germanism results. Where that is not the case, the waves of Americanism soon overwhelm the second and third generations. 'The mission of Germanism' in America, about which some speak so loudly, can consist in nothing other than a modification of the American spirit, through the German, while the nationalities melt into one. In a few years the old patriarchs in pleasant little Augusta will be dead and their successors must be carried away by the universal movement."

The Civil War was an important factor in Americanizing recent immigrants. The war itself proved an economic boon for the many immigrant farmers; their sons served in the Union Army; the long duration of the war, the anxieties about its outcome and about the fate of family members, anxieties which the newcomers shared with the old settlers, tightened the ties between the immigrants and the new country and detached them more and more from their old home lands. In the Ode which James Russell Lowell recited at the Harvard Commemoration on July 21, 1861, he spoke of the American nation as

> She that lifts up the manhood of the poor,
> She of the open soul and open door,
> With room about her hearth for all mankind! [29]

In the patriotic speech which Schurz delivered almost half a century later on June 15, 1893, during German Day at the Chicago World's Fair he warned his fellow citizens that however fervent their sympathy might be with the aspirations and struggles of the old home, they must never allow "their sense of duty towards their new fatherland to become shaken by the idea of leading this Republic away from the secure path of its traditional and wise policy, nor to attempt to involve it in the quarrels or conflicts of interest of the old Europe." He praised the American Germans because "never have they tried to mingle European politics with those of America." Speaking six years later at a banquet in honor of his seventieth birthday in New York on March 2, 1899, Schurz repeated his warning against injecting any German concern or "the German vote" into American politics and against any attempt to influence American policy in favor of what to most of his hearers was the land of their birth. "It may well be said of the German-Americans," Schurz stated, "that however warm their affection for their native land, they have never permitted that affection to interfere with their duties as American citizens, and least of all, to seduce them into any design or desire to use their power in American politics for foreign ends." [30]

Schurz' warnings to the immigrants were in agreement with the tradition underlying the American nation of nations, the common loyalty to the one American idea and the common devotion to the future, which united them. But later in the nineteenth century, a period of immense nationalist and political agitation throughout Europe, it became often difficult for some immigrants to follow the warning. Many, especially in the first generation, still felt a natural attachment to the land of their birth; many had left it out of a deep dissatisfaction with the nationalist and political conditions there; they continued to follow with ardent sympathy the former homeland's nationalist and political struggles and to identify themselves with them. All that was understandable and legitimate. Yet—and this was understandable and legitimate too—it aroused a sharp and antagonistic reaction among the older settlers. There were other equally understandable though much less legitimate reasons for this antagonism. Many immigrants appeared unprepared for the American way of life. Some Americans did not believe in, or underestimated, the assimilative power of the American idea. As early as 1838, one of the first great American writers, James Fenimore Cooper, wrote: "The great immigration of foreigners into the country, and the practice of remaining, or of assembling, in the large towns, renders universal suffrage doubly oppressive to the citizens of the latter. The natives of other countries bring with them the prejudices of another and an antagonist state of society; or what is still worse, their reaction; and it is a painful and humiliating fact, that several of the principal places of this country are, virtually, under the control of this class, who have few convictions of liberty, beyond those which arise from a love of licentiousness, who are totally ignorant of its governing principles, and who, in their hearts and language, are hostile to the very people whose hospitality they enjoy. Many of these men cannot even speak the language of the land, and perhaps a majority of them cannot read the great social compact, by which society is held together." [31]

When in the decades after the Civil War the immigration from southern and eastern Europe rapidly increased, a new angle was given to the anti-immigration sentiment by a school of American historians and political scientists who, influenced by and partly trained in Germany, thought to discover the origin of American liberty not in the English constitutional development and in the English seventeenth century revolutions but in the ancient Germanic forests and in alleged Teutonic racial traits which supposedly united Germany, England and the United States.[32] An American magazine, *Galaxy*, important and influential in its day, published in 1877 an article "A Dream of Anglo-Saxondom." Its author was convinced that in fifty years the Anglo-Saxons would possess "almost a monopoly of the undeveloped resources of the globe," and that among the Anglo-Saxons the United States for many generations to come would be the chief seat of the race and its unique qualities.[33] This emphasis in America on the excellence of the Teutonic race was only part of the general trend, which was fashionable in the middle of the nineteenth century in England as well as in the United States. In England its foremost champions were Thomas Carlyle, Charles Kingsley and the historian Edward Augustus Freeman. Of them Carlyle was deeply pro-German and alien to the liberal and democratic main trend of British nineteenth century thought.[34] Kingsley on the other hand regarded the English as "the only real Teutons left in the world," but he was deeply convinced that English—and thereby American—liberty had its roots not in a specifically English development starting in the thirteenth century and reaching its maturity in the seventeenth, but went back "to the bogs and moors of Jutland," from which the English brought their constitution with them to Britain as a Teutonic inheritance.[35] The more extreme adherents of this school claimed that the superiority of the three Teutonic peoples—Germans, English and Americans—was based not only on race but also on the Protestant religion and its belief in liberty, which they contrasted with Latin (and Roman Catholic) moral levity and inclination for dictatorship (many of them wrote in the period when Louis Napoleon assumed supreme power in France to the enthusiastic acclaim of the masses). Freeman was convinced that the history of liberty started in the German forests with Arminius who liberated the Germans from the Romans, and continued on to Hampden and to Washington. "In Caesar's day . . . the history of ourselves, as distinguished from the history of our future home, is to be sought for, not by the Thames and the Severn, but by the Rhine and the Weser. . . . We have our part in the great deliverance by the wood of Teutoburg; Arminius, 'liberator Germaniæ,' is but the first of a roll which goes on to Hampden and to Washington." [36]

None has better pointed out the fallacies in this identification of the English with the Germans than Matthew Arnold when he wrote in 1861 about the French and the English: "It is in vain that we call the French Celts and ourselves Teutons: when nations have attained to the greatness of France and England their peoples can have no profound identity with any people beyond their own borders. Torrents of pedantry have been poured forth on the subject of our Germanic origin; in real truth, we are at the present day no more Germans than we are Frenchmen. By the mixture of our race, by the Latinization of our language, by the isolation of our country, by the independence of our history, we have long since lost all vital connection with that great German stem which sixteen centuries ago threw out a shoot in this island." [37] The fundamental difference in the development of liberty in Germany on the one hand, in England and the United States on the other hand—a difference of which the German historians and political scientists were clearly conscious—remained often strangely unperceived by American and English writers in the nineteenth century. Even Emerson, deeply read in Carlyle, was not entirely free from this bias. Bancroft, the great historian of American democracy, profoundly admired Bismarck and his newly established German empire. When he was American minister to Prussia he wrote from Berlin to Secretary of State Hamilton Fish on November 29, 1870: "In my former reports I have led you to expect for United Germany the establishment of the most liberal government on the continent of Europe and all that I may have led you to expect seems likely to be realized. In one sense the new government is a child of America; but for our success in our civil war it would not have been established. Our victory in that strife sowed the seeds of the regeneration of Europe." Bismarck's transformation of Europe and his reversal of the liberal trend then sweeping Europe are here regarded by the spokesman of American democracy as a sign of Europe's democratic regeneration.[38]

The Germanic angle played only a subordinate role in a book which was very widely read in the 1880's, *Our Country* by Josiah Strong. More than by Teutonic considerations Strong was influenced by Darwinism. He saw in immigration the cause for the acute economic and social crisis in the United States and a possible threat to the great future of the country. He was not hostile to immigrants, he welcomed them into the fold of Americanism if only they really wished to enter it. "There is among our population of alien birth an unhappy tendency toward aggregation, which concentrates the strain upon portions of our social and political fabric . . . If our noble domain were tenfold larger than it is, it would be still too small to embrace with safety to our national future, little Germanies here, little Scandinavias there, and little Irelands yonder . . . Our safety demands the assimilation of these strange populations, and the process of assimilation will become slower and more difficult as the proportion of foreigners increases . . . We may well ask whether this in-sweeping immigration is to foreignize us or we are to Americanize it." [39] Strong was a midwesterner deeply interested in social reform and progressive movements. In 1898 he founded the League for Social Service. He was one of the pioneers of social and progressive Christianity. In his zeal for social reform, in his fervor for an active Christianity, in his appeal to the common man, Strong resembled his German Protestant contemporary Adolf Stöcker. But their concepts of nationalism differed fundamentally. Both believed in race and succeeded in fusing this belief, as the Danish theologian and nationalist Grundtvig and so many other Christian spokesmen in the Age of Nationalism did, with Christianity. But to the German Protestant preacher, nationalism was identical with a narrow racialism, with monarchical authoritarianism, with anti-democracy, anti-capitalism and anti-Semitism. To the American the Anglo-Saxon race stood for individual libertry and democracy; he had no doubt that the principal center of Anglo-Saxon life and influence had shifted from England to the United States, and that the latter was developing the highest type of Anglo-Saxon civilization; he was in no way a racialist in a narrow or exclusive sense; he was convinced that the marked superiority of the Anglo-Saxon race in the United States over that in the mother country was "due, in large measure, to its highly mixed origin." [40] Strong did not reject the nation of many nations, formed on the basis of the English, and in this case even the Puritan, tradition. He accepted its mingling of races, its enhancement by immigration. But he warned against the overflow of immigrants living under conditions which made their assimilation to the American idea almost impossible and which thus might create an obstacle to the fulfillment of America's destiny. Many trends of American national thought fused in Strong's writings: its progressivism and futurism; its emphasis upon the progressive Middle West and the supposed morality and democracy of its rural pioneers as against the "rabble ruled" big cities—Strong saw the danger, inherent according to him, in metropolitan agglomeration and the concomitant rabble rule increased by immigration, a situation which Jefferson would have denounced as emphatically as Strong did; its faith in education and Christianity; its confidence in the United States as the light of democratic mankind in its manifest destiny; and finally, a new element added in the latter part of the nineteenth century, the Darwinian ingredient of the survival of the fittest.

But immigration was growing even more rapidly after Strong's appeal against the little Germanies and the other segregative settlements, half-voluntary and half-imposed—not by law but by circumstances. Was the melting pot really working? Did the immigrants become Americans or did they remain attached to their homelands? Was there more space for new immigrants? Even as liberal a scholar as Woodrow Wilson wrote in his *History of the American People* that in the last decades of the nineteenth century "there came multitudes of men of the lowest class from the south of Italy and men of the meaner sort out of Hungary and Poland, men out of the ranks where there was neither skill nor energy nor any initiative of quick intelligence; and they came in numbers which increased from year to year, as if the countries of the south of Europe were disburdening themselves of the more sordid and hapless elements of their population." A quarter of a century later, another famous liberal American historian opposed further immigration. "We, like European nations, are approaching a saturation of population," Frederick Jackson Turner warned in 1925.[41] But even if there was still space left—and Turner underestimated the non-spatial frontiers of the United States—was the American idea strong enough to form and maintain the nation of many nations? Would it not show its weaknesses and discords in time of national strain? Was not the international situation everywhere, in Europe as well as in Asia, rapidly changing from the apparent security of the Pax Britannica of the nineteenth century into an era of new and dangerous international challenges and threats? A British student of nationalism remarked during the Balkan wars of 1912–13 that "nationality strikes its roots deep, and is happily [!] hard to kill. A single illustration may show its power. In the autumn of 1912 the English-speaking people of the United States, basking complacently in the thought that they were annexing new citizens from Southern Europe at the rate of a million a year, were startled to learn that thousands of newly made 'Americans' were taking ship to the Balkan peninsula to offer their lives to the old countries. Tens of thousands more, who would not go themselves, sent money. The people of the United States awoke to the strange reality that, in spite of all the visible and invisible agencies of 'assimilation,' their country was not one nation but a congeries of nations such as the world has never seen before within the limits of a self-governing State. America had, in fact, become almost a school of [foreign] nationality." [42]

The First World War accentuated the difficulties and fears. In an article "The Square Deal in America" Theodore Roosevelt wrote: "There is no room for the hyphen in our citizenship . . . We have room in this country for but one flag, the Stars and Stripes, . . . for but one loyalty, loyalty to the United States, . . . for but one language, the language of Washington and Lincoln, the language of the Declaration of Independence and the Gettysburg Address, the English language. . . . This is one of the demands to be made in the name of the spirit of American nationalism. The other is equally important. We must treat every good American of German descent or any other American, without regard to his creed, as on a full and exact equality with every other good American, and set our faces like flint against the creatures who seek to discriminate against such an American, or to hold against him the birthplace of himself or of his parents . . . We must shun as we would shun the plague all efforts to make us separate in groups of separate nationalities. We must all of us be Americans, and nothing but Americans; and all good Americans must stand on an equality of consideration and respect, without regard to their creed or to the land from which their forebears came." [43]

Roosevelt was in the American tradition when he put equal emphasis on the unity of the nation and on the fact of absolute non-discrimination against all Americans irrespective of their ethnic descent or religious faith. A writer of an entirely different personal, political and social complexion than Theodore Roosevelt, Randolph Bourne, a radical *homme de lettres* who died young, observed toward the end of World War I: "No reverberatory effect of the great war has caused American public opinion more solicitude than the failure of the 'melting-pot.' The discovery of diverse nationalistic feelings among our great alien population has come to most people as an intense shock." [44] Bourne, too, was in the American tradition when he stressed the futurism and the universalism of the American national idea. "Let us speak," he wrote, "not of inferior races, but of inferior civilizations. We are all to educate and to be educated. These peoples in America are in a common enterprise. It is not what we are now that concerns us, but what this plastic next generation may become in the light of a new cosmopolitan idea." But Bourne misunderstood the "new cosmopolitan idea" which he postulated as the foundation of American nationality. The foundation of American national life was not a new cosmopolitanism but the universalization of the English tradition of liberty, which the early settlers had brought with them. With a difference in evaluation, Bourne noticed himself: "The early colonists came over with motives no less colonial than the later. They did not come to be assimilated in an American melting-pot. They did not come to adopt the culture of the American Indian. They had not the smallest intention of 'giving themselves without reservation' to the new country. They came to get freedom to live as they wanted to. They came to escape from the stifling air and chaos of the old world; they came to make their fortune in a new land. They invented no new social framework. Rather they brought over bodily the old ways to which they had been accustomed. Tightly concentrated on a hostile frontier, they were conservative beyond belief. Their pioneer daring was reserved for the objective conquest of material resources. In their folkways, in their social and political institutions, they were, like every colonial people, slavishly imitative of the mother-country. So that, in spite of the 'Revolution,' our whole legal and political system remained more English than the English, petrified and unchanging, while in England itself law developed to meet the needs of the changing times." [45]

But the newly arisen doubts about America's power to assimilate ever increasing immigrant multitudes led in the 1920's to the first sharp restriction of immigration. This attitude conformed to the general mood of the period. The First World War had all over Europe aroused nationalism to an unprecedented degree. Ethnic and linguistic nationalism, so alien to the American tradition, triumphed. Federal solutions which in the mid-nineteenth century were debated in Europe were definitely abandoned. New nation-states arose, ancient frontiers were changed, border territories were bitterly disputed—this over-heated nationalism with its revival of past passions and ancient symbols increased the fear in America that the new immigrants would bring with them deep rooted allegiances and antagonisms. Moreover, the war had made possible in eastern and southern Europe the establishment of regimes which challenged the validity of free Western civilization. Under Lenin's leadership Russia organized opposition to the principles for which the United States stood; under the influence of communism, intensified nationalism, assuming the new name of fascism in central and southern Europe, stressed governmental authority, national uniformity and the total subordination of the individual to the state. Under these circumstances new immigrants might be less inclined than they were in the nineteenth century to embrace and cherish the American idea; they might easily become outposts of national movements hostile to, or contemptuous of, American democracy.

During the war the loyalty of some German-Americans had seemed doubtful; reported acts of sabotage had deeply stirred public opinion. In an address in 1917, "Children of the Crucible," Theodore Roosevelt appealed to German-Americans "to give up all other allegiances" and to stand with their fellow-Americans as "a mighty and united people, facing a future of glorious promise." [46] The suspicion aroused by German attitudes was not new. More than ten years before the outbreak of the war, on April 23, 1903, John Hay had written to President Roosevelt: "It is a singular ethnological and political paradox that the prime motive of every British subject in

America is hostility to England, and the prime motive of every German-American is hostility to every country in the world, including America, which is not friendly to Germany." Hay's statement was in both its aspects an overstatement, yet there was an element of truth in it which deeply worried the American people during the war. It led them to rethink the problems of immigration in general. Leading American sociologists like Professor Edward Alsworth Ross of the University of Wisconsin marshalled the facts to prove the disastrous economic, social, political and moral effects of unchecked immigration, the triumph of low-standard elements over the high-standard elements in the United States, a situation which Ross compared to that in the dying Roman world. "I am not of those," he wrote in 1914, expressing the viewpoint of many midwestern progressives, "who consider humanity and forget the nation, who pity the living but not the unborn. To me, those who are to come after us stretch forth beseeching hands as well as the masses on the other side of the globe. Nor do I regard America as something to be spent quickly and cheerfully for the benefit of pent up millions in the backward lands. What if we become crowded without their ceasing to be so? I regard it as a nation whose future may be of unspeakable value to the rest of mankind, provided that the easier conditions of life here be made permanent by high standards of living, institutions and ideas, which finally may be appropriated by all men. We could have helped the Chinese a little by letting their surplus millions swarm in upon us a generation ago; but we have helped them infinitely more by protecting our standards and having something worth their copying when the time came." [47]

A more extreme point of view was expressed ten years later by another progressive sociologist, Henry Pratt Fairchild, who went so far as to regard race and nationality as "the two universal foundations of group unity," identifying nationality with race. "The only way," he wrote, "in which we can escape the evils and dangers of non-assimilation is by reducing the problem to so small a compass that it makes little difference whether assimilation is accomplished in the first generation or not. . . . Among the nations of the world America . . . has a role to play which no other nation can play. Foremost in this role is the development of true democracy. . . . Any program or policy which interferes in the slightest degree with the prosecution of this great enterprise must be condemned as treason to our high destiny. . . . Any force that tends to impair our capacity for leadership is a menace to mankind and a flagrant violation of the spirit of liberalism. Unrestricted immigration was such a force. It was slowly, insidiously, irresistibly eating away the very heart of the United States. What was being melted in the great Melting Pot, losing all form and symmetry, all beauty and character, all nobility and usefulness, was the American nationality itself." In the name of democracy and liberalism Dr. Fairchild approved a restricting regulation of immigration.[48]

After the war, and the disastrous growth of nationalism and extremism in Europe—and a few decades later in Asia—the question was no longer that of the loyalty of some German-Americans, but a growing doubt whether mass immigration after the war could be assimilated as it had been in the nineteenth century. In spite of their overstatements, the warnings by the two American sociologists contained a kernel of truth. On the other hand, Professor Horace M. Kallen presented the case for a cultural pluralism going far beyond anything envisaged by the American national idea. He practically demanded the introduction of the rights of national minorities as they existed in central and eastern Europe, on the basis of an ethnico-linguistic nationalism unknown to the Anglo-American tradition. He saw America as "a democracy of nationalities, cooperating voluntarily and autonomously through common institutions in the enterprise of self-realization through the perfection of men according to their kind. The common language of the commonwealth, the language of its great tradition would be English, but each nationality would have for its own emotional . . . life its own peculiar dialect or speech, its own . . . aesthetic and intellectual forms. . . . Thus 'American civilization' may come to mean the perfection of the cooperative harmonies of 'European civilization'—the waste, the squalor and the distress of Europe being eliminated—a multiplicity in a unity, an orchestration of mankind." There was some justification in this view, too, a balance against the extreme views of Ross and Fairchild, but this cultural pluralism of a multiplicity of autonomous nationalities seeking *their* self-realization in America underestimated the importance of the historical roots of American nationalism, its unifying character, its unique and assimilative power. American civilization could not mean—and had no right to claim to be—the perfection of the cooperative harmonies of European civilization: it was a civilization sui generis, rooted in a common Western background and in a political tradition common to all English-speaking peoples, but it was a distinct national civilization which had undertaken, with great success, the task of assimilating many more racial strains and immigrant groups and with a far greater speed than British or French civilization had had to.[49]

The unrest created in the United States by the First World War was intensified by the doubts about the wisdom of American participation, by the misunderstanding of America's interest in the peace treaties, by the assumption first and then rejection of world responsibility, by the new and unexpected circumstances facing the United States in the 1920's. This atmosphere gave rise to a number of "patriotic" societies, of which the most important was the Ku Klux Klan. The original Ku Klux Klan was one of the secret societies formed in the South after 1865 as a protest against the Reconstruction. All of them rapidly faded out of existence after 1870. The Ku Klux Klan was revived in 1915, no longer on a sectional but on a national basis, as powerful in the Middle West as in the South. It wished to promote "real patriotism" and "pure Americanism." It grew rapidly after 1919, partly as a protest against the apparently sudden decline of traditional mores and morality in the wake of the First World War. Old standards and securities of private and public morality seemed to evanesce rapidly in a bewildering world. The Ku Klux Klan was a continuation of the Know-Nothing movement, a reaction of old-stock Protestant American nativism and its moral and social traditions inherited from Puritan and frontier days. It pretended to fight corruption and abuse of justice and to protect the purity of womanhood; by a strange dialectic it was apparently able to combine the proclaimed profession of the Fatherhood of God and the Brotherhood of Man with a struggle to uphold white supremacy and, in the days of Prohibition, the enforcement of law and decency against racketeering gangsterism, with the application of illegal, indecent violence. It was directed against Negroes, Catholics and Jews, and indirectly against immigration. The course of the Ku Klux Klan followed closely that of the Know-Nothing movement. In the general but transitory post-war disorientation the Ku Klux Klan grew fast and became a power in the elections of 1924 and 1926; it rapidly disintegrated after 1928. The depression which set in two years later did not revive it. The Ku Klux Klan, vigorously investigated by the authorities, remained dead. The many other patriotic societies which mushroomed after 1918 for a very brief time amounted to nothing, their combined membership never surpassing 25,000.

In the light of the history of American nationalism, the regulation of immigration after 1920 was as justified as the Civil War had been. In view of the immigrant masses in the first years of the twentieth century the melting pot—a fundamental trait of American national-ism—required time to operate. The immigration laws should have aimed at the right selection, distribution, and incorporation of a continuing though much diminished stream of immigrants. The ac-tual laws from the first in 1924 to that of 1952 fell far short of this goal. Nevertheless the curtailment of immigration accelerated, or made possible, the continuing successful process of incorporation and assimilation. The attitude of the immigrant groups at that time was well expressed in 1937 by one of the prominent foreign born citizens of the country, Aleš Hrdlička, an anthropologist of Czech origin, when he declared of America: "It received them without any sentiment, without any care, often, perhaps, with outright neg-lect and selfishness. But it gave them freely of the precious new air of spiritual liberty. It dealt with them perhaps at times rudely, but frankly. It gave them a chance, a chance to educate themselves and their children, a chance to progress in every direction if they were willing and capable. What wonder that with all the initial difficulties and even sufferings, so many of the immigrants became deeply grateful to the country of their adoption, became fused with it like so many wholesome grafts on a healthy virile tree, and became within less than a generation true, loyal Americans."

In the Second World War and in the difficult decade which fol-lowed—difficult for its demand upon the Americans completely to readjust their way of thought to their new position as a nation among nations—the American people were united to a degree unknown in the First World War and in all the preceding wars which America had fought. The foreign policy of the administration—Democratic or Republican—enjoyed a national support which neither Abraham Lincoln nor Woodrow Wilson had ever known. In a war in which the national survival itself of Germany, Italy and Japan seemed at stake, far beyond any threat involved in the First World War, the American citizens of German, Japanese and Italian descent behaved with a remarkable loyalty. The only discordant note was introduced not by them but by the highhanded governmental action against American citizens of Japanese descent.[50] Only homogeneous Britain showed a similar unity of purpose and loyalty. Future historians may rather claim that the American nation was too unified in its backing of all administration policies—especially of President Franklin D. Roosevelt's actions and opinions after 1940—and that there was too little inclination for critical consideration and dissent. The cohesion of the American nation in liberty is so great that it can stand not only diversity but—different in that from the ancient polis and from Rousseau's ideal fatherland—even a large measure of civic apathy on the part of its citizens. For a free nation can neither be an entirely uniform nation nor an entirely politicized nation. Contrary to the opinion of many democratic reformers, it is no misfortune if not every citizen cares to vote, as long as everybody can vote and as long as nobody is forced to vote.

Although many German nationalists predicted that in times of strain racial antagonisms would destroy American unity, an assumption similar to that of Marxism according to which the class conflict would divide United States society into irreconcilable camps, the catastrophe did not occur. This cohesion of a nation of many nations is largely due to the educational system of the United States which —to use the words of Professor William Yandell Elliott—with all its weaknesses and alarming defects, has succeeded in integrating the products of many lands into a basic sense of "belonging." As far back as 1798 Benjamin Rush, a Pennsylvania physician and a fervent advocate of female education and of "progressive" ideas, conceived "the education of our youth in this country to be particularly necessary in Pennsylvania, while our citizens are composed of natives of so many different kingdoms in Europe. Our schools of learning, by producing one general and uniform system of education, will render the mass of the people more homogeneous, and therefore fit them more easily for uniform and peaceable government." Dr. Rush went too far in his Jacobin enthusiasm, both in the direction of uniformity and in that of nationalism. His demand for a national system of education was only slowly realized, and then in much milder form than he had insisted upon. Diversity, freedom of choice, a willingness to experiment, and respect for universal and humanitarian considerations, have characterized the American educational system.[51]

Nevertheless, the schools were a strong unifying force. They did not escape the defects of a classless, democratic society where every endeavor is made to keep the career open to talent, and where the tendency exists to err in admitting to higher institutions of learning too many rather than too few. The classical discipline of learning, the hard and serious pursuit of grammar and mathematics, are unduly slighted; less emphasis is put on an awareness of, and gratitude to, the heritage of the past than on an orientation in the contemporary world and on the building of a better future. These serious shortcomings conform to the optimistic and futuristic character of American society; it is a trend which with the democratization of western European society and education is beginning to make itself felt in Britain and France, in Italy and Germany. Therein, too, the United States has anticipated the general trend of modern Western development; therefore its shortcomings are nowhere as conspicuous as in the American system.[52] But there are better sides to the picture too: in the American schools on the whole the dread is lacking, which so many Europeans retain as the main impression from their school days; the schools have performed their task of Anglicization so well that the children of immigrants no longer wish to talk the language which they hear their parents speak at home; and the American colleges work hard to make up for the glaring deficiencies which many students bring with them from their twelve years of elementary and secondary school training. With all their scholastic weaknesses, the schools emphasize the potentialities of human dignity, the equality of opportunity and reward to the talented, and a basic sense of brotherhood and of community responsibility. A conscious effort is made to teach the children the sense of "belonging." Later on in the rich profusion of voluntary and spontaneous group life in America, most grown-ups find an opportunity for partnership and sharing in joint enterprises, for striking roots within a free society based upon mobility, which faces the need of ever new adjustments to the dizzying speed of the most advanced technology. In such a society, which is without parallel, it might appear difficult to strike roots. Yet all the immigrants, all the ethnic strains, have fully developed the sense of "belonging," of being here at home, and nowhere else. In spite of the call from Israel, few American Jews left their country to settle in a land where their ancestors probably lived two thousand years ago; the creation of in-chapter five

A nation among nations

"The United States may be a world in itself, but it
is also a part of a larger world. There is no doubt that
its power for good and for evil is very great. How that
power is to be used is of consequence to all humanity . . . the moral for Americans . . . is the old one
that greatness brings responsibilities. These they will
have to face, for it is now too late for them to return
to the simple life of their earlier history. They will
do well, therefore, to take to heart the words of the
President [Theodore Roosevelt]: 'We have no choice,
we people of the United States, as to whether or not
we shall play a great part in the world. That has been
determined for us by fate, by the march of events.
We have to play that part. All that we can decide is
whether we shall play it well or ill'."

ARCHIBALD CARY COOLIDGE
The United States as a World Power
(New York: Macmillan, 1908), pp. 15, 373 f.

The Republic of many Republics prospered by striking a difficult balance between the rights of the individual states and the strength of the federal structure. Likewise the nation of many nations had to keep an equilibrium between the wide unguarded gates of an open society and the assimilating power of the Anglo-America tradition. States' rights and immigration have been essential and constitutive elements of American nationalism to a degree unknown elsewhere. Yet there were times in history when they were curtailed, though this curtailment, at least in the case of the rights of the states, ran counter to the very principles on which the United States was founded. The attempt to curtail states' rights kindled the bitterest conflict in American history, whereas the curtailment of immigration could be carried through with infinitely less cost. In both cases, however, the principles involved—the diversity and autonomy of constituting states and the fusion of diverse ethnic strains in a melting pot—remained intact; they were only controlled as far as it seemed necessary for the preservation of the Union and its character. This preservation allowed the United States to play its twentieth century role as a nation among nations, a role which fell upon the United States through its character as a frontierland of English liberty and of the modern West, and through the course of recent history. The diversity of nationalism everywhere expresses itself above all in international relations. In the United States this stage, though vaguely indicated long before, was reached only after the middle of the second century of its national existence.

Canning's famous words calling the New World to redress the balance of the Old have come true to a degree which Canning hardly expected. Speaking on the King's message relative to the affairs of Portugal on December 12, 1826, before the House of Commons, Canning pointed out that it would be disastrous to try to regulate the balance of power in Europe according to the situation as it prevailed at the end of the seventeenth century, the time of William III. He did not reject the principle but he wished to apply it flexibly according to changing circumstances. "Is the balance of power a fixed and unalterable standard?" Canning asked. "Or is it not a standard perpetually varying, as civilization advances, and as new nations spring up, and take their place among established political communities? . . . Thus, while the balance of power continued in principle the same, the means of adjusting it became more varied and enlarged." The occupation of Spain by France in 1823, Canning noted, did not call for British action, as it would have called in previous times, but there was one condition attached which alone would allow Britain to view the situation with relative unconcern: "Contemplating Spain, such as our ancestors had known her, I resolved that if France had Spain, it should not be *Spain with the Indies*. I called the New World into existence, to redress the balance of the Old." [1] Canning certainly overstated his case, but he did not prove a poor prophet. In the twentieth century the New World was called upon to redress the balance of power in the Old World. By that time the United States had become the leading partner of two groups of nations with which, by its origin and character, it has been indissolubly associated: the commonwealth of the English-speaking peoples and the North Atlantic Community.

As early as the eighteenth century a number of writers, enlightened enthusiasts and sober observers alike, predicted this then almost incredible future. It fascinated or haunted the imagination of many Europeans throughout the nineteenth century. The foremost among them was Tocqueville who in the 1830's concluded the first volume of his great work with a well known vision of the future, the worth of which could be appreciated only more than a century later. He insisted against American isolationism that in the modern age nations were being driven closer together than ever before, even against their will. "The consequence is that there is less difference at the present day between Europeans and their descendants in the New World, in spite of the ocean which divides them, than there was between certain towns in the thirteenth century, which were separated only by a river. If this tendency to assimilation brings foreign nations closer to each other, it must a fortiori prevent the descendants of the same people from becoming aliens to each other. The time will therefore come, when one hundred and fifty millions of men will be living in North America, equal in condition, . . . owing their origin to the same cause, and preserving the same civilization, the same language, . . . the same manners, and imbued with the same opinions, propagated under the same forms. The

rest is uncertain, but this is certain; and it is a fact new to the world,
—a fact which the imagination strives in vain to grasp."

From this affirmation of the indissoluble ties between the peoples
on the two shores of the North Atlantic Tocqueville proceeded to a
vision of the world of the 1950's: "There are at the present time
two great nations in the world, which started from different points,
but seem to tend towards the same end. I allude to the Russians and
the Americans. Both of them have grown up unnoticed; . . . and
the world learned of their existence and their greatness at almost
the same time. All other nations . . . have stopped, or continue to
advance with extreme difficulty; these alone are proceeding with
ease and celerity along a path to which no limit can be perceived.
The American . . . combats the wilderness and savage life; the
Russian, civilization with all its arms. The conquests of the Americans are therefore gained by the plow share; those of the Russian
by the sword. The Anglo-American relies upon personal interest to
accomplish his ends, and gives free scope to the unguided strength
and common sense of the people; the Russian centers all the authority
of society in a single arm. The principal instrument of the former is
freedom; of the latter, servitude. Their starting point is different,
and their causes are not the same; yet each of them seems marked
out by the will of heaven to sway the destinies of half the globe."

Similar, though less well known statements abound throughout
the nineteenth century. They were more often voiced by Europeans
than by Americans, who were too preoccupied with their continental
affairs to allow their indulging in any global fantasies. Such a fantasy was expressed with a queer mixture of scholarship and a naive
flight of imagination in the book *The New Rome or the United
States of the World*, which a German and a Pennsylvania farmer of
German origin wrote together in 1852. The New Rome was, of
course, the United States; its constitution, the authors believed, was
in the near future to broaden into a universal constitution fusing
all nations into one people. On the 29th of January, 1852, the authors
reported, a congress of Germans held in Philadelphia formed the
"American Revolutionary League for Europe," and discussed a resolution, "that in the opinion of the present congress, every people,
upon throwing off the yoke of its tyrants, ought to demand admission into the league of states already free, that is, into the American
Union; so that these states may become the nucleus of the political

organization of the human family, and the starting point of the World's Republic." This resolution was not adopted in Philadelphia but a second congress, held at Wheeling eight months later, unanimously adopted the resolution; the League changed its name to the "Peoples' League of the Old and New World," and inscribed on its banners the principle of universal annexation in the name of human liberty. The annexationist views of the authors of *The New Rome* were in any case quite extensive: first and foremost, the whole of Northern America down to the Isthmus of Panama—"This garden of the world may be said, without exaggeration, to be dying for want of annexation"—and then England and all her colonies—"The stupendous greatness of England is fictitious, and will only become natural when that empire shall have found its real center here. That center is in the United States." According to the two authors, the New Rome would also universalize the English language, which in their opinion was manifestly destined for all mankind.[2]

The two German-Americans whose fantasy was fired by the disillusionment of the European revolutions of 1848 thought only of the New Rome which they placed in Washington—to them emigration to the United States seemed the only political action left to freedom loving Germans; they disregarded the Third Rome which the Russians, deeply convinced of its mission and finality, placed in Moscow. Tocqueville avoided the comparison of either America or Russia with Rome, but many European minds in the middle of the nineteenth century were conscious of the threat of Moscow as the Third Rome.[3] The German poet Heinrich Heine who commented from Paris on French political developments for a German newspaper wrote on June 3, 1840, of "the all-powerful Czar of Russia, the Emperor and Pope of all who recognize the only holy, orthodox Greek Faith; he is its Messiah in armor, who is to free it from the yoke of the unbelievers, the cannon-thunder god, who will some day plant his banner of victory on the towers of the great mosque of Byzantium. Yes, that is their political as well as religious faith and they dream of a Russian-Greek-Orthodox world-supremacy which shall spread forth its arms from the Bosphorus over Europe, Asia, and Africa. . . . The words of Napoleon at St. Helena, that very soon in the future the world will be an American republic or a Russian autocracy, are a very discouraging prophesy. What a

prospect! In the most favorable case, to die as republicans of mo-
notonous *ennui!* Poor posterity!" [4]

An Austro-Hungarian minister of war voiced a similar fear of a
partition of Europe between the United States and Russia when
he tried to persuade Emperor Francis Joseph in 1870 to launch a
preventive war against Russia: "Sooner or later we have to wage
this struggle, the sooner the better. . . . If we postpone it we shall
find Russia growing stronger with every year because she is proceeding feverishly with her armament and her building of railroads. . . . We must weaken this giant and confine him to Asia,
otherwise the earth will sooner or later be divided up among two
powers, the North Americans and the Russians." [5] Around the same
time the liberal French historian Jules Michelet expressed similar
apprehensions regarding Russia's threat to Europe, but he envisioned
an entirely different role for North America and its relationship to
Europe. In 1871 he called upon the United States to lead a congress
of Western European peoples against the danger from the East:
"I solemnly call upon young America. Let her justify our hope, let
her be deaf to all petty interests, . . . let her be devoted to the great
general interests of human progress closely associated with the cause
of liberty which she has supported so recently and which she has
made so gloriously victorious." [6]

Whereas Heine, General Kuhn, and Michelet, three Europeans
so different in origin and in their station of life, expected in the
middle of the nineteenth century a coming struggle over Europe
between the United States and Russia, an American naval officer,
Commodore Matthew C. Perry, the man who opened up Japan on
behalf of the United States, foresaw a similar clash over the Far
East. In a lecture delivered before the American Geographical and
Statistical Society on March 6, 1856, Perry predicted a "fierce and
final battle" between Russia and America. His warning appeared at
the time so little newsworthy that it was not reported in the *New
York Times* until March 6, 1956, a century later: "It requires no sage
to predict events so strongly foreshadowed to us all," Perry declared.
"To me it seems that the people of America will, in some form or
other, extend their dominion and their power [to the eastern shores
of Asia] and that eastward and southward will her great rival stretch
forth her power to the coasts of China and Siam; and thus the Saxon

and the Cossack will meet once more, in strife or in friendship, on another field. Will it be friendship? I fear not! The antagonistic exponents of freedom and absolutism must thus meet at last, and then will be fought that mighty battle on which the world will look with breathless interest; for on its issues will depend the freedom or the slavery of the world, whether despotism or rational liberty must be the fate of civilized man. I think I see in the distance the giants that are growing up for that fierce and final encounter: In the progress of events that battle must sooner or later inevitably be fought." [7]

Whatever future role some writers or officers foresaw for the United States in world affairs, the American people in the nineteenth century were very much averse to assuming any world role, either in Europe or in the Far East. American expansionism in the first half of the century was vigorously pushed by the bellicosity of the Western settlers, rough and undisciplined frontiersmen remote from the control or the feeling of responsibility of the central government; but for geographic reasons this expansion did not lead to any major conflict which would involve America as a nation among nations. Manifest destiny was then understood in the limited sense of imperial expansion over the North American continent.[8] This imperial expansion, like that of Britain, did not proceed according to any plan. It was frequently the result of private or individual actions and it was often pushed by unforeseen circumstances beyond the original intention; it never came about without arousing sharp opposition, either by sectional interests, or more frequently for moral reasons.

Such was the case as early as 1802 when Western settlers threatened to provoke war by attacking New Orleans in order to control the transportation on the Mississippi River, a waterway which was then thought vital for shipping the products of the new West to the nearest port. Jefferson anticipated the settlers' moves by buying the Louisiana Territory from France; in so doing he made use of the opportunity offered by the destruction through yellow fever of Napoleon's army sent against Toussaint l'Ouverture in Haiti. Originally Jefferson wished to buy only the mouth of the Mississippi River, but Napoleon, in order to weaken Britain, proposed a wider deal: he was willing to sell the whole territory though this measure violated his treaty with Spain and lacked the confirmation by the

French Senate required for such transactions by the French constitution. Thus the immense territory of 900,000 square miles between the Mississippi River and the Rocky Mountains was bought by the United States for the insignificant sum of about $15,000,000. This acquisition, the result of a deal with a dictator without regard for international obligations, laid the foundation not only for the flowering of manifest destiny but for the territorial disputes that led to the catastrophe of the Civil War—west of the Mississippi new territories were formed, the control of which was later at stake between the North and the South. The geopolitical belief that it was necessary to maintain the unity of the whole Mississippi River basin under one government added to the conviction of the need for the maintenance of the Union.

But imperial expansion never went unchallenged by "Little Americans." There were sectional protest voices raised against the acquisitions west of the Mississippi and later against the expansion into Mexico.[9] Yet more important were the many protests motivated by ethical reasons. Thus Longfellow regarded the Mexican War as a "shabby" and "disgraceful" affair and was proud when his brother Sam prayed in the pulpit for "our country in her hour of shame." Like the British, the American attitude to war and expansion was always ambivalent. Both people disliked army life and high brass; though they have been excellent soldiers and could be highly pugnacious at times, they have always rejected the military ideal which has been venerated by the Germans and French. The origin of this anti-militarist attitude may perhaps be found in the social and evangelistic character of Anglo-American Reformed Christianity which tried to permeate all political life with its ideals; the tradition of the Glorious Revolution which jealously maintained civilian and parliamentary supremacy over the military establishment certainly also had a share in this general attitude. Yet anti-militarism was in no sense identical with pacifism. It could, at times, lend a note of crusading morality and bellicosity to American (or British) involvement in war. Julia Ward Howe's "Battle Hymn of the Republic" with its magnificent somber rhythm is an outstanding example of this Christian and moralistic battle spirit.

An English visitor at the beginning of the nineteenth century and an American historian one hundred years later have both commented on the complexity of America's attitude toward war. "As to the assertion, that the people of America hate the war," William Cobbett, the famous radical editor, wrote about the War of 1812, "I must say that I have seen no proof of such hatred. The Americans, being a reflective people, and a people resolutely bent upon preserving their freedom, have a general hatred of war, as being, generally speaking, hostile to their freedom. But in the choice of evils, if war should appear the least evil, they will not fail to take it—and, indeed, they have taken it—for, in America, it is really the people who declare war—the congress is the real representative of the people— there are no sham elections—no buying and selling of votes and of false oaths—but the members are unbought, uncorrupted, unenslaved agents of the people, and if they cease to speak the sentiments of the people who elect them, they are put out of the congress at the end of a very few months. It is, therefore, not only false, but stupid, to affect to believe that war is unpopular, and the government is odious in the eyes of the people. All its members are chosen by them—and if it ceased to please them, it would soon cease to exist. Nothing, therefore, can be so absurd as to suppose that a measure so important as that of war has been adopted against the will of the people." [10]

"Though Americans praise peace and find it greatly to their interest they are in a chronic state of expectancy of war," a leading American historian wrote in the period between the wars of 1898 and 1917. "Living in a territory which is unassailable by any military force that could be transported to our shores, recognized throughout the world as one of the half-dozen most powerful nations, free from direct interest in the problems which beset European powers, the American people love to talk about war; and by their annexations in the Pacific have involved themselves in controversies which may lead to war. This warlike spirit arises partly from a genuine patriotism, a belief in the United States, a confidence in its principles, and a desire to make them known among all nations. Nevertheless, the outward demonstrations of patriotism, such as the excessive enthusiasm shown for military heroes, are in many instances simply the great American people worshipping the great American people." But though they be "warlike and patriotic, the Americans are still unwilling to take those steps which the experience of mankind has shown are necessary for a bellicose people. Tocqueville, seventy years ago, devoted a chapter to 'Causes which render democratic armies weaker than other armies at the outset of a campaign, and more formidable in protracted warfare.' The difficulty is that Americans like armies much better than they do soldiers. It is not simply an English fashion which causes American military and naval men to put off their uniforms, except when on official duty; it is because people dislike distinctions between gold lace and black broadcloth. With reluctance do Americans admit even the necessity of entrusting their armies and navies to expert soldiers, technically educated; it seems like an undemocratic distinction." [11]

Manifest destiny guided the Americans not only toward territorial expansion; it was also a means for spreading democracy and its blessings into new vast spaces. Many Americans of the 1840's were convinced that in their war against Mexico they were fighting for law and civilization. "Every patriot who clamored for Mexico's provinces would indignantly deny any desire to exploit a neighbor's territory. The righteous but ill-informed people of that day sincerely believed their democratic institutions were of such magnificent perfection that no boundaries could contain them. Surely a benevolent Creator did not intend such blessings for the few; expansion was a divinely ordered means of extending enlightenment to despot-ridden masses in near-by countries! This was not imperialism, but enforced salvation. So the average American reasoned in the 1840s when the spirit of manifest destiny was in the air." [12] And this reasoning was at that time not without some foundation. Like other imperial powers the United States expanded into territories which made no real national resistance because their populations had not yet reached the state of integration of modern nationhood. That was true of Mexico in the middle of the nineteenth century as it was then of India or Algeria. Mexico was disorganized; an almost permanent civil war raged within its frontiers; the failure of the Mexican government to maintain order and to protect life and civilized procedures facilitated and invited imperial expansion. That situation changed radically in the twentieth century. With the change, imperial expansion—even any thought of it—of the United States into Mexico or intervention into Mexican affairs has completely come to an end.

Some of the early American expansionists preparing the War of 1812 sounded like the firebrands of the French Revolution of 1792 in their attempt to lay the foundations for their war with the courts of Europe. "The occasion is now presented," Representative Peter B.

Porter from New York, Chairman of the Committee on Foreign Relations, reported to Congress, "when the national character misunderstood and traduced for a time by foreign and domestic enemies should be vindicated. If we did not rush to the field of battle like the nations who are led by mad ambition of a single chief or the avarice of a corrupted court, it proceeded not from a fear of war but from our love of justice and humanity. The proud spirit of liberty and independence which sustained our fathers in the successful assertion of their rights against foreign aggression is not sunk. . . . The patriotic fire of the Revolution still warms in the American breast with a holy and inextinguishable flame and will conduct this nation to those high destinies which are not less the reward of dignified moderation than of exalted valor." Henry Clay, on December 31, 1811, passionately cried out: "Shall we bear the cuffs and scuffs of British arrogance? . . . By a continuance of this peace we shall lose our commerce, our character, and a nation's best attribute, our honor. A war will give us commerce and character; we shall enjoy the proud consciousness of having discharged our highest duty to our country." [13]

It was, however, only in the 1840's that an aggressive American nationalism with broad expansionist goals represented by the young radicals of the Democratic party tried to carry the nation forward to high imperial destinies. John Louis O'Sullivan founded the *United States Magazine and Democratic Review* in October, 1837, "to strike the hitherto silent strength of the democratic genius of the age and of the country." The new periodical became a mouthpiece of cultural nationalism too and gathered most of the prominent American writers in its pages.[14] It was widely read abroad and at home it helped to return the Democrats under James K. Polk to power. O'Sullivan wholeheartedly supported President Polk's aggressive policy against Mexico. In an article "Annexation," he defended in 1845 the annexation of Texas and bitterly denounced all those who doubted the legitimacy of the war or of American imperial expansion. Texas, he wrote, "is no longer to us a mere country on the map. She comes within the dear and sacred designation of Our Country; no longer a *pays*, she is a part of *la patrie;* and that which is at once a sentiment and a virtue, Patriotism, already begins to thrill for her too within the national heart." He accused Britain, "our old rival and enemy," and France of trying to thwart our expansion, thus "limiting our greatness and checking the fulfillment of our manifest destiny to overspread the continent allotted by Providence for the free development of our yearly multiplying millions." O'Sullivan claimed that in the annexation of Mexican territory by the United States "all the censures due to wrong, perfidy and folly, rest on Mexico alone." He was convinced that California would soon detach herself from Mexico and that a transcontinental railroad would make our "Empires of the Atlantic and Pacific flow together into one." In 1847 he went even further. "The Mexican race now see," he wrote, "in the fate of the aborigines of the north their own inevitable destiny." They must be either amalgamated and assimilated or they must utterly perish. A few months later O'Sullivan praised the occupation of territory by the citizens of the United States as the great movement of the age; the foundations of the future empire will not have been laid, he wrote, until every acre of the North American Continent is occupied by citizens of the United States.[15]

O'Sullivan enlarged his point of view in an article "The True Title" which he wrote in support of President Polk's desire to terminate the agreement of 1818 with Great Britain which provided for the joint occupation of the Oregon country. O'Sullivan rejected any rights based on law and tradition, on treaties and agreements, as against the "natural" rights of nations. America's claim to Oregon was, in his opinion, based on the right "of our manifest destiny to overspread and to possess the whole continent which providence has given us for the development of the great experiment of liberty and federated self-government entrusted to us. . . . The God of nature and of nations has marked it for our own; and with His blessing we will firmly maintain the incontestable rights He has given and fearlessly perform the high duties He has imposed." The Old Testament fierceness of this article marked the climax of the manifest destiny theory.[16] In Congress, however, this new startling theory of international law, though upheld by supporters of the Democratic administration, was denounced by Robert C. Winthrop, who represented Massachusetts in the House from 1840 to 1850. In a speech in the first session of the 29th Congress, he characterized manifest destiny as the revelation of a new right opening "a new chapter in the law of nations or rather, in the special laws of our own country, for I suppose the right of a manifest destiny to spread will not be admitted to exist in any other nation except the universal Yankee nation." Therein, Winthrop erred. Manifest destiny with its right to override treaties and traditions was not specifically American. Under other names a similar feeling of exuberant democratic nationalism animated the "progressive forces" throughout Europe in the 1840's and was to inspire similar revolutionary forces a century later in Asia. The God-given rights of the peoples were to make short shrift of the established order, of long-standing boundaries, of legal obligations. In that sense, nationalism, especially in its populist and radical forms, represented a profoundly revolutionary force.[17]

Much of the radical nationalism of the period—and of later periods too—believed not only in its divine right of expansion but also in the burden of its mission of spreading peace and civilization. These American blessings were to be carried at that time not so much to Asia as to Europe. "Europe is antiquated, decrepit, tottering on the verge of dissolution," Stephen Douglas, a leader of Democratic Young America and United States Senator from Illinois, remarked. "It is a vast graveyard." Radical intellectuals in Europe and America were convinced that peoples were deeply peace-loving and virtuous, whereas kings and aristocrats—or at some later stages, plutocrats— were mainly responsible for wars. This misconception of history which originated largely in the later eighteenth century with Rousseau and Herder and was propagated by Marx and Mazzini colored much of American thinking and not only among the general public. Even students of diplomacy and history shared it. Thus John Hay wrote from Vienna in 1868 about the enormous armaments; he believed them to represent the great calamity and danger of the Europe of his day. "Why then is this awful waste of youth and treasure continued?" he asked, and answered his own question with typical innocence: "I believe from no other motive than to sustain the waning prestige of kings. . . . With the disappearance of armies, the welfare of the people will become the mainspring of national action," and the power of the people will destroy the danger of war. That the nationalist passions of the peoples might threaten peace and cause wars in order to fulfill what the people regarded as their manifest destiny or their national exigencies apparently did not enter Hay's mind. Yet thirty years later, when nationalist passions aroused by the popular press had driven the United States into a war, Hay felt no qualms about the desirability of the war. "We are all very happy over Dewey's splendid Sunday's work at Manila," he wrote from Paris in 1898. "I detest war, and I had hoped I might never see another, but this was as necessary as it was righteous. I have not for two years seen any other issue." [18]

In 1895, before the war with Spain started, two well informed observers of the American and international scene who were both in favor of war, rightly saw in plutocrats or in big business interests a force opposing, and trying to prevent, war. Theodore Roosevelt wrote then to Lodge that "This country needs a war," but "the bankers, brokers, and Anglomaniacs, generally," favor "peace at any price." Henry Adams expressed the same thought with a characteristic anti-Semitic twist. Convinced of the necessity of limiting Russian ambitions by armed power, he bitterly complained of the pacifism of big business in London and in New York. "I regret that England and America should be now so imbecile in foreign matters, but the Jew business of money lending is not conducive to vigorous politics, and Russia can sweep us both out of her path without a squeal. We have even reached the point now where—in this country at least—our cities like Boston and New York think it bad form to have any foreign policy at all." [19]

Walt Whitman was not blind to the danger of populist nationalism and its democratic passions. "We fear our unmatched strength may make us insolent. We fear that we shall be too willing to avenge our injuries by war—the greatest curse that can befall a people and the bitterest obstacle to the progress of all those high and true reforms that makes the glory of this age above the darkness of the ages past and gone." Nevertheless Whitman fervently approved the Mexican War and justified it in the interest of mankind by the claim that the territory of so enlightened a people as the Americans "should be extended—the farther the better." Years later Whitman admitted that the war with Mexico had been a great wrong.[20] Some American radicals wished to go even beyond the continental limits and carry on American expansion under the garb of America's duty to help movements for national independence and republican constitutions abroad. Young America supported enthusiastically Louis Kossuth, the Hungarian nationalist leader, irrespective of the fact that the triumph of his independence movement involved the subjection of the non-Magyar nationalities in Hungary. In this agitation sincere democratic enthusiasm, misconceptions of history, and economic and nationalist self-interest were strangely and inextricably intermingled. One of the most prominent leaders of Young America was George M. Sanders of Kentucky who promoted grandiose business schemes to be realized by jingoism. There is no reason to wonder at the fact that "his faith in the liberal institutions of his country and its mission to extend them was apparently genuine." He became editor of the *Democratic Review* in 1852 and argued that republics established through American intervention in central Europe would necessarily adopt free trade and thus provide markets for American surplus produce. During his brief tenure as American consul in London in 1853 he pleaded for the support of the Spanish republicans in a not entirely disinterested way, for the United States was to receive Cuba as its reward. Stephen A. Douglas made generous though vague declarations in favor of self-determination of all oppressed nationalities in Europe and at the same time strongly endorsed the expansion of the United States southward and westward and the capture of the commerce of the Pacific.[21] A similar confusion of national and commercial self-interest, of democratic idealism and historical misunderstandings characterized American sympathies with "anti-colonial" movements in the twentieth century.[22]

No wonder that in the middle of the nineteenth century Young American ideological imperialism alarmed some European observers. In the summer of 1852 Emile Montégut wrote that it was not only republican ardor which drove the Americans to expand. "C'est une ardeur bien plus fatale, l'ardeur du sang et du tempérament propre aux peuples jeunes, à laquelle vient se joindre la convoitise égoiste et raffinée des nations vieillies." The United States combined, the French author believed, the vices of youthful savagery and of aged over-civilization, sharpened by "le pressentiment obscur et fatidique d'une grande mission providentielle." [23] In its Chronique de la Quinzaine, *La Revue des Deux Mondes* pointed out in the fall of the same year that Young America and Stephen A. Douglas hoped and worked for United States intervention in all the conflicts between the peoples and their governments. "Rien ne peut rendre l'ardeur sanguine, l'esprit de rapacité, les pensées de convoitise, en un mot, la faim et la soif de cette politique vorace, insatiable, qui, selon un proverbe vulgaire, a les yeux plus gros que le ventre." One month later the same periodical discussed the strength which the universal suffrage was lending to the "new democratic policy of conquest and expansion," which seemed to the French observer more and more to triumph and dominate in America. The young nation appeared to him to have abandoned the prudence of the founding fathers. The democratic locomotive was seen roaring full speed ahead, and the French observer thought the United States would be fortunate if the influence of the young radicals would not overheat the engine. His apprehensions were not borne out: common sense and prudence prevailed and the expansionist agitation ebbed off as so many inflammatory crises in American life do. Neither Canada nor Cuba was annexed. The United States kept clear of involvement in European politics. Even its foreign policy in the Western Hemisphere hardly occupied any large place in American thought.[24]

The Monroe Doctrine, proclaimed in the president's annual message to Congress on December 2, 1823, underwent many changes of interpretation and application. Originally, it was only aimed against European armed intervention in the American republics. It aroused very little interest at the time. Neither President Monroe nor the Congress gave any hint that the document would exercise an immense influence on future American foreign policy. In Baltimore, however, which had then a flourishing trade with South America, the local press in its issues of September 3, 1823, underlined the importance of the doctrine. The *Baltimore Patriot* declared that "every American heart will respond" to the sentiments expressed in Monroe's state paper, "to the support of which every American arm will be extended." The *Federal Gazette* greeted the presidential message as the worthiest since the days of Washington, "calculated to promote the beneficial interests not only of the people of the United States but of mankind in general." [25] But for a period of more than twelve years after 1826, when it was briefly mentioned in the debate on the First Pan-American Congress called at Panama, it was never once invoked.[26]

Only at the end of 1838, Caleb Cushing referred to President Monroe's message in discussing the blockade of the Mexican port of Tampico by the French navy. Cushing, a fervent imperialist, was then Congressman from Massachusetts, and later, as United States Commissioner to China, negotiated in 1844 the first treaty between the two countries, firmly insisting upon American extraterritorial rights. He joined the annexationist Democratic group of Young America, fought in the war against Mexico, and as an important member of the administration of President Franklin Pierce, did his utmost to annex Cuba and to provoke Britain. But in 1838 the United States was not yet in the grip of the extreme nationalists; the Monroe Doctrine was at that time so little known even to the informed part of the American public that the *Columbian Centinel* of Boston found it necessary in its editorial of January 4, 1839, to recall to the reader the "remarkable passage" in the presidential message of 1823. "We do not consider," the editorial went on, "that President Monroe ever intended to carry his sympathy so far, as to commit this government in favor of making common cause with our southern neighbors in every dispute with European nations. . . . Such a committal would have amounted to a treaty of alliance, offensive and defensive. But even if a former president had intended such an alliance, an intimation of the kind would not have been binding upon his successors,—much less on Congress." William Ellery Channing went even further: he attempted to prove that the principles set down in Monroe's message should prevent the United States from interfering in the affairs of the then independent nation of Texas.[27]

Official American foreign policy, even under President Polk, was little influenced by the expansionist clamors of the Young American radicals. In the *Democratic Review* of January, 1846, Caleb Cushing attacked Polk for acquiescing in British and French intervention to preserve order in La Plata. The Clayton-Bulwer Treaty of 1850, negotiated by Secretary of State John Middleton Clayton, a Quaker, and the British minister Sir Henry Lytton Bulwer under the presidency of Zachary Taylor, whose generalship in the Mexican War had carried him to the White House, was a model of statesmanlike moderation. It pledged the United States and Britain jointly to guarantee the neutrality of any canal built across the Isthmus, not to fortify it and not to acquire any colonies in Central America. Naturally the *Democratic Review* attacked the treaty; its nationalism was not satisfied by American foreign policy even under the Democratic administration of President Pierce. Like Caleb Cushing, Pierce had enlisted in the Mexican War of 1847 as a volunteer, as President he followed a vigorous foreign policy which was directed against Britain and aimed at the acquisition of Cuba and Hawaii; he also sought a strengthened military establishment. "Occupied for a long period of years," the *Review* complained in February, 1853, "in the discussion of our internal policy we have neglected to exercise the primary function of our national government." Yet the following decades were, from the point of view of radical nationalism, even worse: the anxieties of the approaching Civil War and then the rewards of a rapidly expanding economy directed the American mind entirely toward domestic problems. Americans had a deep conviction of their mission as the most progressive and freest government in the world but they expected to fulfill this mission by staying within their geographic confines and "to lead in the manner of the stars with their kindly light, by the passive radiation of their brilliant example." [28]

President Johnson expressed this hope in his fourth message to Congress on December 8, 1868: "The conviction is rapidly gaining ground in the American mind that with the increased facilities for inter-communication between all portions of the earth, the principles of free government, as embraced in our constitution, if faithfully maintained and carried out, would prove of sufficient strength and breadth within their sphere to influence the civilized nations of the world." Five years later Ulysses S. Grant, in his second Presidential inaugural address, March 4, 1873, followed the same line: "It is my firm conviction that the civilized world is tending toward republicanism, our government by the people through their chosen representatives, and that our own great Republic is destined to be the guiding star of all others. . . . I believe that our great Maker is preparing the world, in his own good time, to become one nation, speaking one language, and when armies and navies will no longer be required." [29] The anti-annexationist mood went so far that when the people of Santo Domingo asked for admission as a territory of the Union, the Congress objected to this demand though President Grant favored its acceptance. In 1881, Secretary of State James Gillespie Blaine attempted to go beyond the negative features of the Monroe Doctrine and to unite all American nations under the leadership of the United States as the "elder sister," but failed through complete lack of popular support or interest. Under the influence of Henry Clay, whom Blaine admired, he wished to expand the "American system" into a hemispheric co-prosperity sphere, "America for the Americans." This move was mainly directed against Britain and partly inspired by the desire to win the Irish vote for the Republican Party. Blaine demanded exclusive United States

control of any canal across the Isthmus, but when Grover Cleveland
became President, he quickly reverted to the former policy opposing the domination of the vital waterway by any single power.
Blaine's policy was attacked as being blustering and aggressive and
as creating British-American tensions. Nor did the country follow
Blaine's policy of preparing the annexation of Hawaii. Blaine's ambitions were only realized in the decade following his death when
the nineteenth century closed and a new era of international relations started.[30]

In the nineteenth century the United States and Britain both
lived through a period of "splendid isolation" and liberal pacifism,
yet both had to face certain strategic realities and responsibilities
at given times. The result was that few people earnestly thought
about foreign policy and that the foreign policies of the two nations did not show any great consistency: the people were constantly
torn between the desire to lead their prosperous and comfortable
lives undisturbed and the frequent inducements to act either to
preserve their way of life or to bring its blessings to others. Splendid
isolation came to an end simultaneously in both countries in 1898,
with the Spanish-American War in the one case and the Boer War
in the other. This change was not due, as has been sometimes said
in the case of the United States, to the closing of the frontier, but to
a new wave of expansionism and vitalism which was characteristic
of the whole Western world. This spirit was reflected in Henry
Cabot Lodge, the biographer of Alexander Hamilton, Daniel Webster, and George Washington, a Senator from Massachusetts for
many years, and Theodore Roosevelt's close advisor in foreign affairs.
In 1895 he wrote that "From the Rio Grande to the Arctic Ocean
there should be but one flag and one country. . . . We should
build the Nicaraguan Canal. . . . We should control the Hawaiian
Islands, . . . the island of Cuba, still sparsely settled and of almost
unbounded fertility, will become to us a necessity. . . . The great
nations are rapidly absorbing for their future expansion and their
present defense all the waste places of the earth. It is a movement
which makes for civilization and the advancement of the race. As
one of the great nations of the world, the United States must not fall
out of the line of march." [31]

The most important spokesman in America of this general movement of the Western world was Theodore Roosevelt, who in many

ways formed the counterpart of Joseph Chamberlain in England, both in his zeal for popular reforms and in his new assertive nationalism. In the Spanish-American War of 1898, which Roosevelt did so much to bring about, manifest destiny led the United States far beyond the continental limits of a land empire. Through it America started on the road to acquiring a dominant position in the Caribbean and in the Pacific, growing into the greatest naval power on the earth, and succeeding to the role and responsibilities which the British Empire had held in the nineteenth century. This happened at the very moment when the South African war and its consequences marked the beginning of the decline of Britain's imperial power and self-confidence and the inauguration of its policy of a liberal transformation and abandonment of empire. From that time on, more than ever before, British policy was determined to proceed only in closest collaboration with the United States. The treaty signed by Secretary of State John Hay and Lord Pauncefote on November 18, 1901, the first important treaty negotiated under the presidency of Theodore Roosevelt, abrogated the Clayton-Bulwer Pact of 1850. In that way Britain renounced her position of equality with the United States in the Caribbean and on the Isthmus. The road was now open to the building of a canal which, though an international waterway of great importance, was under the exclusive control of the United States. At the same time, the third great event setting the stage for the international relations of the twentieth century announced itself: the emergence of the Far Eastern problem, which took the place which the Middle Eastern problem had occupied in the nineteenth century. The reason for the emergence of these problems was in both cases the same: great ancient empires—the Ottoman Empire and the Chinese Empire—had entered a state of rapid disintegration and the disposition of their inheritance became a central concern of world importance. During the nineteenth century Britain had preserved the integrity of the Ottoman mainland against threats by Russia. After the easy Japanese victory over the once so powerful Chinese Empire in 1894, it seemed only a question of time until China would suffer the fate of the Ottoman Empire. The sick man on the Bosphorus was joined by the sick man on the Yang-tse. In this latter case the United States took over the role of preserving the integrity of China against threats by Russia and Japan. Thus at the turn of the century, the United States entered

—often against its desires and inclinations—upon the role of a world power; a role foreseen by some visionary observers in the nineteenth century.

In both nations—the United States and Britain—many citizens opposed the Spanish-American War and the South African war and the policy of expansion. In Britain, the Liberal party came to power as the result of the wide-spread protest against the Boer War and started the course of revolutionary imperial transformation—in South Africa, in Ireland, in India—which set the model for the course followed later by the United States in the Philippines and in Puerto Rico. Among the many voices raised in the United States against the new imperialism was that of Carl Schurz. In an article "Manifest Destiny" in *Harper's Magazine* of October, 1893, he protested against the intended annexation of Hawaii and warned against the building of a large navy. "When our maritime commerce was most flourishing, we had no navy worth speaking of to protect it, and nobody thought that one was needed," Schurz wrote, forgetting that it was the existence of the British navy and its control of the Atlantic which made this fortunate position possible for the United States. In another article, "About Patriotism," in *Harper's Weekly* of April 16, 1898, Schurz regarded no delusion as more dangerous to the honor and the liberty of a free people "than the one that the needless or wanton clamoring for war on every occasion of foreign embroilment is a sign of patriotic spirit."

Roosevelt and the popular press took the point of view opposite to that of Carl Schurz. "To Roosevelt, the conduct of foreign affairs was essentially simple. Right was right, and the United States defined and enforced the rules of the international game; arbitration of disputes was laudable, except when America was a party to the issue. Peace was secondary to honor, and America defined honor. The Monroe Doctrine was the corner stone of American diplomacy or belligerency; and before President Roosevelt had concluded his interpretations, it had been changed almost beyond recognition." [32] Yet as a statesman, Roosevelt undoubtedly showed a better understanding of the changing international scene and of America's responsibilities than most of his contemporaries. In 1901 he declared in Minnesota that "To us is given the privilege of playing a leading part in the century that has just opened. . . . Whether we wish it or not, we cannot avoid hereafter having duties to do in the face of other nations. All that we can do is to settle whether we shall perform these duties well or ill." [33]

During his presidency Roosevelt toned down some of the blustering spirit of adventurous enterprise and learned more to appreciate the complexities of the international situation. He was the first American statesman to realize fully that the relative strength of the European powers was of fundamental importance to the United States and that in the Far East the safety of American interests rested "upon a balance of power between Russia and Japan and that of these two powers, Russia was the more dangerous." [34] Roosevelt was also the first to advocate before the Nobel Prize Committee the formation of a league to enforce peace. "It would be a master stroke," he said, in Christiania, Norway, on May 5, 1910, "if those great powers honestly bent on peace would form a League of Peace, not only to keep the peace among themselves, but to prevent, by force if necessary, its being broken by others. . . . The combination might at first be only to secure peace within certain definite limits and certain definite conditions, but the ruler or statesman who should bring about such a combination would have earned his place in history for all time and his title to the gratitude of all mankind." [35] It was a historical tragedy that seven years later personal hostility estranged Roosevelt and Woodrow Wilson and prevented their cooperation. Wilson's noble but abstract idealism would have gained from an admixture of Roosevelt's sometimes rough realism.

This realism was often obscured by Roosevelt's fervent activism and his at times almost bloodthirsty nationalism. The latter was to him a matter of "robust" morality and he considered it the only foundation upon which "a vigorous civilization" could be built; "every civilization worth calling such," he exclaimed, "must be based on a spirit of intense nationalism." This statement corresponded to the fashionable social Darwinism and vitalistic biologism of the period, but not to historical truth; neither the civilization of thirteenth century Christianity nor of eighteenth century Enlightenment was based on a spirit of nationalism. [36]

Roosevelt was of course not alone among American progressives of the period in voicing an extreme nationalism. Not by accident was Rudyard Kipling's famous poem "The White Man's Burden" intended primarily for Americans; it was written soon after the end of the Spanish-American War in December, 1898, and first published at the beginning of the following year in New York papers. So much was America then affected by "ideas about far flung lines of empire that even the gentle, amiable William Allen White" declared in his *Emporia* (Kansas) *Gazette* on March 20, 1899, that Yankee domination was the civilizing salvation for the Cubans as well as for the Chinese.[37] Among the midwestern progressives, Albert Jeremiah Beveridge was probably the most outspoken herald of a revived concept of manifest destiny in which several elements merged: geopolitical concepts of providentially shaped geographic or continental limits; the conviction of the superior ability and morality of the Americans; the excellence of democracy and its universal mission to extend its blessing; the advanced stage of the American economy and technology which would make the desert bloom and bring little used or much abused land to full economic fruition. The Darwinian survival of the fittest provided some of the ideological justification which in older times the will of God had supplied. In his famous March of the Flag speech in Indianapolis in 1898, Beveridge called Jefferson "the first imperialist of the Republic," with whom the march of the flag began, a march carried on by Jackson who heard and obeyed the same call as did Jefferson. Two years later Beveridge again appealed to Jefferson and to Chief Justice John Marshall—who was his idol and whose definitive biography he wrote—as authorities for the duty of extending "our empire,—the empire of liberty and law, of commerce and communication, of social order and the Gospel of our Lord—the star of empire of the civilization of the world." [38]

Roosevelt's imperialism changed the Monroe Doctrine into a theory of the positive right of the United States to intervene in any Latin American country where the government was unstable or disorderly. "Brutal wrong-doing or an impotence which results in a general loosening of the ties of civilized society," Roosevelt wrote to Elihu Root on May 20, 1904, "may finally require intervention by some civilized nation and in the Western Hemisphere the United States cannot ignore this duty." Similar turmoils in Asian or African lands had provoked European intervention in the nineteenth century.[39] Roosevelt applied this nineteenth century doctrine to the Western Hemisphere. Though his administration resisted strong demands for repudiation of the promise to grant Cuban independence, the Platt Amendment of March 2, 1901, imposed severe restrictions on this independence and entitled the United States not only to maintain naval bases on the island but also to intervene there in case of domestic disturbances. The amendment was abrogated in 1934 at a time when the trend started by Britain after 1905 of granting self-government and independence to dominions and colonies had set the example for a similar course to be followed by the United States.[40]

Without Roosevelt's blustering nationalism, other Americans of his time recognized the new position of the United States among the nations. Around the turn of the century, Henry Adams foresaw the breakdown of the British Empire with all the consequences of a great system of universal order and civilization disintegrating, and the ensuing conflict between America and Russia. "For, to anyone who has all his life studied history," he wrote in 1900, "it is obvious that the fall of England would be paralleled by only two great convulsions in human record, the fall of the Roman Empire in the fourth century and the fall of the Roman Church in the sixteenth." With the shield of imperial Britain removed, the United States would come face-to-face with Russia. Adams repeated Tocqueville's prediction of the future role of the two countries but he was convinced of America's being at least temporarily ahead. "America and Russia. There are the two future centers of power, and of the two, America must get there first. . . . The sum of my certainty is that America has a very clear century of start over Russia, and that western Europe must follow us for a hundred years, before Russia can swing her flail over the Atlantic." [41] A few years later Henry Adams drew the necessary conclusions from his observations; he clearly recognized the need of a North Atlantic Community. "We have got to support France against Germany, and fortify an Atlantic system beyond attack," he wrote to Mrs. Cameron as early as August 27, 1905, during the first Moroccan crisis, "for if Germany breaks down England or France, she becomes the center of a military world, and we are lost." Twelve years later, on June 8, 1917, two months after the United States had entered the war, Adams wrote his old English friend Gaskell: "Meanwhile, here we are, for the first time in our lives, fighting side by side and to my bewilderment I find the great object of my life thus accomplished in the building up of the great community of Atlantic powers, which I hope will at least make a precedent that can never be forgotten. We have done it once and perhaps we can keep it up." He went on to reflect that it was not common Anglo-American intention which brought the North Atlantic community into being but the threat of German military force. Henry Adams's hopes were disappointed. The lesson taught by the war of 1914 was not sufficient to make the English-speaking peoples realize the changes in their world position. A more profound experience was needed, which only the totalitarian attack on democracy provided.

Captain Alfred T. Mahan clearly foresaw the need of such an experience. He wrote in July, 1894, an article entitled "Possibilities of an Anglo-American Reunion" for the *North American Review* in answer to Andrew Carnegie's question about how to achieve a formal political connection between the United States and the British Empire for the advancement of the general interests of the English-speaking peoples. Mahan advised against a federal union proposed by other writers and against an immediate close alliance, because public opinion was not yet ripe for it. "Let each nation be educated," he wrote, "to realize the length and breadth of its own interest in the sea; when that is done, the identity of these interests will become apparent. This identity cannot be established firmly in men's minds antecedent to the great teacher, Experience; and experience cannot be had before that further development of the facts which will follow the not far distant day, when the United States people must again betake themselves to the sea and to external action, as did their forefathers alike in their old home and in the new." [42] Mahan was right. By the middle of the twentieth century Experience had taught the two nations to recognize the desirability of that fraternal association which Henry Adams had demanded at the beginning of the century.[43]

In the small chorus of American voices which at the turn of the century recognized the changing international scene and the new role imposed upon the United States was Woodrow Wilson, then a professor of jurisprudence and political economy, on the threshold of a career which eleven years later was to carry him into the White House. In 1901 he wrote in an article of "a new era [that] has come upon us like a sudden vision of things unprophesied," a new order, fundamentally different from that of the eighteenth and nineteenth centuries. "The affairs of the world stand in such a case, the principles for which we have battled the long decade through are now put in such jeopardy amidst the contests of nations, the future of mankind faces so great a peril of reactionary revolution, that our own private business must take its chances along with the greater business of the world at large. We dare not stand neutral." Wilson believed that the cause of individual liberty was at stake, and that America, its champion, would not long be able to uphold it if the world were permitted to lose faith in the cause; for the United States was the chief defender of individual liberty and had been schooled like no other nation in practical proficiency and self-confidence. As a result, the Americans were prepared to face the new tasks set before the whole Western world. "Themselves through all their history a frontier," Wilson wrote, "the English colonies in America grew into a nation whose life poured still with strong tide along the old channel. . . . England sought colonies at the end of the earth to set her energy free and give vent to her enterprise; we, a like people in every impulse of mastery and achievement, had our own vast continent and were satisfied. . . . It is only just now that we have awakened to our real relationship to the rest of mankind. Absorbed in our own development, we had fallen into a singular ignorance of the rest of the world . . . we have acquired a false self-confidence, a false self-sufficiency, because we have heeded no successes or failures but our own." The twentieth century, Wilson believed, would force the Americans out of their isolation. "The East is to be opened and transformed whether we will or no; the standards of the West are to be imposed upon it; nations and peoples which have stood still the centuries through are to be quickened, and made part of the universal world of commerce and of ideas which has so steadily been a-making by the advance of European power from age to age. It is our peculiar duty, as it is also England's, to moderate the process in the interests of liberty: to impart to the peoples thus driven out upon the road of change, . . . the drill and habit of law and obedience which we long ago got out of the strenuous processes of English history; secure for them, when we may, the free intercourse and the natural development which shall make them at least equal members of the family of nations." [44]

One year later, as president of Princeton University, his alma mater, Woodrow Wilson delivered an address on the Ideas of America in which he foresaw his country's and his own future—the country's active participation as a nation among nations, and the role of its President as its leader in foreign affairs. "We have come to full maturity with this new century of our national existence," he declared, "and . . . the day of our isolation is past. . . . Moreover, the center of gravity has shifted in the action of our federal government. It has shifted back to where it was at the opening of the last century [when] foreign affairs, the sentiment and policy of nations overseas, dominated our politics and our Presidents were our leaders. And now the same thing has come about again. Once more it is our place among the nations that we think of; once more our Presidents are our leaders. . . . It is by the widening of vision that nations, as men, grow and are made great. We need not fear the expanding scene . . . Let us lift our thoughts to the level of the great tasks that await us, and bring a great age in with the coming of our day of strength." [45]

Little more than a decade later Woodrow Wilson was in the position to apply his newly announced principles concerning the United States—a nation among nations in a new and rapidly changing world—and concerning the President—a leader of his nation in international affairs and its spokesman before the world. Woodrow Wilson was a man endowed with some remarkable insights into the complexities of contemporary international relations but, by his own background and by the unpreparedness of his people, he was unable to follow through a policy consistent with these insights. The course of history forced decisions upon him which started the United States on the road foreseen by Tocqueville. Theodore Roosevelt and Woodrow Wilson, different in so many ways, shared the feeling that they and their people stood at the threshold of a new era—an era in which the American people would have to play an ever increasing role. In the same spirit of a new era, a British journalist, William Thomas Stead, a contemporary of Roosevelt and Wilson, wrote in 1901 a book with the significant title *The Americanization of the World or the Trend of the Twentieth Century.* He prefaced it with a quotation from the famous British liberal and free trade leader, Richard Cobden, who had declared in 1835: "We fervently believe that our only chance of national prosperity lies in the timely remodeling of our system, so as to put it as nearly as possible upon an equality with the improved management of the Americans."

Around 1900 Stead raised issues which half a century later have become obvious—he spoke of the Americanization of European literature and art, marriage and society, habits of life and ways of consumption. He even spoke of an "American invasion" which was being bitterly resented by many Europeans "as if the Americans bearing gifts in their hands were bent upon doing us the greatest possible injury." He found continental Europe even more frightened than England; most hostile to this Americanization, Stead found, were the Germans who wished to rally the continent against the United States, under the slogan "Europe for the Europeans," with Africa and Asia constituting the European reserves. But Stead regarded such European solidarity a vain dream. Addressing himself especially to the British, Stead put before them a momentous choice. "If they decide to merge the existence of the British Empire in the United States of the English-speaking World, they may continue for all time to be an integral part of the greatest of all world powers, supreme on sea and unassailable on land. . . . That is one alternative. The other is the acceptance of our supersession by the United States as the center of gravity in the English-speaking world, the loss one by one of our great colonies, and our ultimate reduction to the status of an English-speaking Belgium." Stead realized that this choice would be felt by many Englishmen as an affront. To all such irate champions of England, Stead replied, "that, as the creation of the Americans is the greatest achievement of our race, there is no reason to resent the part the Americans are playing in fashioning the world in their image, which, after all, is substantially an image of ourselves."

In the British edition of the book, Stead added a preface in which he wrote: "The advent of the United States of America as the greatest of world powers is the greatest political, social, and commercial phenomenon of our times. . . . It is only when we look at the manifold manifestations of the exuberant energy of the United States and the world-wide influence which they are exerting upon the world in general and the British Empire in particular, that we realize how comparatively insignificant are all the other events of our time." Stead resumed here one of the great themes sounded first by Tocqueville about the future leadership of America. But he did not envisage, as Tocqueville did, an equally important role for the Russians nor any Russian-American antagonism. On the contrary, Stead believed in Russia's willing acceptance of United States

leadership. He noted in the United States the absence of Russopho-
bia, which was widespread in nineteenth century England, and he
pointed out that the Russian minister of communications who had
built the Siberian transcontinental railway had served his appren-
ticeship in Pennsylvania and retained in his personal appearance
and his manner of doing business the impress of this apprentice-
ship.[46]

The turning point for the Western world and for the United
States was the war of 1914. It linked the destinies of the two shores
of the North Atlantic again as closely as they had been in the eighteenth century. But few foresaw at the time the consequences of the
war: it marked the end of the predominance of Western ideas, and
the rise of communism, fascism, and Asian nationalism—movements
adumbrated before 1914 but for which the war provided the condition necessary for their actual growth. Not the war itself, however,
but the self-abandonment and disunity of the Western democracies
after the war enhanced the strength of the anti-Western movements
to such a degree that they reversed a trend which had been steadily
gaining in momentum from the seventeenth century on. Though the
Europeans were not aware of it, and continued their struggle to
maintain a European balance of power, bidding for European
hegemony as if no fundamental change had happened, the end of
the war marked also the political eclipse of Europe. It was a misfortune for both Europe and the United States that neither realized
it or wished to acknowledge it. Yet in 1917 only the entrance of the
United States into what had been until then a war for the maintenance of the balance of power in Europe, saved Europe from the
consequences of a German victory on the eastern and western fronts
and from German hegemony over the whole continent.

Woodrow Wilson could not have reestablished the European
balance of power in 1918 even if he had wished. His understanding
of foreign affairs before the war was slight. In his message to Congress in December, 1913, he confidently stated that "many happy
manifestations multiply about us of a growing cordiality and even
of unity and interest among the nations, foreshadowing an era of
settled peace and good will." The report which his then close advisor in foreign affairs, Colonel Edward M. House, sent him from
Berlin on May 29, 1914, must have come as a shock to Wilson: "The
situation is extraordinary. It is militarism run stark mad. Unless

some one acting for you can bring about a different understanding, there is some day to be an awful cataclysm: no one in Europe can do it. There is too much hatred, too many jealousies. . . . England does not want Germany wholly crushed, for she would then have to reckon alone with her ancient enemy, Russia; but if Germany insists upon an ever-increasing navy, then England will have no choice. The best chance for peace is an understanding between England and Germany in regard to naval armaments, and yet there is some disadvantage to us by these two getting too close." [47]

Before 1914 as before 1939, England tried hard to maintain the European balance of power and to arrive at an understanding with Germany. Sir Eyre Crowe expressed official British policy in his famous memorandum of January 1, 1907.[48] To a later generation his words clarify the fundamental similarities of the situations preceding the two German bids for European hegemony, though as in all historical instances, the great differences in both cases should not be overlooked.[49] Sir Eyre maintained that at the beginning of the twentieth century "the vague and undefined schemes of Teutonic expansion ('die Ausbreitung des deutschen Volkstums') are but the expression of the deeply rooted feeling that Germany has by the strength and purity of her national purpose, the fervor of her patriotism, the depth of her religious feeling, the high standard of competency, and the perspicuous honesty of her administration, the successful pursuit of every branch of public and scientific activity, and the elevated character of her philosophy, art, and ethics, established for herself the right to assert the primacy of German national ideals. And as it is an axiom of her political faith that right, in order that it may prevail, must be backed by force, the transition is easy to the belief that the 'good German sword' which plays so large a part in patriotic speech, is there to solve any difficulties that may be in the way of establishing the reign of those ideals in a Germanized world."

The British diplomat absolved the Germans of wishing war, but he pointed out that since the dismissal of Bismarck German policy had provoked general apprehension by its lack of a clear and well defined line. Many of its methods anticipated those used again before 1939.[50] Sir Eyre described these methods as diplomatic blackmail, to which Britain yielded out of fear of some vague but perhaps dreadful consequences in the event of her refusal. Such a relationship made for almost perpetual friction, notwithstanding the pretense of friendship. "The generally restless, explosive and disconnected activity of Germany," Sir Eyre wrote, in relation to other states, found its explanation partly in the same attitude toward them and "partly in the suggested want of definite political aims and purposes. A wise German statesman would recognize the limits within which any world-policy that is not to provoke a hostile combination of all the nations in arms must confine itself. He would realize that the edifice of Pan-Germanism, with its outlying bastions in the Netherlands, in the Scandinavian countries, in Switzerland, in the German provinces of Austria, and on the Adriatic, could never be built upon any other foundation than the wreckage of the liberties of Europe. A German maritime supremacy must be acknowledged to be incompatible with the existence of the British Empire, and even if that Empire disappeared, the union of the greatest military with the greatest naval Power in one State would compel the world to combine for the riddance of such an incubus. . . . Whilst each of these grandiose schemes seems incapable of fulfillment under anything like the present conditions of the world, it looks as if Germany were playing with them all together simultaneously, and thereby wilfully concentrating in her own path all the obstacles and oppositions of a world set at defiance. That she should do this helps to prove how little of logical and consistent design and of unrelenting purpose lies behind the impetuous mobility, the bewildering surprises, and the heedless disregard of the susceptibilities of other people that have been so characteristic of recent manifestations of German policy."

In spite of this vague German restlessness, England tried before as after the war of 1914 to maintain a European balance of power, and therefore a strong Germany. "So long as England remains faithful," Sir Eyre wrote, "to the general principle of the preservation of the balance of power, her interests would not be served by Germany being reduced to the rank of a weak Power, as this might easily lead to a Franco-Russian predominance equally, if not more, formidable to the British Empire. There are no existing German rights, territorial or other, which this country could wish to see diminished. Therefore, so long as Germany's action does not overstep the line of legitimate protection of existing rights she can always count upon the sympathy and good will, and even the moral support, of England. Further, it would be neither just nor politic to ignore the claims to a healthy expansion which a vigorous and growing country like Germany has a natural right to assert in the field of legitimate endeavor." But after 1917 the return to a European balance of power, though the British attempted it,[51] was impossible. Europe was no longer a self-sufficient power system. This system collapsed as the result of two events which were not of Wilson's doing—Russia's turning against Europe in Lenin's anti-Western and anti-democratic counter-revolution and one year later the disintegration of the Habsburg Empire, which had formed a pivotal element in the European balance of power.

Woodrow Wilson's attitude toward the war and its issues was, like that of most Americans, ambivalent and not clearly defined; when he finally decided to enter the war he did it for contradictory and never fully clarified reasons. Morally, he came more and more to believe that in the war of 1914 the Germans stood for values and interpretations of history and human nature opposed to the Anglo-American political ideas—ideas which Wilson had frequently expressed in his articles and speeches. In his vision of the future he beheld not a balance of power in Europe or elsewhere, but a world-wide system based upon the strength of public opinion and the moral nature of man, accepting democracy as a universally valid pattern. In his second Inaugural Address on March 5, 1917, Wilson declared, "The greatest things that remain to be done must be done with the whole world for stage and in cooperation with the wide and universal forces of mankind, and we are making our spirits ready for those things. . . . We are provincials no longer. The tragic events of the thirty months of vital turmoil through which we have just passed have made us citizens of the world. There can be no turning back." These moral and ideological considerations of a global nature were tacitly supported by Wilson's realistic grasp of the fact that the United States could not afford to have the eastern shore of the Atlantic and the British Isles fall under the control of one great military power.

This consideration was perhaps best expressed in an editorial of the *New Republic* in February, 1917, which envisaged consequences yet unseen by Woodrow Wilson: "If the Allied fleet were in danger of destruction, if Germany had a chance of securing command of the seas, our navy ought to be joined to the British in order to prevent it. The safety of the Atlantic highway is something for which America should fight. Why? Because on the two shores of the Atlantic Ocean there has grown up a profound web of interest which joins together the western world. . . . If that community were destroyed we should know what we had lost. . . . The passing of the power of England would be calamitous to the American national interest. . . . [America would] be morally and politically isolated. What we must fight for is a common interest of the western world, for the integrity of the Atlantic Powers. We must recognize that we are in fact one great community and act as a member of it. . . . By showing that we are ready now . . . to defend the western world, the corner stone of federation would be laid." [52] The vision of the *New Republic* was soon dimmed and the expectations Woodrow Wilson cherished when he led America into the war were soon frustrated. The reasons for this failure have often been discussed. American domestic politics and personal animosities played their role; no chapter of human history is without its woeful tales of individual insufficiencies and partisan intrigues, but they were not responsible for America's deserting the war which she helped to decide and the peace which she helped to make.

The over-idealization and over-moralization of the reasons for which the United States had entered the war had roused an expectation that a new and better world would emerge from the war such as no peace treaty could ever have satisfied. This attitude was deeply engrained in America's missionary idealism and in her distrust of "decadent" Europe and "imperialist" Britain. Woodrow Wilson shared these traditional attitudes to a large degree, as did later Franklin D. Roosevelt. Wilson refused to join the Allies: the United States kept aloof and became only an "associated" power. "One would hardly have judged from his [Wilson's] speeches," an American historian wrote looking back upon the events about three decades later, "that the Allies knew anything about courage and sacrifice and suffering, or that some of the Allied leaders also had ideas. We Americans, it seemed, were to be freedom's chief, if not first and only champion." [53]

Wilson's Americanism contained a large element of Walt Whitman's nationalism, identifying the Ego with the American people, or at least the right-thinking American people, and the American people with the cause of world freedom. Whitman embodied the

ideal in the Poet, and Wilson in the President, as the leader of the
United States and of world democracy.[54] Wilson's supreme confidence in himself and in his people militated against his effective
guidance of domestic and world affairs. He supposed that Americans and people everywhere shared his political and moral ideas—
that the people left to themselves in self-determination would abandon their "wicked" statesmen and espouse the cause of peace and
reasonableness as understood in the liberal world, and above all, in
the United States. He never took into account the revolutionary
character of nationalism in the twentieth century or the desire for
collective power which inspired "awakening" masses. In his speeches
urging United States participation in the war, President Wilson did
not stress the strategic American interest in supporting Britain and
the Allies; he put moral reasons into the foreground so that the
Allies appeared to fight for egoistic motives of national self-preserva-
tion or self-aggrandizement, whereas the Americans could easily
persuade themselves that they were knights in shining armor fighting for universal peace and justice. In Wilson's mind the League
of Nations was to emerge as the expression of typical American
idealism to be imposed upon a half-reluctant Old World.

But Wilson was not alone in urging a league of nations. In the
fall of 1916 the British Foreign Office had submitted a memorandum
to the Prime Minister in which it proposed a league of nations in a
more sober and helpful mood than did Wilson. "We are under no
illusion that such an instrument will become really effective until
nations have learned to subordinate their personal and individual
ambitions and dreams for the benefit of the community of nations.
. . . If America could be persuaded to associate itself to such a
league of nations, a weight and influence might be secured for its
decisions that would materially promote the objects for which it
had been created." [55] Nor was the league of nations idea alien
to Wilson's leading adversary in the Senate, the Republican chairman of its Foreign Affairs Committee, Henry Cabot Lodge. With
a realism which recalled the better insights of his friend Theodore
Roosevelt, Lodge wrote on December 2, 1918, in a memorandum to
Henry White that it was absolutely vital that the terms of peace
should be determined by the United States and the Allies first and
then imposed upon the German government, and that the terms
must be of a nature to make it impossible for Germany to try a

second time for European or world hegemony. "The League of Nations to preserve and enforce peace presents a conception," Lodge wrote, "which must appeal to every right-thinking man," but he insisted that the provisions for such a league must not be made a part of the peace treaty. "Any attempt to do this would not only delay the signature of the treaty of peace . . . but it would make the adoption of the treaty, unamended, by the Senate of the United States . . . extremely doubtful." [56] Yet Wilson thought of himself as the only proponent of the League—overlooking the fact that in Paris the French insisted upon a real League with police power to enforce peace, an idea rejected by the American and British delegations. The Americans received no clear guidance from Wilson: he failed to convey the understanding that it was not a question of moral idealism but of their own national self-interest to stay with the Allies and with the peace. In 1919 Americans still judged worldwide issues in domestic, and largely in traditional domestic, terms. It could not be otherwise. As Professor Daniel J. Boorstin has pointed out, "Changes in national thought occur not by mutation but by evolution. Old ideas do not suddenly become obsolete; rather they gradually become irrelevant. And in all societies people are slow to discover the irrelevance of their traditional vocabulary." [57]

Woodrow Wilson himself went to the peace conference of Paris full of the traditional American prejudices. On his way to Europe he still clung to the illusion that among the statesmen who were to gather at Paris he alone would really represent the people of his country. In reality, Georges Clemenceau and David Lloyd George were the spokesmen for their countries to a degree that Wilson, after the Congressional elections of November, 1918, could no longer claim. The disillusionment of the American people with his idealism set in before the terms of the Treaty of Versailles were drawn up. The misunderstanding of the treaty fanned the disillusionment. As early as March 17, 1919, a writer in the then influential weekly *Nation* contended that in all history there had been no treaty which more readily deserved to be regarded as an international crime "than the amazing document which the German representatives are now asked to sign." He pointed to Wilson as the man primarily responsible for the evils of the treaty. [58] The *New Republic* published later in serial form John Maynard Keynes' fateful book on *The Economic Consequences of the Peace*, which presented the case for the belief that American moral idealism was no match for the evil schemers of old world politics.[59]

Contrary to Keynes' opinion, Woodrow Wilson had not been taken in by his European colleagues nor had he shown the disastrous incompetence "in the agilities of the council chamber" with which Keynes charged him. Wilson grew through his experiences in Paris to new stature. He came there in touch with the realities of the world situation and he began to understand them and their implications long before the majority of his countrymen did. In the addresses which he delivered after his return on his western tour in September, 1919, he presented a convincing argument for the treaty and for America's participation in its execution. "If America should not take the leading part in this new enterprise of concerted power," Wilson warned, "the world would experience one of those reversals of sentiment, one of those penetrating chills of reaction, which would lead to a universal cynicism . . ." This happened. The "lost generation" feeling became characteristic of the 1920's throughout the Western world and helped the anti-Western movements to achieve successes undreamt of before, by promising to fill a vacuum. A period of "debunking" set in, the ideals of liberalism and democracy were "unmasked" as hollow pretexts for national egotism and economic interests. There seemed to be no difference between the conduct and war aims of the Germans, who interpreted 1914 as a struggle against Western liberalism, and the conduct and war aims of the Western democracies.

Under the impact of this disillusionment, the history of the world for the many students who concentrated more and more on "current affairs," seemed to start with 1919; they regarded the international crisis of the 1930's as a consequence of the peace treaties following the war. But the Treaty of Versailles and its weakening of Germany were not the root of all evil. As if the strength and unity of Germany in 1914 and again in 1939 had helped to promote peace. As if a Treaty of Versailles had preceded and "caused" World War I. Nor were the totalitarian mass movements, communism and fascism, products of "unjust" peace treaties. They were the result of an insufficient democratization or Westernization of countries which, by adapting totalitarianism, rejected the difficult Western ways of life and hoped to destroy the Western concept of liberty. Communism rose in Russia long before the peace treaty of Versailles. In fact it

was this treaty and the victory of the Western democracies which
liberated Russia from German domination and from the consequences of the peace treaty of Brest-Litovsk which a victorious
Germany had imposed on a defeated Russia in March, 1918. Fascism
arose in one of the victor nations which in spite of its important territorial gains cared more for imperial grandeur than for individual
liberty. The first open attack against the League of Nations and its
system of security came from another victor nation which, like Italy,
preferred imperial traditions and glory to the unwanted importation of the burden of individual liberty. The rise of communism and
fascism was made possible by World War I but these movements
were not products of harsh peace treaties.

Woodrow Wilson not only foresaw the era of disillusionment and
its disastrous consequences for the Western world; after his return from Paris he also viewed the world political situation real-
istically. "The terms of the treaty are severe, but they are not unjust," he said in his address at Columbus, Ohio, on September 4,
1919. "I can testify that the men with me at the Peace Conference
at Paris had it in their hearts to do justice and not wrong. . . . And
I wish to testify that they exercised restraint in the terms of this
treaty. They did not wish to overwhelm any great nation, . . . and
throughout this treaty every term that was applied to Germany
was meant, not to humiliate her, but to rectify the wrong that she
had done." Wilson opposed the prevailing American opinion that
Allied victory in itself and the donning by the German Reich of a
republican garb would assure peace. This wide-spread illusion was
understandable: Germany was defeated and disarmed; the Kaiser's
regime was replaced by what appeared a democratic republic accepting Western ways; Bolshevism in Russia was for the time being
rendered harmless by the collapse of the system of militant war
communism and by the retreat to a partial re-introduction of the
capitalistic system. Britain and France seemed strong—perhaps too
strong. Was peace not assured? And should war come, could not
America, peace-loving and idealistic, stay out of the conflict? Wilson
said no; he saw further than most of his countrymen. "The passions
of this world are not dead," he warned. "The rivalries of this world
have not cooled. They have been rendered hotter than ever." Only
collective security and the cooperation of the victorious democracies

could preserve peace. Wilson was convinced that "Germany would not have gone into this war if she had thought Great Britain was going into it, and she most certainly would never have gone into this war if she dreamt America was going into it. . . . Unless there is this assurance of combined action before wrong is attempted, wrong will be attempted just as soon as the most ambitious nations can recover from the financial stress of this war." If America fulfilled Germany's dearest wish and disassociated herself from those along whose side she fought in the war, Wilson was certain that within twenty-five years the United States would have to fight Germany again at the side of the same allies and on the same battle ground. This happened exactly twenty-five years after Wilson predicted it. He even foresaw that the new German war would start by Germany's *Drang nach Osten.* The road to the east, he declared, was Germany's road to world domination. "If you do not close it," he insisted, "we have no choice but some day or other to enter into the same sort of war as we have just gone through." [60]

The lack of cooperation among the democracies made the resumption of Germany's renewed bid for hegemony possible. Clemenceau and Lloyd George declared on April 23, 1919, that Germany felt sure that the union of her enemies would never survive their triumph. "She based her schemes no longer on the conquest of Europe, but on its political and perhaps its social disintegration." [61] Therein German and Communist propaganda converged after 1918. It took the bitter lesson of a Second World War to make the American people—and the other democracies—understand what Woodrow Wilson had tried to explain in the late summer of 1919. This high price of Experience to be paid by the democracies was also anticipated by Wilson in 1919. "If this treaty should be refused," he said, "if it should be impaired, then amidst the tragedy of the things that would follow, every man would be converted to the opinion that I am now uttering, but I do not want to see that sort of conversion. I do not want to see an era of blood and chaos to convert men" to an understanding of the changing realities of the world of nations. Alas, the democracies had to go through that bitter experience. Perhaps if nation-wide broadcasting had been in operation in 1919 as it was twenty-five years later, history might have taken another course. Woodrow Wilson might have swayed his countrymen by radio addresses delivered from the

White House to many millions, without having to spend all his energy to reach relatively small gatherings in far-off cities and submitting to a strain under which he broke down.

Woodrow Wilson was not the only one to foresee the tragedy which was to befall a confused democratic world, where people had set their minds on not seeing and not understanding the forces of history and therefore eagerly listened to those who demonstrated either that all people were good and peace-loving or that cooperation among democracies would threaten democracy. In 1917 Thorstein Veblen, and in 1918 Norman Angell demanded a union of the Western democracies as the indispensable condition for their survival.[62] But only Woodrow Wilson had the authority and the personal appeal to present to the world at large the message and the challenge of an order which would make the world safe for the survival and growth of democracy. Under his leadership the United States for the first time tried to intervene in shaping mankind's future, no longer only by the mild radiance of its example, but by active participation. The man who in so many respects was the last great Victorian figure of the Anglo-American community, did rise above the nineteenth century outlook with its apparent security based upon the pax Britannica, the global advance of the white race, and the growing acceptance of liberal constitutional principles. This world of security seemed in 1914 at its zenith; by 1918 it had received a deep wound; yet neither Americans nor Western Europeans had then the slightest notion of what the rise of communism, fascism, Asian and African nationalism and imperialism, would mean within a few years for the West. No wonder the American people repudiated Woodrow Wilson. What he vaguely foresaw ran counter to their whole traditional experience.

Even the more realistic French, did not foresee it. They clearly understood the German danger, but they understood only the German danger. They knew—and by this knowledge they anticipated what the seafaring democracies were to learn in 1940—that the Rhine was a frontier to be guarded by the whole West. In 1919 the French asked for a North Atlantic alliance in the interest of a world in which democracy could be safe—a safety precious for a free Germany too, and perhaps first of all for her. Trusting in Anglo-American promises of such an alliance—promises which were quickly repudiated—Clemenceau, for many decades the dedicated and lonely spokesman

in France for Franco-Anglo-American friendship, was willing to re-
nounce the military control of the Rhineland. But the French pleaded
in vain when they declared in 1919 that the safety of France was an
Anglo-American concern if and when a power from the east should
attack the West. "In order that the maritime Powers may play a useful part on the Continent against any aggression coming from the
East, they must have the assurance that French territory will not be
overrun in a few days. In other words, should there not remain
enough French ports for the Overseas Armies to debark their troops
and war supplies, should there not remain enough French territory
for them to concentrate and operate from their bases, the Overseas
Democracies would be debarred from waging a continental war
against any power seeking to dominate the Continent. They would
be deprived of their nearest and most natural battleground. Nothing
would be left to them but naval and economic warfare." Suppose, the
French wrote in 1919, that Germany, mistress of the Rhine, wished
to attack Poland or Czechoslovakia. Would she not be able to hold
in check the Western nations coming to the aid of Germany's eastern
neighbors? Similarly the French warned in 1919 that it was not
enough "to know that final victory would rest with us in the case of
a new German aggression. We cannot allow, between aggression and
victory, the invasion of our soil, the systematic destruction, the mar-
tyrdom of our fellow citizens in the north and east as in 1914." This
North Atlantic interdependence of freedom's interests has by 1957
become visible to many more people than it was in 1917.

In the same year when, through Woodrow Wilson, the United
States stepped forth to assume the leadership of the free world, a
similar claim to world leadership was raised by Lenin on behalf of
Russia and of Communism. The bi-polarization of the world which
Tocqueville had foreseen in 1832, announced itself for the first time
in 1918. Lenin's and Wilson's appeals were both based on the promise of peace and on the slogan of national self-determination. It is
curious that Lenin, who otherwise felt deep contempt for the individual or corporate liberties evolved in the liberal West, fully endorsed only one among them—national self-determination, in which
he recognized a mighty revolutionary instrument. As far back as December, 1918, Robert Lansing pointed out the possible dangerous
implications of too broad an application of the Mazzinian doctrine of
national self-determination, a doctrine which Mazzini wished to

apply, however, to Europe alone and from which he excluded Asia and Africa. "When the President talks of self-determination," Lansing wrote, "what unit has he in mind? Does he mean a race, a territorial area, or a community? Without a definite unit which is practical, application of this principle is dangerous to peace and stability. . . . The phrase is simply loaded with dynamite. It will raise hopes which can never be realized. It will, I fear, cost thousands of lives. In the end it is bound to be discredited, to be called the dream of an idealist who failed to realize the dangers until too late to check those who attempt to put this principle in force. What a calamity that the phrase was ever uttered! What misery it will cause!" [63] Lenin had no scruple about proclaiming national self-determination as a guiding principle for the ordering of the international community. He was convinced that totalitarianism could control the use and application of this slogan according to its needs. Its dangerous explosive force was to be reserved for the disintegration of the Western world alone. In a similar way National Socialist Germany used the slogan later.

Though Wilson and Lenin seemed to express the same appeal, they started, as Tocqueville had seen, from opposite points. Wilson's call stemmed from the liberal tradition of the modern North Atlantic world: with it the United States assumed the leadership for which geography and history had prepared it. Lenin's call came at the very same moment, when under his leadership Russia turned away from its brief and fruitful contact with the modern West. He tried to rally Asia and Germany for a struggle against the Western democracies which had won the war only to lose, by disunity, the fruit of their hard-won victory.

The situation in which Washington and Moscow faced each other in 1918, trying to sway the destinies of half the globe or perhaps the whole globe, lasted only a short time. The United States voluntarily withdrew into isolation; Russia was forced by its weakness to abandon all active attempts to decide the course of history. The contrast went further: the Russians expected that after careful preparation a favorable moment for their assuming world leadership would sooner or later arrive; the American people hoped that the day of United States leadership would never dawn. For two decades the Russians and the Americans followed policies of isolationism. Stalin inaugurated his Five Year Plan in 1928 under the slogan, "Socialism in one country"; in the United States the depression, which set in the following year, strengthened the concentration on domestic issues and increased the doubts about the viability of the free enterprise system. Distrust of Britain, midwestern progressivism, the belief that the participation in another war might destroy democracy at home, fear of dark financial machinations thriving in wars—these factors combined to enforce isolationism and neutralism in the United States. This mood found its climax in the neutrality legislation during Franklin D. Roosevelt's first term, and in the America First Committee during his second term when he himself had moved away from the isolationism of his earlier years.[64]

Much of the isolationist sentiment in the United States centered on the moral repudiation of the Treaty of Versailles. Yet most Americans overlooked the fact that the administration of President Harding negotiated in 1921 a separate peace treaty with Germany which hardly differed from the Versailles Treaty; it fully accepted its articles which were deemed harsh, and claimed for the United States all the benefits deriving from Versailles. It rejected only its universal and humanitarian features; the United States did not assume any of the responsibilities which counterbalanced the advantages received. Thus the United States succeeded in getting the best of both worlds: the profits derived from a peace treaty generally condemned, and the moral satisfaction from its condemnation. Midwestern progressivism continued to see Britain as the arch-villain, and for obvious reasons many citizens of Irish or German descent shared this point of view. "You have here," Senator William E. Borah of Idaho declared in 1919, "a League of Nations composed of the great and dominant powers of the earth, some of whom are now engaged in oppressing and decimating weak nations and innocent peoples, and with those people you ask me to form a permanent combination and bring this Republic down to that level of debauchery and shame." The Senator, who was Chairman of the powerful Senate Foreign Relations Committee from 1924 to January 19, 1940, shared the popular prejudice that all British and European history consisted of incessant wars and sordid deeds—whereas America was exempt from these vices. Was not American honesty and decency rewarded in the 1920's by fabulous prosperity, whereas the Europeans even refused to honor their war debts? Some Europeans answered that American prosperity was bought by European blood and suffering, and that the insistence upon repayment of the war loans which had made the common victory possible was a sign of Uncle Sam's rapacity and hypocrisy. Faced with this reaction, many Americans felt that the Europeans, instead of being grateful for generous help, misunderstood and disliked their transatlantic cousins. The gulf between the United States and western Europe seemed deeper in the 1920's, after a war fought in common, than in the two decades preceding the war. The first attempt at North Atlantic cooperation which Henry Adams had welcomed turned out a failure. Neither side was prepared for it.

The 1930's with their economic depression and with the gathering war clouds over Asia and Europe hardened the isolationist attitude in the United States. In April, 1934, Hiram W. Johnson, veteran Senator from California, sponsored the Debt-Default Act which closed the American markets to the selling or buying of securities issued by governments in default of payment of their American debts and even prohibited private loans to them by Americans. In the following years the neutrality legislation took shape: out of a misinterpretation of the First World War it tried to keep America out of any future war—and in an ever more interdependent world abandoned victims of aggression resolutely to their fate. Comforting reasons were always found to point out the grievous shortcomings of the prospective victim and thus to excuse the aggressor. The legislation, inspired by Senator Gerald P. Nye's hearings before the Special Committee Investigating the Munitions Industry, intensified American smugness and strengthened the conviction that America's sublime will to peace and its fortunate geographic position guaranteed its security. Senator Nye's fervent belief that the evil machinations of British imperialism and the armament manufacturers' greed for profits had misguided America into the war was shared by most Americans. This state of mind lessened the understanding of the moral issues involved in the crisis of the 1930's and thus fundamentally weakened American democracy. Communist and pro-fascist spokesmen gained the ear of some American youth. Did not the "young" nations with their energy represent the wave of the future against the decadent democracies? Were not the "have-nots" right to demand their place in the sun? Isolationists emphasized that one should not needlessly irritate and antagonize nations with whom one otherwise could live in peace and that one should not meddle with what really was not one's concern. Americans, the isolationists said,

must treat the nations on both sides of the conflict with perfect im-
partiality, irrespective of the principles for which the various conflicting nations stood. Many Americans refused to support Britain
and France; they called them "so-called democracies" and were
ready to abandon them to their just fate. Yet the very same Americans
were often willing to defend the apparently superior democracy of
the Latin American republics.[65]

The isolationism of the democracies in the 1930's allowed the
fascist powers one success after the other—and threatened in the
middle of the 1940's to allow the communist powers to advance similarly step by step. The anti-democratic nations were confident that
each step would take the world by surprise, that it would be regarded
as an isolated event, maybe as a last event, and that it would be
deemed not of sufficient importance to arouse concerted resistance
on the part of the united democracies. In their isolationism the democratic nations criticized the inadequate response of fellow democracies to aggression, but rarely recognized the implications of their
own refusal to take the risk of cooperation in such a resistance. In
1939 when Britain and France finally decided to resist German aggression without having been attacked themselves, public opinion in
the United States which had until then voiced sharp moral dissatisfaction with British and French "peace-mindedness," shrank from
any active cooperation with them and self-righteously took refuge in
America's superior love of peace. A spurious "pacifism," not based
upon a Christian realism of self-denial but upon an escapist illusion
of self-indulgence, supported this isolationist attitude. The principle
of non-resistance to evil degenerated into a denial that evil exists,
into an appeal to accept or to excuse the evil and to condone injustice.
Thus instead of bearing witness to the verities, pacifism became one
of the instruments which could be used and abused by the aggressor
nations for the destruction of the verities.[66]

Leftist writers further confused the American public by represent-
ing the struggle in Europe as a conflict between two imperialisms.
They compared the Stalin-Hitler pact of August, 1939, with the
Munich four-power pact of September, 1938. Yet the Munich pact
was concluded to prevent war; it was inspired by a consuming
though misguided desire for peace on the part of Britain and France.
Neither of them sought any aggrandizement at Munich. The Russian-
German pact on the other hand was intended to make war possible

if not inevitable—a war designed by the agreement of the two partners for their own aggrandizement. Hitler and Stalin were both equally hostile to and contemptuous of the "bourgeois" West, though each thought of himself as the greatest leader in the war against the West. So blind were the Germans and Hitler then, that by their pact of friendship with communism they opened to the Russians for the first time since 1920 the road to westward expansion. That the British Conservative government of the day had no intention of unleashing Hitler against Russia—such "machiavellian" plans were imputed to it by communist propagandists in the United States—can be deduced from the fact that in 1939 Britain guaranteed Poland against German aggression; Poland was not only a bulwark against Russian expansion; it was also a shield protecting Russia against the German *Drang nach Osten.* Thus Britain's guarantee of Poland also protected Russia against Germany, for only by destroying Poland could the Germans invade Poland's eastern neighbor. This invasion followed the destruction of Poland, a destruction in which the Germans were helped by the Russians themselves: as it was German folly which ultimately brought the Russians to Berlin, so it was communist folly which opened for Germany the road into eastern Europe and brought the Germans to the gates of Moscow and Stalingrad. By their agreement of 1939 the Communists played the very same role of facilitating German plans (ultimately aimed at Russia herself) as semi-fascist Poland under Colonel Joseph Beck had played in its agreement with Germany in January, 1934 (to which Poland ultimately fell victim). As long as the pacts lasted, Poland (from 1934 to 1939) and the communist world movement (from 1939 to 1941) behaved like fervent supporters and moral defenders of the German National Socialist regime and helped to undermine the Western defenses, upon whose strength Russian and Polish survival ultimately rested.

The close cooperation between Communists and Fascists against the "plutocratic" democracies was the outstanding fact of the propaganda war between August, 1939, and June, 1941. Whereas from the moment they seized power Communism and Fascism began preparations for the war which they proclaimed inevitable and which they brought about, the victorious democracies found themselves after the First World War in a state of moral and psychological

disarmament. Thus they were unprepared not only to prevent the
Second World War but even to wage it successfully through unity
of purpose until that fateful summer of 1940 when Winston Churchill
and the English turned the tide and gave the Americans the chance
to understand, to act, and to survive. In those critical months Churchill proclaimed the need for Anglo-French unity and for an Anglo-
American fraternal association. But the United States did not, as the
British had done, enter the war without being directly attacked.
They waited until no choice was left to them. In fact the year 1940
marked in many ways the climax of ultra-nationalist American isolationism. The prevailing sentiment of the time was well diagnosed by
a leading scholar of American foreign policy who concluded an
article "The United States as a World Power" by insisting that
"There is today [1940] a tendency to follow George Washington's
advice for aloofness from Europe (and Asia) and Henry Clay's
enthusiasm for a peaceful and defensive inter-American system." [67]

American isolationists saw in the war of 1939 not a deliberate
challenge against the Western way of life—a challenge which the
Western powers had tried hard not to accept and certainly not to
provoke—but one of the perennial squabbles in which Europe loved
to indulge. The real divide, these Americans believed, did not separate National Socialist Germany and liberal Britain, but Europe as
a whole and the Western Hemisphere. They acknowledged neither
the North Atlantic community of traditions and interests nor the fact
that Latin American nationalism drew its inspiration from an "anti-
colonialism," directed not primarily against Europe but against
"Yankee imperialism." Nationalism in the modern sense made itself
felt in Latin America only in the twentieth century, simultaneous to
the awakening of Asian nationalism. In both cases this nationalism
derived from a desire for rapid industrialization as a precondition of
an accretion of power and it was stimulated partly by "uprooted"
intellectuals and partly by the armed forces. The most characteristic
Latin American nationalist program, that of the Alianza Popular
Revolucionaria Americana (APRA) followed consciously the model
of the Kuomintang; it demanded resistance to United States imperialism; the political and economic federation of Latin America
against the colossus of the north; the internationalization of the
Panama Canal; the nationalization of all land and industrial re-

sources; and finally the solidarity of all "oppressed" classes and peoples, a grouping to which the United States obviously did not belong.[68]

In 1940 only a minority of Americans believed in an active North Atlantic cooperation against totalitarian aggression. President Franklin D. Roosevelt gave the people only scant leadership in foreign affairs. He had earned the gratitude of the nation and of the whole world for the unprejudiced and daring experimental way in which he met the confusion and despondency caused by the depression. Applying unorthodox and, to many old-timers, "un-American" means he led the people back to a renewed faith in Americanism. He acted not out of preconceived theories but out of an instinctive understanding of the American people and of the American scene. But he had not the same understanding of the wider world of nations. He never took the people fully into his confidence; he did not explain to them that they were facing a time of great danger and supreme trial. As late as May 28, 1940, he was still telling the press that "there was no reason for the country to become 'discombooberated' in apprehension of what may come to pass. The women of the country would not have to give up their cosmetics, lipsticks and chocolate sodas in consequence of the preparedness program." The Draft Law Extension was almost defeated in 1941, a few months before Japanese aggression, because President Roosevelt publicly insisted that war was not imminent, and thus gave support to the widespread desire for taking things easy. He never outgrew some popular American prejudices. He regarded Soviet Russia as an experimental democracy, dedicated to goals similar to those of the United States and equally opposed to "imperialism" and "colonialism." Henry Wallace, then Roosevelt's vice president, hailed the "political" democracy of the United States and the "economic" democracy of the Soviet Union as equal bulwarks of a future peace. Like Wallace, Roosevelt distrusted British imperial machinations more than communist plans and ideology.[69] Yet, even in the international field, Roosevelt's experimental and pragmatic genius stood him in good stead when he initiated such daring innovations as the destroyer deal and lend lease aid.

In 1940 few voices were raised for American participation in the war. After having published several articles advocating American isolationism, *Harper's Magazine* printed in its issue of January, 1940, an article "War and the Verities" by Elsworth Barnard, a spirited affirmation of America's moral obligation to democracy abroad as well as at home. "The first question for America," Mr. Barnard wrote, "is not whether we *can* keep out of war but whether we *ought* to. . . . The war is not a mere clash of rival imperialisms, a mere far off quarrel in which nothing is involved except the selfish, material interests of the combatants; it is, instead, an irreconcilable conflict as to what shall be the ultimate principle governing the relations between states." Against the frequently heard argument that Britain and France, as well as the United States, have in former centuries annexed territories by force of arms, and that, therefore, none of them had any right to oppose similar acts by Germany today, Dr. Barnard pointed out that the statement was true but that it would be hard to find a more glaring non-sequitur than the conclusion. "According to this reasoning, the fact that the Stone Age ancestors were probably cannibals would make it unreasonable and immoral for any of us to oppose a revival of cannibalism today." The fall of France in June, 1940, made some isolationists who had regarded their neutralism as an expression of a hardboiled "realism," immune to "propaganda," realize America's interest in the maintenance of a strong Britain. Walter Lippmann asked himself what it was that had prevented this generation of "realists" from being realistic until it was very nearly too late. "It is," he answered, "that the postwar generation have been duped by a falsification of American history. They have been miseducated by a swarm of innocent but ignorant historians, by reckless demagogues, and by foreign interests, into believing that America entered the other war because of British propaganda, the loans of the bankers, the machination of President Wilson's advisors, and the drummed-up patriotic ecstasy. They have been told to believe that anyone who challenges this explanation of 1917 and insists that America was defending American vital interests is himself a victim or an agent of British propaganda." [70]

The Japanese attack on Hawaii in December, 1941, brought the United States into the war. Yet even then Congress did not declare war upon National Socialist Germany nor did President Roosevelt ask for it. It was left to Hitler in his contempt for the national cohesion of the United States to declare war, and Mussolini followed him. Thus the United States entered the war and became an ally of Britain, which out of her own decision had declared war on National Socialist Germany, and of the Soviet Union, which like the United States had been drawn into the war by outright aggression. But even while Americans actively participated in the war, their thinking lacked clarity about the issues of the war. Many put Britain and Russia on an equal footing as far as their relationship to the United States and the forthcoming peace was concerned. Some Americans distrusted Britain more than Russia; few only understood the meaning of Russian communism. The confusions of the 1950's with its communist scare can be explained by the lack of understanding and the lack of responsible leadership in the years of the Second World War. In 1945 many Americans inclined again toward isolationism. The sudden realization of the threat of communism, of America's continuing responsibility in a prolonged world crisis, the end of which no one could foresee, understandably led to a passing period of fright which gave to Senator Joseph McCarthy the opportunity of occupying for a short time the center of the American political stage as twenty years before Senator Gerald P. Nye had done.[71] The trend denounced as McCarthyism was reversed with remarkable ease; the excesses committed under it hardly reached the degree which similar waves of fear produced previously in American history—at the time of the French Revolution; during the Civil War under Abraham Lincoln; and in 1919 under Woodrow Wilson. The Cassandras who saw in McCarthyism the end of American democracy misread the character and history of American nationalism. An American historian who called the years between 1945—the end of the Second World War—and 1955 —when the United States had consciously accepted its role as the leading member of the North Atlantic community—the crucial decade, concluded his analysis of this time of indecision and contradiction on a hopeful note. By the end of the decade, he wrote, "the American people could approach the oncoming years and the oncoming decisions with the help of what they had brought about and a reassuring pride. They had brought about a consensus in their thinking which was ready for the world of the Nineteen Fifties. They would know the pride of a people who sorely tempted to a frightened petulance had in the long run reacted with good sense and not without courage and generosity." [72]

Much has been accomplished, which to American citizens and to foreign observers alike would have seemed impossible only twenty years ago: President Truman's courageous and far-sighted decision in March, 1947, to replace the British at their own wish in their historical role of defending Turkey and Greece against Russian aggression; the outpouring of economic aid under the plan named after its sponsor, General George Marshall, then Secretary of State; above all, the establishment of a community of armed forces of the United States and its allies in peacetime and the signing of the North Atlantic Pact in Washington on April 5, 1949. Through it the nations on the two shores of the North Atlantic have started to realize that in the twentieth century with its unpredictable dangers and crises, they have strategic interests, moral ideas and political traditions in common. At the signing of the pact, President Truman called it a "simple document, but if it had existed in 1914 and in 1939, supported by the nations who are represented here today, I believe it would have prevented the acts of aggression which led to two world wars. . . . The nations represented here are bound together by ties of long standing. We are joined by a common heritage of democracy, individual liberty and the rule of law." What the American people refused to do in the 1930's, the generation of the 1950's was willing to undertake. It is possible that in the coming times of world-wide strain and stress the Atlantic Pact will outgrow the old notions of sovereignty and isolation which have dominated the Western community. A long road still lies ahead before the West will fully realize its mutual interdependence in an age in which the survival of Western civilization is at stake. Even "the two countries which should be the two pillars of the Western community, the United States and Britain, have failed not only to accord their views on the kind of unity they want; but also to coordinate their diplomatic, economic and military policies. The difficulties of reconciling the interests of the United States and the British Commonwealth with its informality of association and aversion to rigid commitments are great and numerous; the difficulties of reconciling the interests of the English-speaking peoples with the nations of continental Europe are staggering. But to admit defeat would be to accept the decline and fall of the West. Western unity is not one of several alternatives. It is the one and only alternative to defeat.[73]

In the 1950's the remarkable prophesy written one hundred

twenty years earlier by Tocqueville has been fulfilled. The nations
of western Europe have declined as he foresaw, a process intensified by two great wars. The newly rising nations and empires of
Asia, which Tocqueville could not anticipate, have not had time to
consolidate the power for which they are longing, even at the expense of the welfare and the liberties of their peoples, and which
one day may be theirs. In the meantime, as Tocqueville expected,
the two nations representing opposite starting points and principles
—the United States and Russia—stand out in assuming the role
of world leadership. This situation was adumbrated in 1918 but
hardly any one counted upon its reappearance. As a result of the disunity of the Western world, of the self-abandonment of democracy,
and of the hubris of German (and Japanese) world hegemonial aspirations, American and Russian forces met, unexpectedly, along the
Elbe River and on the Manchurian border, circling and dividing
the earth. The Communists have always proclaimed that the world
is divided into two irreconcilable hostile camps: Russia eagerly
assumed in 1917 the leadership of the communist camp; the United
States reluctantly assumed in 1947 the leadership of the democratic
West, the destruction of which the Communists regarded as the
condition of their own victory and of mankind's salvation.

But it would be a mistake to read into Tocqueville's remarkable
prediction any statement of a permanent or inevitable polarization
of the world between the two giant powers. The Communists have
always believed in a bi-polar world in which their angelic hosts
oppose and ultimately will defeat the devil represented by all those
who differ from them. The power constellation in the world of the
1950's seems to confirm the existence of a polarity in the world;
some Americans in an understandable desire for the oversimplifica-
tion of a bewildering and complex situation accept the polarity.
But in reality, no such "two worlds" exist. After 1941 most Americans succumbed to a similar simplification: they concentrated exclusively on the defeat of Germany and Japan and hoped that there-
after all peoples would be "democratic" and "peace-loving." In
the 1950's many Americans tried to see in communism the only
obstacle to a peaceful world and to accept the unwarranted thesis
that all "liberated" peoples would by necessity become democracies
after the American image. But the defeat of fascism has not made
Western democracy acceptable to all peoples; the disappearance

of communism will not make all peoples like Western democracy. In view of the multiplicity of traditions and ways of life on this earth, such a development is neither desirable nor possible. The modern West represents one, but not the only valid form of human civilization. The peoples who do not wish—or whose background and centuries-old traditions do not incline them—to accept Western ways, are not thereby pro-communist, as some Americans assume. These people have a right to be different, neither communistic nor democratic, neither in the Russian nor in the American camp.

There is no validity to the chosen people idea inherited from the Hebrews nor to the Hegelian concept that in each age one leading nation represents the spirit of the age. History is too complex for any monistic or dualistic interpretation. The world is enriched by intellectual and cultural diversity; on the power-political plane it is possible to foresee the rise of new power centers which would end the existing bi-polar power distribution. Neither American world leadership nor the concept of a bi-polarized world with America leading one camp, is in the long run desirable or possible; what is needed is the cooperation, with the United States *primus inter pares,* of the Western nations. A union of the West is a goal for its own sake; it is not hostile to, or directed against, other civilizations; on the other hand it would have nothing to fear from any other agglomeration of power; it could, with sympathy and patient urbanity, help others to appreciate the virtues of individual freedom and of rational moderation, which since the Glorious Revolution have formed the true strength of the modern West.

The West which for three centuries was in control of the globe and of civilized progress is now facing a difficult reassessment of its relationship to the rest of the world. The Western nations—above all the United States and Britain—have to face this reassessment together. As long as they exert the Western virtues of political restraint and public morality, they can hope to turn the destructive and inflammatory passions of twentieth century nationalism and socialism—provided they are not totalitarian—into more constructive and civilized channels. Western nineteenth century imperialism was a legitimate and fruitful movement until the end of the First World War. By then its time was over: it had aroused among Asians and Arabs a nationalism which, a product of Western influence, emancipated Asia and the Arab lands from Western control. In World

War II the wave of nationalism reached Africa. The first to understand the implications of this tremendous and rapid transformation
of the world was Lenin: he hoped to build an anti-Western union
out of Russian communism and Asian-African nationalism, the
greatest threat to the West's survival. In the West the British were
the first to counter this plan by extending their liberal tradition to
the "colonial" peoples and helping Arab, Asian and African nationalism. When in the fall of 1956 in support of Israeli aggression
against Egypt the French and British invaded Egypt, the overwhelming majority of public opinion throughout the free world—in
the United States, in Canada, in Scandinavia—which viewed this
step with dismay, was supported by many voices raised in Britain—
proving the power of liberalism—against the invasion. These voices
testified to Britain's moral vigor and sense for political practicabil-
ity.[74] American leadership in the United Nations thwarted communist
strategy for organizing the whole non-Western world against the
West; it restored respect for Western public morality and reinvigorated the United Nations. The creation of a United Nations
force, proposed by Canada and supported by the United States, was
the first step ever undertaken in the almost forty years since Woodrow Wilson launched the idea of collective security to bring his
ideal somewhat nearer to realization. The end of 1956 saw the
United States successfully opposing the Soviet bid—first voiced by
Lenin—for swaying the destinies of the by far larger half of mankind. The world in the second half of the twentieth century is rapidly growing more and more different from that known in the second
half of the nineteenth century. The West's relationship to the outside world has to change rapidly too.

Yet mid-twentieth century circumstances have not changed the
fundamental character of American nationalism which goes back
to the eighteenth century. It is still based on the outlook of the
English-speaking peoples of the seventeenth and eighteenth centuries. In the middle of the twentieth century "the American was
still optimistic, still took for granted that his was the most favored
of all countries, the happiest and most virtuous of all societies, and,
though less sure of progress, was still confident that the best was
yet to be. . . . The persistence of fundamental philosophical beliefs and assumptions was as tenacious as that of practices, habits
and attitudes. Puritanism lingered on, not so much as a search for

individual salvation or as a celebration of the virtues of thrift and industry but as a recognition of the dignity of the individual and of his duty to achieve both spiritual and material prosperity. . . . The America that would shape the unknown future was an America whose character had been forged in the known past; and if the lineaments of that character had not yet hardened into fixed patterns, they were at least recognizable and familiar." [75]

The First World War, in which all the aspirations and contradictions of the Age of Nationalism came to a head, intensified nationalism in the United States as it had done everywhere. The effect was originally, as in preceding great periods of war—the Napoleonic wars at the beginning of the Age of Nationalism and the various civil wars in its middle period—a strengthening of self-conscious isolationism. The war produced, as Amy Lowell wrote, "a more poignant sense of nationality than has recently been the case in this country of enormous spaces and heterogeneous population." Since the war the Americans felt themselves no longer colonies of this or that other land, Miss Lowell continued, "but ourselves, different from all other peoples whatsoever." [76] This isolationism was possible in Western Europe and in North America because the common basis of their way of life still appeared unbreakable and unassailable. But when liberal democracy in Europe began to retreat in the 1930's before the new phenomenon of totalitarianism, the United States began to re-examine the origins and the nature of the principles on which traditionally its liberal government rested.[77] This re-examination led to the rediscovery of the eighteenth century roots of American civilization and nationalism. Even America's championing of democracy abroad in the middle of the twentieth century could find its precedent in the missionary democratic idealism of the 1840's. It changed, however, its methods and direction. It shed some of its naive illusions and gained in historical understanding. It now became, "perforce, in an age of violence and revolution, the mainspring of a realistic policy in international affairs." [78]

At the same time the differences between the way of life in the United States and in Western Europe, which seemed wide in the middle of the nineteenth century, have considerably narrowed down in the middle of the twentieth century. The welfare state in Britain, which began with the reform legislation of the Liberal cabinet after 1905 and was fully developed by the Labor cabinet after 1945,

and the New Deal in the United States, which started in the 1930's,
are fundamentally similar in purpose and structure. In both cases
their social legislation has been fully accepted and even expanded by
the Conservative government which came to power in Britain in
1950 and by the Republican administration which took over in the
United States in 1953. The similarity of the changes in the way of
life goes even further: In the twentieth century Britain and the
United States simultaneously adopted identical policies for their
armed forces, though these new policies contradicted long-cherished
traditions. After the First World War both nations abolished universal military service, which they had introduced during the war;
then they reintroduced it just before they entered the Second World
War and continued it after the war, although in each case with the
same misgivings and with the same hope of abandoning it sooner or
later as a peace-time institution. To the process of the Americanization of western Europe, a process obvious to everyone since T. W.
Stead wrote about it at the beginning of the century, corresponds a
less obvious but steady process of the Europeanization of the United
States. Measures which a short time ago would have been regarded
as un-British or un-American, have become part of the British and
American ways of life without changing the fundamental character
of the nationalism of these two peoples. Even the frequently heard
complaint that American or British life in the middle of the twentieth century has been characterized by a sharp decline of individualism or by a much greater conformity seems without validity.
Emerson or Thoreau and Mill's "On Liberty" expressed a century
ago similar bitter complaints about conformism and about the disappearance of true individualism in the United States and in Britain of their time.[79]

In the eighteenth century the consciousness of the unity of the
Western world was still alive. The Age of Nationalism which followed the Napoleonic wars brought with it an emphasis on the self-
centered nation and its autonomous growth. This isolationism led
to a distortion of perspective and to the over-valuation of the distinctiveness of national history and of national character. After 1914,
the experience gained in wars and revolutions of unprecedented
magnitude led men to understand the interdependence of the nations sharing Western civilization, a civilization that has been the
most dynamic so far known to history, and the first one to exercise a

world-wide influence. It has revitalized all other civilizations with which it has come into contact. Through its history and its geography, the United States has been the most "modern" and most "Western" nation. It revealed, perhaps more than other North Atlantic nations, the potentialities and hopes, the dangers and frustrations, the daring and the self-doubting of the *homo occidentalis aevi contemporanei*. The study of American national thought and of its specific contribution to the common civilization may help toward a better self-understanding of modern Western man and of the history of Western ideas. Nor is it a study devoid of practical and immediate relevance. In the present age Americans are faced with a situation entirely new to them. Only now has national security become the single most important function of their government—a function hardly acknowledged in the nineteenth century. This shift in emphasis has happened at the very moment when any American action or inaction has come to cause the greatest impact on all nations and when the field of foreign policy, formerly so narrow, has grown to include matters economic, moral, cultural, and psychological, as well as military and diplomatic. In such a situation, nations whom history forces to assume their place among nations need, in order to survive, more than technological armor; they need the inspiration which only the awareness of their traditions and an understanding of their historical context can provide.

Even in the nineteenth century—the Age of Nationalism—modern Western civilization, in spite of its conflicts of interests and growing diversity, preserved a fundamental unity. Yet this unity was never felt as strongly as in the eighteenth century with its stirring intellectual curiosity, its ever-widening horizons of daring exploration and utopian dreams, and the rapid broadening of its geographic orbit. While modern Western civilization then began slowly and painfully to penetrate Russia and the Near East, it took full possession of the wide open areas across the North Atlantic. In the twentieth century, when the validity and even the survival of the North Atlantic civilization were threatened by forces whose great initial successes were helped by Western weaknesses and disunity, the United States had to assume the leadership of the West, a role which some observers had predicted for it a long time ago. Its kind of nationalism, rooted in the eighteenth century, and its character as a republic of many republics and a nation of many nations, seemed to predestine the United States for a role, for which no previous experience had prepared it. In the past the United States has rarely seen itself as one among the Western nations, sharing their problems, paradoxes, aspirations and achievements—often in a form intensified by the vastness of the open spaces and the novelty of an open society. In the last ten years the United States has had to grope for a solution to the crisis which came upon it more unexpectedly and suddenly than that of the 1860's and which may turn out to be an even more severe and certainly a more protracted test, demanding new concepts of union and sovereignty, a rethinking and relearning which involve the discarding of cherished misinterpretations and illusions which, whatever their relevance in the past, have become irrelevant to the new world situation. "The ordeal of the twentieth century—the bloodiest, most turbulent era of the Christian age—is far from over," an American political leader observed in 1952. "Sacrifice, patience, understanding and implacable purpose may be our lot for years to come. Let's face it. Let's talk sense to the American people. Let's tell them the truth, that there are no gains without pains, that we are now on the eve of great decisions, not easy decisions." [80] This outlook appears even more valid in 1957 than it was five years ago. American nationalism faces a continuing difficult reorientation before new expanding horizons. The most serious problem is presented by the transformation of the East, which Woodrow Wilson foresaw in 1901. He then called upon the United States and Britain to cooperate in securing for the newly awakened peoples their full and equal partnership in the world of free intercourse which the North Atlantic civilization had created. This task may appear to strain all intellectual, moral and economic resources of the Western world and of American leadership. But such a situation is not alien to the American tradition; the pioneering spirit survives and tests itself. Its present task is facilitated because it implies, after a long separation during which the two shores of the North Atlantic seemed to draw farther and farther apart, a return to common roots. In this return, American nationalism fulfills itself in the broader community of its North Atlantic origins.

Notes

Notes to chapter one

[1] Alexis de Tocqueville, *Democracy in America*, tr. by Henry Reeve, with an introduction by Daniel C. Gilman, 2 vols. (New York: Century, 1898), vol. I, p. 32.

[2] See Hans Kohn, *The Idea of Nationalism: A Study in Its Origins and Backgrounds* (New York: Macmillan, 1944), pp. 275, 667.

[3] Tocqueville, *op. cit.*, p. 52. The intensely religious outlook of Puritanism, fused with the concept of liberty, has much contributed to the dynamic quality of American civilization. See George M. Stephenson, *The Puritan Heritage* (New York: Macmillan, 1952), and Kohn, *The Idea of Nationalism, op. cit.*, pp. 269 ff., 278 f.

[4] Émile Boutmy, *Éléments d'une Psychologie Politique du Peuple Américain* (Paris: Armand Colin, 1902), pp. 93 f. See also Will Herberg, *Protestant—Catholic—Jew: An Essay in American Religious Sociology* (New York: Doubleday, 1955).

[5] Thomas T. McAvoy, "Bishop John Lancaster Spalding (1840–1916) and the Catholic Minority," *The Review of Politics*, vol. XII (January, 1950), pp. 3–19. Also Father McAvoy's "Americanism and Frontier Catholicism," *ibid.*, vol. V (July, 1943), pp. 275–301; "The Formation of the Catholic Minority in the United States, 1820–1860," *ibid.*, vol. X (January, 1948), pp. 13–34; "The American Catholic Minority in the Later Nineteenth Century," *ibid.*, vol. XV (July, 1953), pp. 275–302; and "Americanism, Fact and Fiction," *The Catholic Historical Review*, vol. XXXI (July, 1945), pp. 133–153. Father McAvoy points out that in the later nineteenth century the prelates in Rome understood American democracy and American conditions hardly better than other Europeans of the period.

[6] *The Works of Orestes A. Brownson*, ed. by Henry F. Brownson (Detroit: T. Nourse, 1882–87), vol. V, p. 102.

[7] *The Private Correspondence of Benjamin Franklin*, ed. by William Temple Franklin (London: Henry Colburn, 1817), vol. I, pp. 195 f.

[8] "The ablest defender of the Revolution—in fact, the greatest political theorist of the American Revolution—was also the great theorist of British conservatism, Edmund Burke. . . . Ours was one of the few conservative colonial rebellions of modern times." Daniel J. Boorstin, *The Genius of American Politics* (Chicago: University of Chicago Press, 1953), pp. 72 f., 70. See also Max Savelle, *The Foundations of American Civilization: A History of Colonial America* (New York: Holt, 1942), and his *Seeds of Liberty: The Genesis of the American Mind* (New York: Knopf, 1948), especially pp. 553–582.

[9] See Kohn, *The Idea of Nationalism, op. cit.*, pp. 177–183. See also the chapter "The Great Mr. Locke, America's Philosopher 1783–1861," in Merle Curti, *Probing Our Past* (New York: Harper, 1955), pp. 69–118. Professor

Curti is also the author of an extensively documented history of manifestations of American nationalism, *The Roots of American Loyalty* (New York: Columbia University Press, 1946).

[10] Carl Becker, *The Declaration of Independence* (New York: Harcourt, Brace, 1922), pp. 79, 231.

[11] Claude G. Bowers, *Beveridge and the Progressive Era* (Boston: Houghton Mifflin, 1932), p. 143.

[12] *The Works of George Berkeley, D.D.*, 2 vols. (London: Thomas Tegg, 1843), vol. II, p. 293.

[13] Adam Smith, *Inquiry into the Nature and Source of the Wealth of Nations*, bk. IV, chap. 7, pt. 3.

[14] C. H. Van Tyne, *The War of Independence: American Phase* (Boston: Houghton Mifflin, 1929), p. 32.

[15] *The Poetical Works of John Trumbull*, 2 vols. (Hartford: Samuel G. Goodrich, 1820), vol. II, pp. 158–159.

[16] See *The Idea of Nationalism, op. cit.*, pp. 280 f. and 669 f. For a similar situation in Switzerland, see Hans Kohn, *Nationalism and Liberty: The Swiss Example* (New York: Macmillan, 1956), pp. 31–34. "In the history of England and the United States of America, the new liberty grows out of the old rights and liberties. It is not established against the old privileges, as it happened in France in the revolution at the end of the eighteenth century; it rather developed in a long though partly also a revolutionary development out of the old order. The thread which was tied in the thirteenth century with the Magna Charta in England could as little be torn as a similar thread in Switzerland." Leonhard von Muralt, *Alte und neue Freiheit in der helvetischen Revolution* (Zurich: Schulthess, 1941), p. 18.

[17] See James Bryce, *The Predictions of Hamilton and De Tocqueville* (Baltimore: Johns Hopkins University Studies in Political Science, 1887), pp. 25 f.: "He has not grasped the truth that the American people is the English people, modified in some directions by the circumstances of its colonial life and its more popular government, but in essentials the same."

[18] See Louis Hartz, *The Liberal Tradition in America* (New York: Harcourt, Brace, 1955). See also Robert E. Brown, *Middle-Class Democracy and the Revolution in Massachusetts, 1691–1780* (Ithaca: Cornell University Press, 1956), and his *Charles Beard and the Constitution* (Princeton, N.J.: Princeton University Press, 1956).

[19] Émile Boutmy, *op. cit.*, p. 100.

[20] Lincoln, *Complete Works*, ed. by John G. Nicolay and John Hay (New York: Century, 1894), vol. I, p. 179.

[21] *The North American Review*, vol. III (May, 1816), p. 20. Isaac Parker (1768–1830) proposed in 1817 the founding of Harvard Law School. *Port Folio*, vol. VI (August, 1815), p. 181.

[22] *The Complete Works of Ralph Waldo Emerson. Centenary Edition*, vol. I, pp. 377 ff.

[23] Samuel H. Beer, "Pressure Groups and Party in Britain," *The American Political Science Review*, vol. L (March, 1956), pp. 1 f.

[24] *Karl Marx and Friedrich Engels, Selected Correspondence 1846–1895*, tr. by Dona Torr (New York: International Publishers, 1942), p. 501. Typically,

Engels believed that the bourgeoisie helped to maintain this condition by playing one nationality among the immigrants against another. *Ibid.*, p. 497.

[25] *Ibid.*, pp. 396 and 449, Engels' letter to Florence Wischnewetsky, June 3, 1886. In his 1892 preface to *The Condition of the Working Class in England in 1844,* Engels saw "a coming class struggle casting its gigantic shadow" over the United States.

[26] Some occasional papers of Fisher Ames (1758–1808) of Massachusetts, who was in 1804 chosen president of Harvard College, but who, because of his failing health, did not accept, were republished in England under the title *The Influence of Democracy on Liberty, Property and the Happiness of Society, Considered by an American, Formerly Member of Congress* (London: John W. Parker, 1835), by Henry Ewbank. In his introduction Ewbank warned against unchecked democracy which he believed a threat to England after the Reform Bill of 1832. Similar fear of excesses of liberty and of its perversion by popular despotism were voiced by conservatives in Switzerland, where liberty was similarly rooted as in the English-speaking nation. See Kohn, *Nationalism and Liberty, op. cit.*, pp. 78–84. On the strength of conservatism see Leonard W. Labaree, *Conservatism in Early American History* (New York: New York University Press, 1948).

[27] Michael Kraus, *The Atlantic Civilization: Eighteenth-Century Origins* (Ithaca: Cornell University Press, 1949), pp. 225, 313.

[28] Bryce, *The American Commonwealth* (New York: Macmillan, 1901), vol. II, p. 311.

[29] See Ray Allen Billington, *Westward Expansion: A History of the American Frontier* (New York: Macmillan, 1949).

[30] See Henry Nash Smith, *Virgin Land: The American West as Symbol and Myth* (Cambridge: Harvard University Press, 1950).

[31] See Hans Kohn, ed., *The Mind of Modern Russia: Historical and Political Thought of Russia's Great Age* (New Brunswick, N.J.: Rutgers University Press, 1955), p. 67.

[32] Fredrika Bremer, *The Homes of the New World: Impressions of America,* tr. by Mary Howitt, 2 vols. (New York: Harper, 1853), vol. II, p. 121. See also Alexander Herzen's attitude in Kohn, *The Mind of Modern Russia, op. cit.*, pp. 158, 186.

[33] See *The Influence of Democracy on Liberty, Property and the Happiness of Society* (*op. cit.* in note 26 above), pp. 42 f. Ames himself knew better; he believed in "what our revolutionists of 1777 called, English Liberty. This they claimed as their birth right, and with good reason . . . yet this glorious distinction of liberty, so ample, so stable, and so temperate, secured by the common law, has been revived and exhibited to popular abhorrence as a shameful badge of our yet colonial dependence on England" (pp. 92 f.). The Englishman Ewbank in his introduction stressed the same point: "In a common origin and a common language, I like to trace brotherhood. . . . The essentials of character are the same in the two nations, and, whatever demagogues may say, all that is truly valuable and excellent in America, excepting such natural advantages as arise from an abundance of fertile soil, and similar causes, is referable to the same origin as the like blessings with ourselves" (p. 5).

[34] Basil Hall, *Travels in North America in the Years 1827 and 1828,* 3 vols. (Edinburgh: Simpkin & Marshall, 1830), vol. II, pp. 167 f.

[35] James Fenimore Cooper, *The American Democrat* (New York: Knopf, 1931), pp. 152, 154. Cooper believed that foreigners influenced American party feuds, and quoted an instance "in which a native-born citizen of the United States of America, the descendant of generations of Americans," became the object of "persecution" at the hands of foreigners acting as the agents of an American party (p. 173).

[36] *The Americans.* By an American in London (London: Frederic Westley and A. H. Davis, 1833), pp. 352, 364.

[37] Michael Forrest, *Travels Through America* (Philadelphia: Johnson & Justice, 1793), pp. 9, 11. K. W. Rowe, *Mathew Carey: A Study in American Economic Development* (Baltimore: Johns Hopkins Press, 1931).

[38] *The Journal of Benjamin Moran: 1857-1865,* ed. by Sarah Agnes Wallace and Frances Elma Gillespie, 2 vols. (Chicago: University of Chicago Press, 1948-49), vol. I, p. 421; vol. II, p. 935.

[39] Royall Tyler (1757-1826), *The Contrast* (Boston: Houghton Mifflin, 1920). See also Harry Hayden Clark, "Nationalism in American Literature," *University of Toronto Quarterly,* vol. II, no. 4 (July, 1933), pp. 492-519.

[40] See *The Idea of Nationalism, op. cit.,* pp. 163-183.

[41] George Bancroft, *History of the United States of America,* 6 vols. (New York: D. Appleton, 1883-85), vol. IV, pp. 3-5.

[42] *Ibid.,* vol. II, pp. 325 f.

[43] See Hans Kohn, *Prophets and Peoples: Studies in Nineteenth Century Nationalism* (New York: Macmillan, 1946), p. 129.

[44] John Spencer Bassett, *The Middle Group of American Historians* (New York: Macmillan, 1917). See also N. H. Dawes and F. T. Nichols, "Revaluing George Bancroft," *New England Quarterly,* June, 1933, and above all Michael Kraus, "George Bancroft, 1834-1934," *New England Quarterly,* vol. VII, no. 4 (December, 1934), pp. 662-686. "The philosophic historians of the eighteenth century," Kraus writes, "in whose traditions Bancroft was largely reared, were not interested in history for history's sake. . . . The idea of progress animated the thought of this school, and Bancroft was an apt pupil. He saw in the United States the goal to which civilization everywhere should aspire" (p. 679). See also Michael Kraus, *The History of American History* (New York: Farrar & Rinehart, 1937).

[45] François Guizot, *Memoirs to Illustrate the History of My Time,* tr. by J. W. Cole (London: Richard Bentley, 1860), vol. III, pp. 161-169.

[46] *The Life and Works of John Adams,* ed. by C. F. Adams, 10 vols. (Boston: Little, Brown, 1856), vol. X, pp. 37, 62.

[47] See Chapter Two, Note 42.

[48] R. B. Nye, *George Bancroft, Brahmin Rebel* (New York: Knopf, 1945), pp. 45, 64.

[49] M. A. DeWolfe Howe, *The Life and Letters of George Bancroft,* 2 vols. (New York: Scribner, 1908), vol. I, p. 186.

[50] From "The Office of the People in Art, Government and Religion, An Oration delivered before the Adelphi Society of Williamstown College in August, 1835," quoted in Nye, *op. cit.,* p. 320.

[51] In my *The Idea of Nationalism,* especially at the beginning of Chapter 6 and at the end of Chapter 8, I tried to see the North American movement as

part of a general Western pattern. See also R. R. Palmer, "The World Revolution of the West, 1763–1801," *Political Science Quarterly,* LXIX, March, 1954.

[52] *Europe, A General Survey of the Present Situation of the Principal Powers with Conjectures on Their Future Prospects* (Boston: O. Everett, 1822). The book was translated into French, Spanish, and German. The German translation was by Ludwig Heinrich von Jacob, professor at the University of Halle. The second book was *America, A General Survey of the Political Situation of the Several Powers of the Western Continent with Conjectures on Their Future Prospects* (Philadelphia: H. C. Carey & I. Lea, 1827). An English edition appeared in London with John Murray in 1828 and a Spanish translation in the same year with Butler in Northampton, Mass.

[53] *America, op. cit.,* p. 11.

[54] *Europe, op. cit.,* p. 225.

[55] *America, op. cit.,* pp. 251 f. "Should a general war unhappily break out among the Christian powers, while the causes which now determine their international relations shall continue to operate, it would necessarily be one in which the United States and Great Britain would both be engaged on the same side." *Ibid.,* p. 252.

[56] *America, op. cit.,* pp. 16 f.; *Europe, op. cit.,* pp. 29, 347, 349, 420; *America, op. cit.,* p. 337. Everett stressed in 1827 the community of interests of the two Americas and saw the British empire as their open and declared ally. He clearly overestimated the rationality of the republican régimes in Latin America (*America,* pp. 171, 272 ff.). Concerning the Western Hemisphere idea, see Arthur P. Whitaker, *The Western Hemisphere Idea: Its Rise and Decline* (Ithaca: Cornell University Press, 1954).

[57] *America, op. cit.,* p. 341; *Present State of Polite Learning in England and America,* An Address to the Phi Beta Kappa Society of Bowdoin College, September 3, 1834, p. 48; *1820—A Poem,* p. 18; *Battle of Bunker Hill,* Address Delivered at Charlestown, Massachusetts, on June 17, 1836, at the request of Young Men Without Distinction of Party, p. 67.

[58] *Europe, op. cit.,* p. 207.

Notes to chapter two

[1] Glyndon G. Van Deusen, "The Nationalism of Horace Greeley," *The American Historical Review*, vol. LV (1950), p. 445.

[2] *Port Folio*, August, 1816, vol. II, ser. 3, p. 188; *The North American Review*, July, 1820, vol. XI, p. 19; *Niles' Weekly Register*, November 11, 1815, pp. 173–177.

[3] See Chapter One, Note 31.

[4] Hervey Allen, *Israfel: The Life and Times of Edgar Allan Poe*, 2nd ed. (New York: Rinehart, 1949), p. 412; Letter of July 2, 1844, to James Russell Lowell, *The Letters of Edgar Allan Poe*, ed. by John Ward Ostrom (Cambridge: Harvard University Press, 1948), vol. I, p. 256.

[5] The tale was written in 1844. *The Works of Edgar Allan Poe*, 10 vols. (New York: Funk & Wagnalls, 1904), vol. V, p. 126. Poe expressed the same view of American democracy as a mobocracy and an "air-conditioned nightmare" in his fantasy "Mellonta Tanta," published in 1846.

[6] Baudelaire, *Oeuvres Complètes* (Paris: Le Nombre d'Or, 1955), vol. I, p. 605, and the critical remarks by Maurice Nadeau, *ibid.*, p. 447. Another great French poet, Stéphane Mallarmé, equally admired Poe. In March, 1866, working on his great poem "Hérodiade," Mallarmé wrote to his friend and fellow poet Henri Cazalis: "I am still going to need three or four winters to finish, but when it is all over, I will have what I always dreamt of: a poem worthy of Poe and just as good as his." Mallarmé, *Selected Prose Poems and Selected Letters*, tr. by Bradford Cook (Baltimore: Johns Hopkins Press, 1956), p. 88. See also Mallarmé's famous poem "The Tomb of Edgar Poe," in Edmund Wilson (ed.), *The Shock of Recognition* (New York: Farrar, Straus, and Cudahy, 1955), pp. 419 f.

[7] Hans Kohn, ed., *The Mind of Modern Russia* (New Brunswick: Rutgers University Press, 1955), pp. 34–56.

[8] In Webster's *American Magazine* (1788). See Kohn, *The Idea of Nationalism*, pp. 300 ff.—there also, pp. 294 ff., on the national poetry of Timothy Dwight, Barlow, and Freneau—and H. R. Warfel, *Noah Webster: Schoolmaster to America* (New York: Macmillan, 1936). On early literary nationalism, see Robert Whitney Bollwell, "Concerning the Study of Nationalism in American Literature," *American Literature*, vol. X (1939), pp. 405–416, and the two doctoral theses written under his direction at George Washington University: Charles William Cole, *The Beginnings of Literary Nationalism in America, 1775–1800* (1939), and James Harold Coberly, *The Growth of Nationalism in American Literature, 1800–1815* (1949), two careful dissertations assembling all the facts. See also Earl Bradsher, "The Rise of Nationalism in American Literature," *Studies for William Alexander Read* (Baton Rouge: Louisiana State University Press, 1940), pp. 269–287.

[9] John C. McCloskey, "The Campaign of Periodicals After the War of 1812

for a National American Literature," *PMLA*, vol. I (1935), p. 262, and Anne Louise Heene, *American Opinion on American Cultural Nationalism as Reflected in American Periodicals, 1790–1830*, Columbia University Master's Essay, 1944, pp. 15–23. On a later period, see John Stafford, *The Literary Criticism of Young America: A Study in the Relationship of Politics and Literature, 1837–1850* (Berkeley: University of California Press, 1952).

[10] "Professor Frisbie's Inaugural Address," *The North American Review*, vol. VI (January, 1818), pp. 224–241.

[11] "The Prospect Before Us," *Niles' Weekly Register*, vol. IX, p. 1 (Sept. 2, 1815). In a footnote on that page, Niles added: "I give it as a deliberate opinion, that the British character, as exhibited by the officers of the army and navy, is more barbarous and cruel than that of any other people." The same issue, Niles pointed out, was the first number "printed on beautiful new type of *American* manufacture. It is with pride we make the declaration that the printing business of the United States is completely independent of the Old World for its materials." In the same article Niles came out for preserving "our beloved country . . . as a *permanent* asylum for the oppressed of all nations."

[12] *Portico*, vol. I (April, 1816), p. 296; *Port Folio*, vol. II, ser. 3 (August, 1816), p. 203; *North American Review*, vol. I (May, 1815), pp. 61–91. Charles Jared Ingersoll (1782–1862) had published anonymously *Inchiquin, The Jesuit's Letters, during a late residence in the United States of America: being a fragment of his private correspondence accidentally discovered in Europe; containing a favorable review of the manners, literature, and state of society of the United States, and a refutation of many of the aspersions cast upon this country by former residents and tourists* (New York: J. Riley, 1810).

[13] *The Analectic Magazine*, vol. VI (September, 1815), p. 257.

[13a] See on David Ramsay (1744–1815), the biographical sketch, by R. C. Hayne in *The Analectic Magazine*, vol. VI (September, 1815), p. 217; Robert Walsh (1784–1859), *An Appeal from the Judgements of Great Britain Respecting the United States of America* (Philadelphia: Mitchell, Ames & White, 1819); George Palmer Putnam (1814–1872), *American Facts* (London: Wiley & Putnam, 1845); Samuel Griswold Goodrich, *Les États-Unis d'Amérique* (Paris: Guillaumin, 1852).

[14] Review of "Aperçu sur la situation politique des États-Unis d'Amérique, par le Général Turreau, ancien Ministre Plénipotentiaire de France aux États-Unis d'Amérique," *North American Review and Miscellaneous Journal*, vol. III (May, 1817), pp. 77 f. General Turreau advised the new nation to abandon its immigration policy and to turn extremely isolationist in that respect. The *North American Review* protested violently against this turning the United States into a second China. It regarded Turreau's proposal as a retrograde step opposed to the spirit of the United States and of the time.

[15] In his article, which was a review of Adam Seybert's *Statistical Annuals of the United States of America* (Philadelphia: 1818), Smith pointed out that so far even American industry and scholarship had produced nothing of importance. Almost half a century after its foundation, the nation still seemed dependent in everything on the mother country. "Finally, under which of the old tyrannical governments of Europe is every sixth man a slave, whom his fellow creatures may buy and sell and torture?" *Edinburgh Review*, vol. XXXIII (1820), pp. 69–80. See also Robert E. Spiller, "The Verdict of Sydney Smith," *American Literature*, vol. I (1929), pp. 3–13, and Henry T. Tuckerman's review

of *A Memoir of Rev. Sydney Smith,* by his daughter Lady Holland, in the *North American Review,* vol. LXXXII (1856), pp. 100–111.

[16] *Journals of Ralph Waldo Emerson,* ed. by Edward Waldo Emerson and Waldo Emerson Forbes (Boston: Houghton Mifflin, 1912), vol. VIII, p. 339.

[17] Oration delivered October 18, 1823, before the American Philosophical Society at the University in Philadelphia. *The Works of W. E. Channing,* 6 vols., 14th ed. (Boston: American Unitarian Association, 1855), vol. I, pp. 245, 248, 252, 261, 262.

[18] Edward Everett, *An Oration Pronounced at Cambridge for the Society of Phi Beta Kappa, August 26, 1824.* Published by request (Boston: Oliver Everett, 1824), pp. 24 f., 37, 49 f., 60.

[19] Cooper, *Notions of the Americans, Picked up by a Travelling Bachelor* (Philadelphia: Carey, Lee & Carey, 1828), vol. II, pp. 107 f., 29, 347. Robert E. Spiller, in his introduction to *James Fenimore Cooper,* American Writer Series (New York: American Book Company, 1936), p. xi, comments on Cooper's claim of American literature's defending or propagating a unified doctrine: "Even a cursory examination of American thought in the early years of national life reveals no such unity." Nevertheless it existed. The unifying force within all the diversity was a common heritage of English liberty and of Western eighteenth century enlightenment, which worked itself out in Anglo-America as nowhere else.

[20] *James Fenimore Cooper,* Spiller ed., *op. cit.,* pp. 27–32. *Home as Found, Sequel to Homeward Bound* (Leather-Stocking Edition, New York: Putnam, n.d.), pp. iv, v, 374, 375.

[21] *The Complete Works of Ralph Waldo Emerson,* Centenary Edition, 12 vols. (Boston: Houghton Mifflin, 1903), vol. VII, pp. 31 f. See on Emerson, John J. Chapman, *Emerson and Other Essays* (New York: Scribner, 1898).

[22] "The Young American," *The Complete Works of Ralph Waldo Emerson, op. cit.,* vol. I., pp. 388 f. Tocqueville, *Democracy in America,* vol. II, bk. IV, chap. VII. William James, *The Varieties of Religious Experience,* 35th printing (New York: Longmans, Green, 1925), pp. 368 f.

[23] Bliss Perry, "Emerson's Most Famous Speech," in *The Praise of Folly and Other Papers* (Boston: Houghton Mifflin, 1923), pp. 81–113.

[24] *Journals, op. cit.,* vol. X, p. 195. Benjamin T. Spencer, "A National Literature, 1837–1855," *American Literature,* vol. VIII, (1936), p. 130.

[25] *The Writings of Henry David Thoreau: Cape Cod and Miscellanies* (Boston: Houghton Mifflin, 1906), pp. 356, 361, 364. *The Complete Works of Ralph Waldo Emerson, op. cit.,* vol. V, pp. 286 f. See also Emerson's letter on this subject, p. 397, where he said that in comparison with the American idea which he unfolded before his English listeners, "they would think French Communism solid and practical."

[26] Alcott in *The Dial,* vol. I (1841), no. 3, p. 359. On Mazzini, see Hans Kohn, *Prophets and Peoples, op. cit.,* chap. 3. On James and Dewey, see Ralph Barton Perry, *Characteristically American* (New York: Knopf, 1949), pp. 46–50.

[27] *United States Magazine and Democratic Review,* vol. I, no. 1 (October–December, 1837), p. 14. See also vol. IX, no. 37, p. 24; vol. VIII, no. 35, 36, pp. 4–9 f.; and vol. XX, no. 105, pp. 267 ff.

[28] McGuffey's *New Fifth Eclectic Reader* (Cincinnati: Winthrop B. Smith, 1857), Lesson LXXVII, pp. 271 f.; McGuffey's *Newly Revised Eclectic Fourth Reader* (*ibid.,* 1853), pp. 313 f.; Richard D. Mosier, *Making the American*

Mind: Social and Moral Ideas in the McGuffey Readers (New York: King's Crown Press, 1947), pp. 41–55, 154. The McGuffey *Readers* sold seven million copies from 1836 to 1850, forty million copies from 1850 to 1870, and sixty million copies from 1870 to 1890. *Ibid.*, p. 168.

[29] Samuel Griswold Goodrich (1793–1860), *Lights and Shadows of American History* (Boston: Thompson, Brown & Co., 1844), pp. 10–20; Jesse Olney (1798–1872), *A History of the United States for the Use of Schools and Academies* (New Haven: Durrie & Peck, 1852), pp. v, vii. See also Bessie Louise Pierce, "The School and the Spirit of Nationalism," *The Annals of the Academy of Political and Social Science*, Philadelphia, September, 1944, pp. 117 ff., and her *Civic Attitudes in American School Textbooks* (Chicago: University of Chicago Press, 1930); Alfred Goldberg, "School Histories of the Middle Period," *Historiography and Urbanization: Essays in American History in Honor of W. Stull Holt*, ed. by Eric F. Goldman (Baltimore: Johns Hopkins Press, 1941), p. 185.

[30] *The North American Review*, vol. LVIII, no. 122 (January, 1844), pp. 3–39. Glyndon G. Van Deusen, "The Nationalism of Horace Greeley," *op. cit.*, pp. 437 f. See also the same author's *Horace Greeley: Nineteenth Century Crusader* (Philadelphia: University of Pennsylvania Press, 1953).

[31] "Hawthorne and His Mosses," in *The Portable Melville*, ed. by Jay Leyda (New York: Viking Press, 1952), pp. 409–414. But see also Melville's entry in his *Journal* at Oxford in 1857, *ibid.*, p. 574.

[32] The Prospectus to the *Stylus* was published in 1843. In two letters of 1846, Poe called the magazine, which never appeared, "the grand purpose of my life." *The Letters of E. A. Poe, op. cit.*, vol. II, pp. 330, 333. The review dealt with the poetry of John Gardiner Calkins Brainard (1796–1828) and appeared in *Graham's Lady's and Gentleman's Magazine*, vol. XX, no. 2 (Philadelphia, February, 1842), p. 119. Poe was its editor for one year, starting in 1841. He explained his resignation as due to his "disgust with the namby-pamby character of the magazine—contemptible pictures, fashion plates, music, and love tales." *The Letters of E. A. Poe, op. cit.*, vol. I, p. 197. He was succeeded as editor by Rufus Wilmot Griswold, who became Poe's literary executor and also his chief detractor. See also Perry Miller, *The Raven and the Whale: The War of Words and Wits in the Era of Poe and Melville* (New York: Harcourt, Brace, 1956).

[33] Review by Franklin Dexter (1793–1857) of a discourse, "Academies of Arts, delivered on May 3, 1827, in the Chapel of Columbia College, before the National Academy of Design on its First Anniversary," by Samuel F. B. Morse (*North American Review*, vol. XXVI, no. 58 [1828], pp. 211, 216). Samuel Finley Breese Morse (1791–1872) was first president of the National Academy of Design from 1826 to 1842; he became more famous as the inventor of the telegraph.

[34] Written in *The Christian Examiner and General Review*, XXXIII (Boston, 1843), pp. 25–33, by John Sullivan Dwight (1813–1893), who for a short time was pastor of the Unitarian Church in Northampton, Massachusetts, and later an important music critic and editor of *Dwight's Journal of Music: A Paper of Literature and Art*.

[35] In a review of "The Life and Letters of James Gates Percival" (1867), *The Writings of James Russell Lowell*, 10 vols. (Boston: Houghton Mifflin, 1894), vol. II, pp. 151 f.

[36] Harry Haydon Clark, "Lowell—Humanitarian, Nationalist, or Humanist?" *Studies in Philology*, vol. XXVII, no. 3 (July, 1930), pp. 411–441. *Longfel-*

low's Works, 11 vols. (Cambridge: Riverside Press, 1886), vol. II, pp. 336 f. Edward Wagenknecht, *Longfellow: A Full-Length Portrait* (New York: Longmans, Green, 1955), pp. 198 f.

[37] *The Writings of James Russell Lowell, op. cit.,* vol. III, pp. 64, 65, 62 f.

[38] *North American Review,* vol. LXXIX, (1849), no. 144, pp. 196–215.

[39] *Annual Report of the American Bible Society,* vol. I (1838), p. 13. See also William Canton, *The Story of the Bible Society* (New York: Dutton, 1904), and H. O. Dwight, *Centennial History of the American Bible Society* (New York: Macmillan, 1916). See also on the peace movement, Merle Curti, *The Learned Blacksmith: The Letters and Journals of Elihu Burritt* (New York: Wilson-Erickson, 1937), and *The American Peace Crusade* (Durham, N.C.: Duke University Press, 1929).

[40] Lenau (Nikolaus Niembsch von Strehlenau) (1802–1850), *Briefe an einen Freund,* ed. by Karl Mayer (Stuttgart: C. Mäcken, 1853), p. 102.

[41] Eduard Castle, *Der Grosse Unbekannte: Das Leben von Charles Sealsfield* (Wien: Manutiuspresse, 1952), p. 408. Ferdinand Kürnberger (1821–1879), *Der Amerikamüde: Amerikanisches Kulturbild* (Frankfurt am Main: Meidinger, 1855). The German interest in the United States was at its zenith in the middle of the nineteenth century. See *Atlantische Studien von Deutschen in Amerika,* 8 vols. (Göttingen: G. H. Wigand, 1853 ff.), and Hildegard Meyer, *Nord-Amerika im Urteil des deutschen Schrifttums bis zur Mitte des 19. Jahrhunderts* (Hamburg: De Gruyter, 1929).

[42] On Sealsfield, see Castle, *op. cit.,* pp. 585, 409, 546. Even Castle with his strong anti-American and antidemocratic bias cannot hide Sealsfield's continuous and deep attachment to the land of his adoption. Sealsfield was convinced that all great powers of his day were on the decline and that only the United States and Russia had a future. Julius Fröbel (1805–1895), *Aus Amerika, Erfahrungen, Reisen und Studien,* 2nd ed. (Leipzig: Dyk, *ca.* 1857), vol. I, pp. 31–41, 50 f., 58 f. See on Fröbel, Kohn, *Nationalism and Liberty: The Swiss Example, op. cit.,* pp. 91 f. William Barton Rogers (1804–1882) was then state geologist in Virginia and became in 1862 the first president of the Massachusetts Institute of Technology. Peter Force (1790–1868) published *American Archives,* covering in nine volumes the documents of 1774–1776. See also Chapter one, Note 47.

[43] On Thoreau, see above, Note 25. Carl Schurz, *Speeches, Correspondence, and Political Papers,* ed. by Frederick Bancroft, 6 vols. (New York: Putnam, 1913), vol. II, pp. 240 ff. On August 5, 1884, Schurz explained his shift from the Republican to the Democratic candidate because he regarded the nomination of James Gillespie Blaine as having "the inevitable effect of sinking the Government for generations to come, perhaps forever, into a depth of demoralization and corruption such as we have never dreamt of before." *Ibid.,* vol. IV, p. 225 f.

[44] *The Poetry and Prose of Walt Whitman,* The Inner Sanctum Edition, ed. by Louis Untermeyer (New York: Simon & Schuster, 1949), pp. 491, 505, 522, 507, 508, 509, 510, 549, 552, 557, 520 f. See also his poems "By Blue Ontario's Shore" (especially 5, 9, 10), "Thou Mother with Thy Equal Brood" (especially 3, 6), and "Song at Sunset," which repeat some of the statements of the prefaces as poetry. On Herder, see Kohn, *The Idea of Nationalism, op. cit.,* pp. 427–451; on Goethe, see Kohn, "The Eve of German Nationalism (1789–1812)," *Journal of the History of Ideas,* vol. XII, No. 2, (April, 1951), p. 256. Whitman was Herderian not only in his cultural folk nationalism but also in his eighteenth century humanitarianism.

[45] Hugh l'Anson Faussett, *Walt Whitman: Poet of Democracy* (New Haven: Yale University Press, 1942), p. 295. See also Henry Seidel Canby, *Walt Whitman, an American* (Boston: Houghton Mifflin, 1943), and Frederic Schyberg, *Walt Whitman*, tr. from the Danish (New York: Columbia University Press, 1951). On "Democratic Vistas," see *The Poetry and Prose of Walt Whitman, op. cit.*, pp. 806, 807, 813, 815, 852, 808, 809, 846.

[46] Marcus Lee Hansen, *The Immigrant in American History*, ed. by Arthur M. Schlesinger (Cambridge: Harvard University Press, 1940), pp. 147–149. See also Rowland T. Berthoff, *British Immigrants in Industrial America* (Cambridge: Harvard University Press, 1953).

[47] Edward Sculley Bradley, *George Henry Boker, Poet and Patriot* (Philadelphia: University of Pennsylvania Press, 1927), p. 316.

[48] Francis Parkman (1823–1893) in the *North American Review*, vol. LXXIV (1852), no. 154, pp. 147–161. But see on the other hand the more judicious review by Henry T. Tuckerman (1813–1871), *ibid.*, vol. LXXXII (1856), no. 171, pp. 319–348, one of the most thoughtful articles on the complex problem of American cultural nationalism.

[49] Donald Davidson, *The Attack on Leviathan: Regionalism and Nationalism in the United States* (Chapel Hill: University of North Carolina Press, 1938), p. 234.

[50] Hamlin Garland (1860–1940), *Crumbling Idols* (Chicago: Stone & Kimball, 1894), pp. 158–161, 189–192. It is worthwhile to note that this book was rejected by American editorial and critical opinion of the day and that Garland himself abandoned his radicalism later, though not his isolationist nativism.

[51] Randolph Bourne (1886–1918), *History of a Literary Radical, and Other Essays*, ed. by Van Wyck Brooks (New York: Huebsch, 1920), pp. 39–43. In his essay "Trans-national America," Bourne warned against "the tight and jealous nationalism of European pattern." The United States represented an international nationalism, "a cosmopolitan federation of national colonies, of foreign cultures, from which the sting of devastating competition has been removed," *ibid.*, p. 288. There is an element of truth in this statement which, however, is incompatible with nationalist pride or cultural chauvinism. See also about this period Richard Hofstadter, *The Age of Reform* (New York: Knopf, 1955).

[52] Howard Mumford Jones, *The Theory of American Literature* (Ithaca: Cornell University Press, 1948), pp. 79, 98, 115.

[53] On Tyler (1835–1900), "the first great historian of the national mind expressed in literature" (p. 175), see Howard Mumford Jones and Thomas E. Casady, *The Life of Moses Coit Tyler* (Ann Arbor: University of Michigan Press, 1933). Tyler's life was a typical example of the nineteenth century Anglo-American scholarly world.

[54] Edward A. Freeman, *Lectures to American Audiences* (Philadelphia: Porter & Coates, 1882), pp. 358, 360, 363. See also Chapter Four, notes 32–36.

[55] Louis B. Wright, *Culture on the Moving Frontier* (Bloomington: Indiana University Press, 1955), p. 223. "We have so long taken English literature for granted, like the air we breathe or the water we drink, that we forget that it has been one of the most enduring and ever present factors in determining the contents of our minds. Whatever we are racially or whatever may be our national origins, we have turned to English literature for our main intellectual sustenances." *Ibid.*, p. 200.

Notes to chapter three

[1] Frederick Jackson Turner, *The Significance of Sections in American History* (New York: Henry Holt, 1932), pp. 23, 37.

[2] Jonathan Elliott, ed., *The Debates in the Several State Conventions on the Adoption of the Federal Constitution as Recommended by the General Convention at Philadelphia in 1787*, 2nd ed. (Philadelphia: Lippincott, 1863), vol. III, p. 365.

[3] *Annals of Congress*, 12th Congress, vol. I (1811–12), p. 427. Plumer quoted in Charles R. Brown, *The Northern Confederacy According to the Plans of the Essex Junto 1796–1814* (Princeton, N.J.: Princeton University Press, 1918), p. 32.

[4] *Boston Gazette*, July 6, 1812. The *New England Palladium*, July 10, 1814, wrote of "the cruel and unnatural war, into which the folly and wickedness of our rulers, entangled in the wiles of Bonaparte, has plunged our ill-fated country." Francis Blake, *Oration Pronounced at Worcester, July 4, 1812* (Worcester, 1812), expressed a general pro-British feeling when he spoke of "an illiberal jealousy of England and an undue attachment to France" guiding the policy "of our rulers," pp. 7 f. David Osgood, *A Solemn Protest Against the Late Declaration of War* (Cambridge, 1812), p. 9, insisted that "those who run to arms without necessity are the scourges of the human race."

[5] Henry Cabot Lodge, *Life and Letters of George Cabot* (Boston: Little, Brown, 1877), p. 340. On the feeling in Massachusetts, see Alden Bradford, *History of Massachusetts* (Boston: publ. by author, 1829), vol. III, pp. 129 f. Theodore Roosevelt, *Gouverneur Morris* (Boston: Houghton Mifflin, 1888), p. 352.

[6] David Osgood, *op. cit.*, p. 10. See also William Plumer, *Address to the Clergy of New England* (Concord, N.H., 1814). Other clergymen like John H. Stevens, pastor in Stoneham, *The Duty of Union in a Just War* (Albany, 1814), p. 16, stressed the duty of unity and full support, and added the anti-British note, "against the common foe who has so long and wantonly oppressed us."

[7] In 1814 the British insisted as little as in 1783. In both peace treaties the Americans secured the desired prize, their unhampered imperial expansion westward. In both cases adroit American diplomacy and British willingness to yield won the peace for the United States. In 1783 the American diplomats won, "even at the risk of angering their French allies and saviours, after military conquest failed. Yet even their repudiation of the Franco-American treaty would not have brought this triumph but for the generosity of Lord Shelburne. 'The deed is done,' he wrote later, 'and a strong foundation laid for eternal amity between England and America.' The vision of an enemy minister and the willingness of American negotiators to place national interest above international ethics secured the trans-Appalachian wilderness for the new republic." Ray Allen Billington, *Westward Expansion, op. cit.*, p. 195.

242

NOTES TO CHAPTER THREE   243

[8] See John C. Carpenter, "The Star-Spangled Banner," *Century*, vol. 48, no. 3 (July, 1894), pp. 358–363, and Albert Mathews, "Uncle Sam," *Proceedings of the American Antiquarian Society*, Worcester, Mass., 1909, pp. 21–65.

[9] Henry Adams, *History of the United States* (New York: Scribner, 1891), vol. IX, p. 220.

[10] See Albert Bushnell Hart, *National Ideals Historically Traced, 1607–1907* (New York: Harper, 1907), p. 64.

[11] John Allen Krout and Dixon Ryan Fox, *The Completion of Independence, 1790–1830* (*A History of American Life*, vol. V) (New York: Macmillan, 1944), pp. 203 f.

[12] Letter to Matthew Lyon, May 7, 1816, in *The Writings of Albert Gallatin*, ed. by Henry Adams (Philadelphia: Lippincott, 1879).

[13] See George Dangerfield, *The Era of Good Feelings* (New York: Harcourt, Brace, 1951). On John Quincy Adams see Samuel Flagg Bemis, *John Quincy Adams and the Foundations of American Foreign Policy* (New York: Knopf, 1949).

[14] Even as late as 1929 Count Hermann Keyserling, in the period after World War I one of the most popular writers on national character, was convinced that "localism alone can produce, in the case of America, a thoroughly authentic type of man," that it alone can lead to an authentic American national culture. "America seems to be subdivided into large provinces of a comparatively unified character, provinces out of which there would undoubtedly have grown in earlier days and under different conditions separate cultures." Count Hermann Keyserling, "Genius Loci—The Civilization of These United States," *The Atlantic Monthly*, September, 1929, pp. 302–311.

[15] See Kohn, *Nationalism and Liberty, op. cit.*, pp. 67–74, 85–88, 96–98. See for the United States the very useful survey by David M. Potter and Thomas G. Manning, *Nationalism and Sectionalism in America, 1775–1877* (New York: Holt, 1949).

[16] Robert C. Binkley, *Realism and Nationalism, 1852–1871* (New York: Harper, 1935), p. xix.

[17] See Kohn, *Nationalism and Liberty, op. cit.*, pp. 99–113.

[18] See also William E. Rappard, "Pennsylvania and Switzerland, the American Origins of the Swiss Constitution," *Studies in Political Science and Sociology* (Philadelphia: University of Pennsylvania Press, 1941), pp. 49–123.

[19] *America in the Forties: The Letters of Ole Munch Raeder*, ed. by Gunnar J. Malmin (Minneapolis: University of Minnesota Press, 1929), pp. 207, 209.

[20] Not in Anglo-America but in Latin America, which lacked the English background, geographically and economically different sections developed into separate nations, in spite of the community of language, of religion, and of Spanish legal and governmental traditions.

[21] Alexis de Tocqueville, *Democracy in America, op. cit.*, vol. II, p. 457.

[22] *Writings*, ed. by H. A. Washington, 9 vols. (Washington: Taylor & Maury, 1853–54), vol. V, pp. 444 f.

[23] February 26, 1825, *Congressional Debates*, 18th Congress, 2nd Session, Washington, 1825, vol. I, pp. 689 ff.

[24] Glyndon G. Van Deusen, "The Nationalism of Horace Greeley," *The American Historical Review*, vol. LV (1950), pp. 432–456.

[25] Quoted in M. A. Fitzsimons, "Brownson's Search for the Kingdom of God: The Social Thought of an American Radical," *The Review of Politics*, vol. XVI (January, 1954), p. 33.

[26] *Writings*, ed. by Albert Ellery Bergh, 20 vols. (Washington, 1903), vol. XVI, p. 113.

[27] See Note 7.

[28] *Annals of Congress*, 11th Congress, 3rd Session, p. 525.

[29] James Z. Rabun in *The American Historical Review*, vol. LVIII, no. 2 (January, 1953), p. 291. See also Harold Schultz, *Nationalism and Sectionalism in South Carolina Politics, 1852–1860* (Durham: Duke University Press, 1950).

[30] *The Works of Rufus Choate*, 2 vols. (Boston: Little, Brown, 1862), vol. II, pp. 415–440. He noted in his speech two divisive factors, one imposed by the federal system, a dual loyalty to state and nation; the other the "terrible phenomenon" sectionalism "which brought into our vocabulary the hateful and illomened words North and South, Atlantic and Western." *Ibid.*, pp. 419, 422.

[31] Charles S. Sydnor, *The Development of Southern Sectionalism, 1819–1848* (*History of the South*, vol. V) (Baton Rouge: Louisiana State University Press, 1948), p. 132.

[32] *The American Democrat* (New York: Knopf, 1931), pp. 165–170. See also Alexander Hill Everett's warning: "And reason good, for it is one thing to love liberty and another to love slaughter, desolation and universal uproar, which would be the consequence of a simultaneous and general emancipation of the blacks." *America, or a General Survey of the Political Situation of the Several Powers of the Western Continent* (London: John Murray, 1828), p. 182.

[33] Quoted by Franklin D. Scott in *The Swedish Pioneer: A Historical Quarterly*, vol. III, no. 1 (Winter, 1952), pp. 2 f.

[34] In the Alabama Convention G. T. Yelverton, who considered slavery as a social, moral, and political blessing, demanded open recognition of the institution in these terms: "This question of Slavery is the rock upon which the Old Government split: it is the cause of secession. Let us leave it no longer doubtful nor in a condition to bring our New Government into new troubles." In its declaration of the causes of secession, the Texas Convention attacked the Northern section for proclaiming the equality of all men regardless of race or color: "We hold as undeniable truths that the governments of the various States, and of the Confederacy itself, were established exclusively by the white race, for themselves and their posterity; that the African race had no agency in their establishment; that they were rightfully held and regarded as an inferior and dependent race, and in that condition only could their existence in this country be rendered beneficial or tolerable." Quoted in Jesse T. Carpenter, *The South as a Conscious Minority 1789–1861* (New York: New York University Press, 1930), p. 246.

[35] Samuel Phillips Day, quoted in Rollin G. Osterweis, *Romanticism and Nationalism in the Old South* (New Haven: Yale University Press, 1949), p. 148.

[36] "Gideon's Water Lappers. A sermon preached in Christ Church, Savannah, on Friday the 8th day of April, 1864, the day set apart by the congress of the Confederate States, as a day of humiliation, fasting and prayer," quoted in E. Merton Coulter, *The Confederate States of America, 1861–1865* (Baton Rouge: Louisiana State University Press, 1950), p. 13. The defense of slavery by the clergy, referring to the Bible and to Greek antiquity, was widespread. In 1850

the Reverend Iverson L. Brooks published in South Carolina "A Defense of the South Against the Reproaches and Encroachments of the North: In which slavery is shown to be an institution of God intended to form the base of the best social state and the only safeguard to the permanence of a republican government." See Charles S. Sydnor, *op. cit.*, p. 338.

[37] J. T. Carpenter, *op. cit.*, pp. 171, 187 f.

[38] *Ibid.*, p. 200.

[39] William Anderson Scott, *Hope of Republics; or the Elements of Permanence in Modern Civilization.* A discourse delivered by the Reverend W. A. Scott, D.D., on Thanksgiving Day, December 21, 1848, in the Presbyterian Church, in Lafayette Square, New Orleans (New York: J. M. Sherwood, 1849), p. 20. Reprinted in Robert Gibbes Barnwell, ed., *The New Orleans Book* (New Orleans, 1851) ["... Extracts from the journals, the pulpit, the bench, and the bar of New Orleans" (p. ix)], p. 52A.

[40] See the two unsuccessful expeditions to "liberate" Cuba in 1850 and 1851 by Narciso Lopez, a Venezuelan adventurer supported by southern expansionists in Mississippi. Samuel Flagg Bemis, *A Diplomatic History of the United States* (New York: Holt, 1942), pp. 314–317. See also about Pierre Soulé of New Orleans in Osterweis, *op. cit.*, pp. 177–181. On the South's inclination to violence, which combined traditions of the American frontier and Old World chivalry, see John Hope Franklin, *The Militant South, 1800–1861* (Cambridge: Harvard University Press, 1956).

[41] See Edward Channing, *A History of the United States*, 6 vols. (New York: Macmillan, 1905–1925), vol. VI, pp. 1, 6–12, 82–84.

[42] J. T. Carpenter, *op. cit.*, pp. 179 ff.

[43] See Margaret L. Coit, *John C. Calhoun: American Portrait* (Boston: Houghton Mifflin, 1950); Charles M. Wiltse, *John C. Calhoun, Nationalist, 1782–1828* (Indianapolis: Bobbs-Merrill, 1944), and *John C. Calhoun, Nullifier, 1829–1839* (Bobbs-Merrill, 1949); Peter F. Drucker, "A Key to American Politics: Calhoun's Pluralism," *The Review of Politics*, October, 1948, pp. 412–426.

[44] Philip May Hamer, *The Secession Movement in South Carolina, 1847–1852* (Allentown, Pa.: H. R. Haas, 1918), pp. 22 f.

[45] Calhoun, *Works, Disquisition, etc.* (Columbia, S.C.: publ. under direction of South Carolina General Assembly, 1851), vol. I, p. 382.

[46] Osterweis, *op. cit.*, pp. 140 f.

[47] Kohn, *Nationalism and Liberty, op. cit.*, p. 100.

[48] See Avery O. Craven, *The Growth of Southern Nationalism, 1848–1861* (*A History of the South*, VI) (Baton Rouge: Louisiana State University Press, 1953), pp. 351 f., 371.

[49] Laura A. White, "Charles Sumner and the Crisis of 1860–61," in Avery Craven (ed.), *Essays in Honor of William E. Dodd* (Chicago: University of Chicago Press, 1935), p. 156.

[50] *Poetical Works* (Boston: Houghton Mifflin, 1891), vol. IV, pp. 88 f.

[51] *Poems of Henry Timrod* (Boston: Houghton Mifflin, 1899), p. 150. This edition by the Timrod Memorial Association of his native city and state (Charleston, South Carolina) called him in the introduction "the Southern poet. ... his song is the voice of the Southland. ... his voice was also the voice of Carolina, and through her of the South, in all the rich glad life poured out

in patriotic pride into that fatal struggle, in all the valor and endurance of that dark conflict, in all the gloom of its disaster, and in all the sacred tenderness that clings about its memories. He was the poet of the Lost Cause, the finest interpreter of the feelings and traditions of the splendid heroism of a brave people" (pp. vii, viii). The name of Timrod's grandfather, a prominent citizen of Charleston of German origin, was first on the roll of German Fusiliers of Charleston, volunteers formed in 1775 immediately on hearing of Lexington.

[52] See Frank L. Owsley, *State Rights in the Confederacy* (Chicago: University of Chicago Press, 1925).

[53] Clement Eaton, *A History of the Southern Confederacy* (New York: Macmillan, 1954). See also Kenneth M. Stampp, "The Historian and Southern Negro Slavery," *American Historical Review*, vol. LVII (April, 1952), pp. 613–624; Thomas J. Pressly, *Americans Interpret Their Civil War* (Princeton, N.J.: Princeton University Press, 1954), and on Lincoln, David Donald, *Lincoln Reconsidered: Essays on the Civil War Era* (New York: Knopf, 1956).

[54] Glyndon G. Van Deusen, "The Nationalism of Horace Greeley," *The American Historical Review*, vol. LV (1950), pp. 432–456; D. M. Potter, "Horace Greeley and Peaceable Secession," *Journal of Southern History*, vol. VII (May, 1941), pp. 145–59.

[55] John Bascom, *Growth of Nationality in the United States* (New York: G. P. Putnam's Sons, 1899), pp. 92 f.

[56] It appeared first in *The Atlantic Monthly* for December, 1863, pp. 665–679; a separate edition was published in Boston by Ticknor & Fields in 1865.

[57] J. R. Lowell, *My Study Windows* (Boston: James R. Osgood, 1871), p. 150.

[58] *Ibid.*, p. 151.

[59] O. W. Holmes, *Oration Delivered Before the City Authorities, Boston, July 4, 1863* (Philadelphia: printed for gratuitous distribution, 1863), pp. 24–26.

[60] *My Study Windows, op. cit.*, pp. 75 f. Lowell continued: "I know one person who is singular enough to think Cambridge the very best spot on the habitable globe. 'Doubtless God could have made a better, but doubtless he never did.'" Lowell meant Cambridge, Massachusetts.

[61] Rollo Ogden, *The Life and Letters of Edwin Godkin*, 2 vols. (New York: Macmillan, 1907), vol. I, pp. 209–219. Godkin emigrated from northern Ireland at the age of twenty-five. American ideas had been "the intellectual food of my youth." *Ibid.*, vol. II, p. 219. He founded *The Nation* in 1865 and opposed in its columns the annexation of Canada.

[62] Elisha Mulford (1833–1885), *The Nation: The Foundation of Civil Order and Political Life in the United States* (New York: Hurd & Houghton, 1870), pp. 108, 324, 340, 358, 362. Mulford quoted with approval (p. 162) from Rothe's *Theologische Ethik*: "The Army must not only be national, but be the nation; the nation insofar as it is capable of bearing arms, in its totality, must form the army."

[63] *The Works of Charles Sumner*, 15 vols. (Boston: Lee & Shepard, 1877), vol. XII, pp. 192, 247 f. The address was delivered before the New York Young Men's Republican Union at Cooper Institute, November 19, 1867. In his discussion Sumner contrasted the loose bonds of noncentralized states with the strength of centralized nations. He offered Germany as an "instructive example," and added, "God grant that the day may soon dawn when all Germany shall

be one!" (p. 204). The day came soon, under Bismarck, and later to a higher degree under Hitler. Sumner might have been astonished if somebody had pointed out that this unified and strong Germany would become disastrous to European peace, to human liberty, and ultimately to the Germans themselves, to their moral standing and their creative genius. In all these respects a case could be made in favor of the loose German Confederation as it existed before Bismarck destroyed it.

[64] Speech, "The New Nationalism," Osawatomie, Kansas, August 31, 1910, *The Works of Theodore Roosevelt*, 20 vols. (New York: Scribner, 1925), vol. XVII, pp. 19 f. Roosevelt went on to demand of the judiciary that it should be interested primarily in human welfare rather than in property. See also Chapter Two, Note 50.

[65] It is a minor point, but not without some pertinence, that the project of a national university, which George Washington had proposed and which among others John Wesley Hoyt (1831–1912), governor of Wyoming Territory and later first president of Wyoming State University, propagated from 1870 on, was as little realized as renaming the Library of Congress the National Library. A national gallery in Washington was only established in 1941 and then entirely thanks to the initiative of a private art collector.

[66] See C. Vann Woodward, *The Strange Career of Jim Crow* (New York: Oxford University Press, 1955).

[67] Russell Warren Howe, "A Talk with William Faulkner," *The Reporter*, March 22, 1956, p. 19. See also Ernest Sondeen, "William Faulkner: His Legend and His Fable," *Review of Politics*, XVIII (January, 1956), pp. 47–68, and Malcolm Cowley, "William Faulkner's Legend of the South," *The Sewanee Review*, LIII (Summer, 1945), pp. 343–361. See on the mood of the South today, Edmund Wilson on James Branch Cabell, a Virginia writer, in *The New Yorker*, April 21, 1956, pp. 129–156, and Robert Penn Warren, *Segregation: The Inner Conflict in the South* (New York: Random House, 1956).

Notes to chapter four

[1] W. T. Stead, *The Americanization of the World* (New York and London: Horace Markley, 1902), p. 148. See also Carl Wittke, *We Who Built America: The Saga of the Immigrant* (New York: Prentice-Hall, 1939).

[2] Quoted in Max Savelle, *Seeds of Liberty: The Genesis of the American Mind* (New York: Knopf, 1948), pp. 567 f.

[3] Letter to George Flower, *The Writings of Thomas Jefferson*, ed. by Albert Ellery Bergh (Washington, D.C.: Auspices of the Thomas Jefferson Memorial Association of the United States, 1903), vol. XV, pp. 139–142. For the point of view of his young years, see in his "Notes on Virginia," *ibid.*, vol. II, pp. 120 f.

[4] Letter to George Flower, September 12, 1817, in Jefferson, *Writings,* ed. by H. A. Washington, 9 vols. (Washington: Taylor & Maury, 1853–54), vol. VII, p. 84. Marcus Lee Hansen, *The Immigrant in American History*, ed. by Arthur M. Schlesinger (Cambridge: Harvard University Press, 1940), pp. 131 f.

[5] James Elliot Cabot, *A Memoir of Ralph Waldo Emerson* (Boston: Houghton Mifflin, 1888), vol. II, p. 789.

[6] Newton Dillaway, *Prophet of America: Emerson and the Problems of Today* (Boston: Little, Brown, 1936), p. 122.

[7] Anon., *Reise von Hamburg nach Philadelphia* (Hanover: Ritschersche Buchhandlung, 1800), p. 143.

[8] *Frontier Parsonage: The Letters of Olaus Fredrik Duus, Norwegian Pastor in Wisconsin, 1855–1858* (Northfield, Minn.: Norwegian-American Historical Association, 1947), p. 32.

[9] Einar Haugen in *Norwegian-American Studies and Records*, ed. by Dr. Theodore Christian Blegen for the Norwegian-American Historical Association, Northfield, Minn., vol. X (1938), p. 2. See also Franklin D. Scott, "Controlled Scholarship and Productive Nationalism," *Nor.-Amer. S. and R.*, vol. XVII (1952), pp. 130–148.

[10] *Nor.-Amer. S. and R.*, vol. I (1926), p. 121.

[11] Reiersen settled in Texas; Storseth settled in the state of Washington. See *Nor.-Amer. S. and R.*, vol. VIII, p. 52, and vol. XIII, p. 158.

[12] Lieber, *Civil Liberty and Self-Government,* 3rd ed., ed. by T. D. Woolsey (Philadelphia, 1874), p. 295. "British institutions and policies appeared to Lieber the zenith of human attainment, vindicated both by reason and by success." C. B. Robsen, "Francis Lieber's Nationalism," *The Journal of Politics*, February, 1946, pp. 57–73.

[13] See Merle Curti, "Francis Lieber and Nationalism" in his *Probing Our Past, op. cit.*, pp. 119–151, especially pp. 127, 137, 139; Frank Freidel, *Francis Lieber, Nineteenth-Century Liberal* (Baton Rouge: Louisiana State University Press, 1948), and B. E. Brown, *American Conservatives: The Political Thought*

of Francis Lieber and John W. Burgess (New York: Columbia University Press, 1951).

[14] *A Compilation of the Messages and Papers of the Presidents, 1789–1902*, ed. James D. Richardson (Bureau of National Literature and Art, 1907), vol. VII, p. 167.

[15] See Gaillard Hunt, *Life in America One Hundred Years Ago* (New York: Harper, 1914), pp. 114 f.

[16] See Ray Allen Billington, *The Protestant Crusade: 1800–1860: A Study of the Origins of American Nativism* (New York: Rinehart, 1952), p. 291. It was feared that the Mississippi Valley "and eventually the entire United States would be won to Catholicism and immeasurably increase the strength of the Papal church and at the same time the despots of the Old World would be relieved from the constant threat of revolutions inspired by the example of freedom and liberty" offered by America. If the Catholics gained control of the Middle West, "supremacy on the American continent and perhaps in the world would be the fruit of victory" (p. 119). The *Home Missionary* wrote in August, 1839: "The cause is the cause of the West—for there the great battle is to be fought between truth and error, between law and anarchy—between Christianity, with her Sabbaths, her ministry and her schools, on the one hand, and the combined forces of Infidelity and Popery on the other."

[17] Oscar Handlin, *Boston's Immigrants, 1790–1865: A Study in Acculturation* (Cambridge: Harvard University Press, 1941), pp. 208 ff. See also on the Irish immigrants, their Irish nationalism and their American acculturation Carl Wittke, *The Irish in America* (Baton Rouge: Louisiana State University Press, 1956).

[18] Billington, *op. cit.*, p. 417. Similar ineffectual nativist movements arose after the Civil War. Their history is told by John Higham, *Strangers in the Land: Patterns of American Nativism, 1860–1925* (New Brunswick: Rutgers University Press, 1955).

[19] Carl Schurz, *Speeches, Correspondence, and Political Papers*, ed. by F. Bancroft (New York: G. P. Putnam's Sons, 1913), vol. I, pp. 58–72.

[20] See Oscar Handlin, *The Uprooted: The Epic Story of the Great Migrations That Made the American People* (Boston: Little, Brown, 1951), and *Adventure in Freedom: Three Hundred Years of Jewish Life in America* (New York: McGraw-Hill, 1954).

[21] Philip Schaff, *America: A Sketch of the Political, Social, and Religious Character of the United States of North America*, tr. from the German (New York: Scribner, 1855), pp. xi, xviii.

[22] *The Works of Herman Melville*, Standard Edition (London: Constable, 1922), vol. V, pp. 216 f. Melville predicted that "the language of Britain" will become through the United States the universal language and "the curse of Babel will be revoked."

[23] André Siegfried, *America in This Century* (New York: Harcourt, Brace, 1956). Better recent studies by Europeans are Guido Piovene, *De America* (Milan: Garzanti, 1953), and by another Italian, long resident in the States, Massimo Salvadori, *Capitalismo democratico: Considerazioni sull'economia Americana* (Rome: Opere Nuove, 1956). German racialists overstressed the danger of racial conflict in the United States and underestimated the cohesive power of the liberal American idea. For that reason they erred about the fighting potentialities of the United States in the two world wars.

[24] Émile Boutmy, *Éléments d'une Psychologie Politique du Peuple Américain* (Paris: Armand Colin, 1902), pp. 95 f. Boutmy stressed (on pp. 97 ff.) the great influence which public opinion, not as in France of a social or intellectual elite, but of the average man, exercises over the individual. But this is balanced by the feeling of the individual in the United States of being, to a large extent, the master of his destiny, less impeded by social barriers than in Europe. "Chacun a le moyen de se faire ce qu'il vaut être, et vaut par ce qu'il s'est fait. Il y a là une forme de félicité ignorée de nos sociétés encombrées, où la difficulté de sortir du rang et le désir de s'en faire tirer conseillent des compromis et des bassesses qui depriment la personne humaine; cette félicité procède d'une exaltation de la personnalité après les victoires faciles que l'homme a remportées par ses seules forces. Il en jouit avec une ivresse orgueilleuse; il en sait gré à la patrie dont l'immensité géographique, les richesses naturelles, les institutions ont ensemble conspiré à étendre et niveler le champ pour un combat dont il a l'honneur et le butin" (p. 102).

[25] Jefferson, *Writings*, ed. by H. A. Washington, vol. VII, p. 27; vol. IV, p. 318. Abraham Lincoln is reported to have told Herndon, "I do not care who my grandfather was, but I care who my grandchildren will be." And George Bancroft was convinced that "the inference that there is progress in human affairs is . . . warranted. . . . The trust of our race has ever been in the coming of better times."

[26] "America, thou art more fortunate than our old continent. Thou hast no ruined castles, no venerable stones. No useless memories, no vain feuds harry thee in thy soul when thou wishest to live in the present. Make something happy out of today! And when thy children start to write, may a kind Providence preserve them from tales of chivalrous knights, robber barons, and ghosts."

[27] Tocqueville, *Democracy in America*, vol. II, bk. I, chap. 17.

[28] Letter to Theodore Petrasch of October 3, 1863, *Intimate Letters of Carl Schurz, 1841–1869*, tr. by Joseph Schafner (Madison: State Historical Society of Wisconsin, Collections), vol. XXX (1928), p. 288.

[29] *Intimate Letters of Carl Schurz, 1841–1869*, op. cit., pp. 382 f. *The Poetical Works of J. R. Lowell*, 4 vols. (Boston: Houghton Mifflin, n.d.), vol. IV, p. 30.

[30] Carl Schurz, *Speeches, Correspondence and Political Papers*, ed. by Frederic Bancroft, 6 vols. (New York: Putnam, 1913), vol. V, p. 182; vol. VI, pp. 43 f. In a letter to Gottfried Kinkel from Philadelphia April 12, 1853, Schurz warned against the schemes of German émigrés to work in America for their homeland. It contradicts "the practical American understanding which little by little becomes operative in the German [immigrant]." Like most first-generation immigrants Schurz felt both the elation and the difficulties of this status. As he wrote, before his immigration, from London on April 19, 1852, to Adolf Meyer, he did not expect to become rich in America but to find there a broader and more fertile field for vigorous uninterrupted activity. On September 24, 1863, he wrote to Theodore Petrasch: "America is the country for striving talent, and the foreigner who studies conditions here fundamentally and knows how to appreciate them can open for himself an even greater career than the native-born. My success surprised even me. I saw my boldest expectations exceeded." When the dream of his youth, German unification, was on the way to its full realization, on February 24, 1868, he wrote to Gottfried Kinkel that

he was too deeply rooted in America to return to Germany, where with his present views and his manner of working he would no longer feel at home. But in a letter to E. L. Godkin on November 23, 1872, he mentioned that at the Republican Convention he declined to make the nominating speech because he was foreign born and did not wish a candidate to appear as his nominee.

[31] Cooper, *The American Democrat* (New York: Knopf, 1931), p. 135.

[32] Edward N. Saveth, "Race and Nationalism in American Historiography: The Late Nineteenth Century," *Political Science Quarterly*, LIV (1939), pp. 421 ff. and his *American Historians and European Immigrants, 1875–1925* (New York: Columbia University Press, 1948). See also Oscar Falnes, "New England Interest in Scandinavian Culture and the Norsemen," *New England Quarterly*, June, 1937; Herbert Baxter Adams, *The Study of History in American Colleges and Universities* (Washington: Government Printing Office, 1887); John Fiske, *American Political Ideas Viewed from the Standpoint of Universal History* (New York: Harper, 1885); John Randolph Dos Passos, *The Anglo-Saxon Century and the Unification of the English-Speaking People* (New York: Putnam, 1903); John William Burgess, *Reminiscences of an American Scholar* (New York: Columbia University Press, 1934).

[33] Howard Mumford Jones, *Ideas in America* (Cambridge: Harvard University Press, 1944), pp. 228 f.

[34] The leading German nationalist historian Heinrich von Treitschke called Carlyle "our loyal friend who recognized lovingly the nobility of our national soul." Treitschke, who was violently anti-English, deeply admired Carlyle. See Kohn, *Prophets and Peoples: Studies in Nineteenth Century Nationalism* (New York: Macmillan, 1946), pp. 125, 196. See also Theodor Deimel, *Carlyle und der Nationalsozialismus, eine Würdigung des englischen Denkers im Lichte der deutschen Gegenwart* (Würzburg: K. Triltsch, 1936), and Wilhelm Vollrath, *Th. Carlyle und H. St. Chamberlain, zwei Freunde Deutschlands* (München: J. F. Lehmann, 1935).

[35] *The Life and Works of Charles Kingsley*, 19 vols. (New York: Macmillan, 1901–03), vol. III, p. 209. See especially Kingsley's lectures, *The Roman and the Teuton*, which he delivered in Cambridge as professor of history.

[36] Edward Augustus Freeman, *The Chief Periods of European History* (London: Macmillan, 1886), p. 64. On Arminius see Kohn, *The Idea of Nationalism, op. cit.*, pp. 144 f., 340, 341, 346.

[37] Frederic E. Faverty, *Matthew Arnold, The Ethnologist* (Evanston: Northwestern University Press, 1951), pp. 22 f.

[38] *Papers Relating to the Foreign Relations of the United States*, transmitted to Congress with the Annual Message of the President, December 4, 1871 (Washington: Government Printing Office, 1871). In the last volume of his *History of the United States* (Boston: Little, Brown, 1874), vol. X, p. 86, Bancroft saw England, the Prussia of Frederick II, and the embryonic United States—Pitt, Frederick, and Washington—working together in the Seven Years' War for human freedom, because British victory over the French gave Frederick "a share in the extension of the Germanic race in the other hemisphere."

[39] Josiah Strong (1847–1916) was born in Illinois, became pastor of the Congregational church in Cheyenne, Wyoming. His book *Our Country: Its Possible Future and Its Present Crisis*, appeared in 1885 and went through many editions and translations. It was published for the American Home Mis-

sionary Society by Baker & Taylor in New York. The above quotation is from pp. 44 f. Strong regarded the Anglo-Saxon race as the representative of two great ideas closely related, civil liberty and spiritual Christianity. "Evidently, it is chiefly to the English and American peoples that we must look for the evangelization of the world" (pp. 159 f.).

[40] *Ibid.,* p. 171. "Then this race of unequaled energy, with all the majesty of numbers and the might of wealth behind it—the representative, let us hope, of the largest liberty, the purest Christianity, the highest civilization—having developed peculiarly aggressive traits calculated to impress its institutions upon mankind, will spread itself over the earth. If I read not amiss, this powerful wave will move down upon Mexico, down upon Central and South America, out upon the islands of the sea, over upon Africa and beyond. . . . Is it manifest that the Anglo-Saxon holds in his hands the destinies of mankind for ages to come? Is it evident that the United States is to be the home of this race, the principal seat of his power, the great center of his influence? Is it true . . . that the great West is to dominate the nation's future? Has it been shown . . . that this generation is to determine the character, and hence the destiny, of the West? Then may God open the eyes of this generation! . . . We of this generation and nation occupy the Gibraltar of the ages which commands the world's future" (pp. 174 f., 179 f.).

[41] Wilson, *History of the American People,* 5 vols. (New York: Harper, 1902), vol. V, pp. 212 f., and F. J. Turner, *The Significance of Sections, op. cit.,* p. 42.

[42] Sir Alfred E. Zimmern, *Nationality and Government, with Other War-Time Essays* (London: Chatto & Windus, 1918), p. 122.

[43] *The Works of Theodore Roosevelt,* 20 vols. (New York: Scribner, 1926), vol. XIX, pp. 301–306.

[44] Bourne, *History of a Literary Radical, and Other Essays,* ed. by Van Wyck Brooks (New York: Huebsch, 1920), p. 266.

[45] *Ibid.* pp. 270 f. Bourne underestimated both the social innovations of the Anglo-Americans and the all-important fact that later immigrants came to be assimilated in the Anglo-American melting pot, and to become imbued with the Anglo-American idea and cultural tradition. It became theirs as fully as it was that of the descendants of the early Anglo-Americans. If the national idea of the United States could fulfill its task of assimilating the influx of immigrants, then they all, settlers of many generations and more recent newcomers, equally "belonged," and shared in this feeling of common "belonging."

[46] *The Works of Theodore Roosevelt, op. cit.,* vol. XIX, pp. 30–47.

[47] E. A. Ross, *The Old World in the New: The Significance of Past and Present Immigration to the American People* (New York: Century, 1914).

[48] Henry Pratt Fairchild, *The Melting-Pot Mistake* (Boston: Little, Brown, 1926), pp. 56, 246, 260.

[49] Horace M. Kallen, *Culture and Democracy in the United States* (New York: Boni & Liveright, 1924), pp. 123 ff. See also John Dewey, "Nationalizing Education," *Addresses and Proceedings of the National Education Association,* vol. LIV (New York, 1916), and Julius Drachsler, *Democracy and Assimilation* (New York: Macmillan, 1920).

[50] See Morton Grodzins, *Americans Betrayed: Politics and the Japanese Evacuation* (Chicago: University of Chicago Press, 1949).

[51] See Kohn, *The Idea of Nationalism, op. cit.,* pp. 304 f.

[52] See Henry S. Commager, "The Problem Isn't Bricks—It's Brains," *The New York Times Magazine,* January 29, 1956.

[53] In *The New York Times Book Review* on February 6, 1956, on p. 19, the Irish-American author Edwin O'Connor, who had written a novel about an Irish-American politician, said in an interview: "As I got into the story [*The Last Hurrah*], I decided I'd better take a trip to Ireland, to see whether they had the same type of politician. . . . The main thing that happened there was I ran into another misconception of Irish-Americans. In Londonderry I wound up in the home of some I.R.A. people. 'What would you do,' they asked, 'if things came to a conflict? If we fought England, what would you in America do?' I had to tell them that all my life I had been associated with Irish Catholics and hadn't heard it mentioned. I had to tell them we wouldn't do anything." In 1857 Julius Fröbel protested the "repatriation" of Negro slaves. "Very many Negroes who were born in the United States and who regard this country as their fatherland, would not leave it voluntarily even for the sake of liberty." *Aus Amerika, op. cit.,* p. 180.

Notes to chapter five

[1] *The Speeches of the Rt. Hon. George Canning*, with a memoir of his life, by R. Therry, 6 vols. (London: James Ridgeway, 1828), vol. VI, pp. 109–111.

[2] Theodore Poesche and Charles Goepp, *The New Rome; or the United States of the World* (New York: Putnam, 1853), pp. 16, 59, 62, 87 f., 99 f., 177. The book was dedicated to Franklin Pierce, President of the United States, "being a guess at the spirit in which he was elected." It hoped that President Pierce would ratify the treaty with King Kamehameha III, bequeathing Hawaii to the American people, "as old Attalus made the Roman people heirs of his kingdom of Pergamus. Is there not something Roman in the walk of this Republic? . . . The annexation of these islands, forming, as they do, an important shipping station between America and Asia, is particularly interesting as marking the extension of America beyond the continent. A people cannot forego its mission, and the mission of the American people is not bounded by oceans" (pp. 20 f.).

[3] See Hans Kohn, *Pan-Slavism: Its History and Ideology* (Notre Dame, Ind.: University of Notre Dame Press, 1953), pp. 84–99.

[4] *The Works of Heinrich Heine*, tr. by Charles Godfrey Leland (London: Heinemann, 1893), vol. VIII, pp. 96 f. The association of American civilization with boredom was not so rare among Western European intellectuals then, and may be found even today. "They have begotten," Carlyle wrote of the Americans in his Latter-Day Pamphlets in 1850, "with a rapidity beyond recorded example, Eighteen Millions of the greatest *bores* ever seen in the world before." *Collected Works of Carlyle*, Library Edition (London: Chapman & Hall, 1870), vol. XIX, p. 26. In 1956 a French intellectual could write even more strongly, "Les quelques ressemblances qui subsistent avec notre vieux monde augmentent les difficultés de porter un jugement—pour tout (!) Européen, forcément défavorable (!)—sur un pays qui paraît avoir survécu à je ne sais quel déluge universel . . . là bas, nous sommes aussi loin de notre monde d'enracinés que de celui des pharaons . . . le grand ennui Americain." Guy Dumux, "L'Été Américain," *Les Lettres Nouvelles*, vol. IV, no. 36 (March, 1956), p. 371.

[5] Field-Marshal-Lieutenant Franz Freiherr von Kuhn (1817–1896) was Austrian minister of war from 1868 to 1874. His conversation with the emperor took place on July 20, 1870. Egon Caesar Conte Corti, *Mensch und Herrscher: Wege und Schicksale Kaiser Franz Josephs I zwischen Thronbesteigung und Berliner Kongress* (Graz: Styria, 1952), pp. 436 f.

[6] Jules Michelet, *Légendes Démocratiques du Nord: La France devant l'Europe* (Paris: Calman Lévy, 1899), p. 480. See also Kohn, *Prophets and Peoples, op. cit.*, chap. 2.

[7] On the little-noticed fierce diplomatic conflicts in the Far East before World War I, see Edward Henry Zabriskie, *American-Russian Rivalry in the*

Far East: A Study in Diplomacy and Power Politics, 1895–1914 (Philadelphia: University of Pennsylvania Press, 1946).

[8] Little will be said here about the nineteenth century because the subject has been treated exhaustively by A. K. Weinberg, *Manifest Destiny* (Baltimore: Johns Hopkins Press, 1935), and by Julius W. Pratt, "The Ideology of American Expansion," *Essays in Honor of William E. Dodd*, ed. by Avery Craven (Chicago: University of Chicago Press, 1935). See also by Pratt, *Expansionists of 1812* (New York: P. Smith, 1949), and *Expansions of 1898: The Acquisition of Hawaii and the Spanish Islands* (Baltimore: Johns Hopkins Press, 1936) and the study by Joseph E. Wisan, *The Cuban Crisis as Reflected in the New York Press* (New York: Columbia University Press, 1934).

[9] See Chapter Three, Note 3.

[10] William Cobbett, *Letters on the Late War Between the United States and Great Britain* (New York: J. Belden & Co., 1815), pp. 85 f.

[11] Albert Bushnell Hart, *National Ideals Historically Traced, 1607–1907* (*The American Nation: A History*, vol. XXVI) (New York: Harper, 1907), pp. 336 ff.

[12] Ray A. Billington, *Westward Expansion, op. cit.*, p. 572.

[13] *Annals of Congress, 12th Congress*, vol. I, 1811–12, p. 376. Porter served in the War of 1812 and received a gold medal for gallantry. He was Secretary of War under John Quincy Adams in 1828. *Life and Speeches of Henry Clay*, 2 vols. (Philadelphia: Leary, Getz & Co., 1860), vol. I, pp. 18 f. During Clay's lifetime, G. Vandenhoff published some of his speeches under the title *The Clay Code, or Textbook of Eloquence* (New York: Shepard, 1844). In his preface he spoke of the one element that "most strongly recommends his oratory to the hearts of his countrymen, his pure, thorough, NATIONALITY. His spirit breathes in every page, pervades every sentence, glows in every line, . . . He is, indeed, heart and hand, might and main, body and soul, American. He loves, he ADORES the land of his birth. . . . Most of all we are struck with his Nationality—his AMERICANISM." See also D. G. Van Deusen, *The Life of Henry Clay* (Boston: Little Brown, 1937).

[14] See Chapter Two, Note 27.

[15] *The United States Magazine and Democratic Review*, vol. XVII, no. 85 (July–August, 1845); vol. XX (February, 1847), p. 100, and vol. XXI (October, 1847), p. 291. About the influence of the *Review* abroad, see the letter of George Sumner to G. W. Greene of November, 1842, quoted in Arthur M. Schlesinger, Jr., *The Age of Jackson* (Boston: Little Brown, 1946), pp. 372 f.

[16] Editorial in the *New York Morning News* of December 27, 1845, which O'Sullivan published together with Samuel J. Tilden. A. K. Weinberg, *op. cit.*, devoted a chapter to this article. See also J. W. Pratt, "John L. O'Sullivan and Manifest Destiny," *New York History*, vol. XIV, no. 3 (July, 1933).

[17] See Lord Acton's "Nationality" (July, 1862) in his *History of Freedom and Other Essays* (London: Macmillan, 1907), pp. 270–300, and the little-known arguments of the French philosopher Charles Renouvier in his *Science de la Morale* (1869) quoted in Kohn, *Prophets and Peoples, op. cit.*, p. 167.

[18] Letter from Vienna on Feb. 5, 1868, in William Roscoe Thayer, *The Life and Letters of John Hay*, 2 vols. (New York: Houghton Mifflin, 1915), vol. I, p. 304. Letter from Paris on May 8, 1898, *ibid.*, vol. II, p. 167.

[19] Letter of Theodore Roosevelt to Henry Cabot Lodge on Dec. 27, 1895, in

Henry Cabot Lodge, *Selections from the Correspondence of Theodore Roosevelt and Henry Cabot Lodge, 1884–1918* (New York: Scribner, 1925), vol. I, pp. 204 f. See also Henry F. Pringle, *Theodore Roosevelt, a Biography* (New York: Harcourt, Brace, 1931), pp. 166 ff. Letter to Charles Milnes Gaskell of June 20, 1895, in *Letters of Henry Adams, 1892–1918*, ed. by Worthington Chauncey Ford (Boston: Houghton Mifflin, 1938), p. 72.

[20] Hugh l'Anson Faussett, *Walt Whitman, Poet of Democracy* (New Haven: Yale University Press, 1942), pp. 47 ff.

[21] Merle Curti, *Probing Our Past* (New York: Harper, 1955), p. 224.

[22] See Hans Kohn, "Some Reflections on Colonialism," *The Review of Politics*, vol. XVIII, no. 3 (July, 1956), pp. 259–268.

[23] Emile Montégut, "Les États-Unis en 1852," *Revue des Deux Mondes*, vol. XV (July 15, 1852), pp. 323, 354. Montégut opposed England and the United States which sacrificed everything to individual liberty to continental Europe with its entirely different traditions, *ibid.*, pp. 325 f.

[24] "Chronique de la Quinzaine," by Charles de Mazade, *Le Revue des Deux Mondes*, vol. XVI (Oct. 15, 1852), p. 407 (Nov. 15, 1852), pp. 792 f.

[25] Laura Bornholdt, *Baltimore and Early Pan-Americanism: A Study in the Background of the Monroe Doctrine* (Northampton, Mass.: Smith College Studies in History, 1949), vol. XXXIV, pp. 128 f.

[26] Dexter Perkins, *The Monroe Doctrine, 1823–1826* (Cambridge: Harvard University Press, 1932), p. 222, and his *The Monroe Doctrine, 1826–1867* (Baltimore: Johns Hopkins Press, 1933), p. 59.

[27] *The Works of W. E. Channing* (Boston: American Unitarian Association, 1849), vol. II, p. 214.

[28] A. Weinberg, *Manifest Destiny, op. cit.*, p. 416.

[29] *A Compilation of the Messages and Papers of the Presidents, 1789–1897*, ed. by James D. Richardson, 10 vols. (Washington: Government Printing Office, 1896–1899), vol. VI, p. 689; vol. VII, p. 221.

[30] See the article on J. G. Blaine (1830–1893) by Carl Russell Fish in *Dictionary of American Biography*, vol. II, and Alice Felt Tyler, *The Foreign Policy of James G. Blaine* (Minneapolis: University of Minnesota Press, 1927).

[31] Published in *Forum*, March, 1895, quoted by Julius Pratt in *New York History*, vol. XIV, no. 3 (July, 1933), pp. 213, 231, 234. See also Chapter Three, Note 63.

[32] Henry Pringle, *op. cit.*, pp. 279 f.

[33] Address at the Minnesota State Fair on September 2, 1901. *The Works of Theodore Roosevelt*, National Edition, 20 vols. (New York: Scribner, 1926), vol. XIII, pp. 474 f.

[34] Pringle, *op. cit.*, p. 379. "When, in the fall of 1906, the yellow peril appeared over the horizon of the Far East, the president made energetic efforts to conciliate Japan. His wrath toward American and Japanese jingoes in the last three years of his administration was as bitter as that of Charles W. Eliot and Carl Schurz in 1898 toward the advocates of war with Spain." *Ibid.*, p. 398.

[35] *The Works of T. H. Roosevelt, op. cit.*, vol. XVI, p. 309.

[36] See Chapter Two, Note 50. Roosevelt's robust nationalism can be found throughout his speeches: see *The Works, op. cit.*, vol. XIX, pp. 321, 372. It was compatible with a lot of "sound" philistinism. Roosevelt declared that the

man who loves other countries as much as his own is as worthless a creature as a man who loves other women as much as his wife.

[37] Mark Sullivan, *Our Times,* 6 vols. (New York: Scribner, 1926–1935), vol. I, p. 50.

[38] Claude G. Bowers, *Beveridge and the Progressive Era* (Boston: Houghton Mifflin, 1932), pp. 69 f., 74 f., 134. Beveridge, who grew up as the son of a poor farmer in Illinois and who entered the U.S. Senate as Senator from Indiana in 1899, fought for equal opportunities, prevention of trust abuses, and conservation of national resources. He was a lifelong passionate defender of labor and of the poor classes and an enemy of corporations and great wealth. See *ibid.,* pp. 387, 394 f., and *passim.*

[39] In 1855 John L. O'Sullivan, the father of manifest destiny, wished to see the British control all of India and the United States the whole Western Hemisphere. In 1906 Elihu Root, as Secretary of State in Roosevelt's second administration, tried to bring about a better relationship with Latin America. In 1912 he was awarded the Nobel Peace Prize.

[40] In his autobiography, Roosevelt advocated future independence for the Philippines. He referred to Cuba with self-congratulatory aplomb and with some historical exaggeration: "When the promise [of Cuban independence] was made, I doubt if there was a single ruler or diplomat in Europe who believed that it would be kept. . . . I know of no action by any other government in relation to a weaker power which shows such disinterested efficiency in rendering service as was true in connection with our intervention in Cuba." *The Works, op. cit.,* pp. 492–494.

[41] Letters to John Hay from Paris, December 4, 1900; to Worthington Chauncey Ford from Washington, February 2, 1899; to Elizabeth Cameron from St. Petersburg, September 1, 1901. *Letters of Henry Adams, op. cit.,* pp. 303, 213, 347. John Hay himself wrote as Secretary of State on Sept. 24, 1899, to Henry White: "As long as I stay here, no action shall be taken contrary to my conviction that the one indispensable factor of our foreign policy should be a friendly understanding with England."

[42] Captain A. T. Mahan, U.S.N., *The Interests of America in Sea Power, Present and Future* (Boston: Little, Brown, 1906), pp. 112 f.

[43] One hundred years before, Jefferson's attitude to this problem was complex and changing. "We see with great concern," he wrote to Sir John Sinclair on June 30, 1803, "the position in which Great Britain is placed, and should be sincerely inflicted were any disaster to deprive mankind of the benefit of such a bulwark against the torrent which has for some time been bearing down all before it." Twenty years later, on October 24, 1823, Jefferson urged President Monroe to "most sedulously cherish a cordial friendship" with Britain because the two together "need not fear the whole world," and because an association with Britain would protect America against any threat from continental Europe. Monroe rejected Jefferson's advice and followed the nationalism of John Quincy Adams, who insisted on going it alone. See also Kohn, *The Idea of Nationalism, op. cit.,* pp. 317–319.

[44] In an article "Democracy and Efficiency," *The Atlantic Monthly,* March, 1901. Woodrow Wilson, *The Public Papers,* 2 vols. (New York: Harper, 1925), vol. I, pp. 403–413.

[45] "The Ideas of America," an address delivered in December, 1901, and printed in *The Atlantic Monthly,* December, 1902. *The Papers, op. cit.,* pp.

441 f. See also Harley Notter, *The Origins of the Foreign Policy of Woodrow Wilson* (Baltimore: Johns Hopkins Press, 1937); Arthur Link, *Wilson: The Road to the White House* (Princeton: Princeton University Press, 1947) and *Woodrow Wilson and the Progressive Era, 1910–1917* (New York: Harper, 1954); Edward H. Buehrig, *Woodrow Wilson and the Balance of Power* (Bloomington: University of Indiana Press, 1955).

[46] William Thomas Stead (1849–1912) was editor of the *Pall Mall Gazette* and later of the *Review of Reviews*. His book, *The Americanization of the World,* was published by the *Review of Reviews*, London, 1902, and by Horace Markley, New York, 1902. See there pp. 346, 396, 2, 161, 179, 180, 181, 182.

[47] *The Intimate Papers of Colonel House: Arranged as a Narrative by Charles Seymour* (Boston: Houghton Mifflin, 1926), p. 249.

[48] Sir Eyre Crowe was Senior Clerk in the British Foreign Office from 1906 to 1912, Assistant Under-Secretary of State from 1912 to 1920, Permanent Under-Secretary from 1920 to 1925. See the memorandum in G. P. Gooch and Harold Temperley, eds., *British Documents on the Origins of the War, 1898–1914*, vol. III, *The Testing of the Entente, 1904–1906* (London: H.M. Stationery Office, 1928), pp. 397–418.

[49] See Ludwig Dehio, *Deutschland und die Weltpolitik im 20. Jahrhundert* (Munich: R. Oldenbourg, 1955), the best interpretative essay on recent German and world history.

[50] An American historian arrived at similar conclusions regarding German policy even under Bismarck. "Contempt for British statesmen he [Bismarck] did feel intensely. For ten years he played on their convictions and aversions, their ignorance and their false assumptions, with uniform success. Each time his trickery became obvious, he relied on English military weakness to prevent hostile action, and on the gullibility of the London government for the possibility of renewed deception; each time England acted as he had foretold. He did not even attempt to hide his contempt. . . . By exposing the weakness of liberal England, he was making more difficult the revival of German liberalism." Raymond James Sontag, *Germany and England, Background of Conflict, 1848–1898* (New York: Appleton-Century, 1938), pp. 233 f., 313–341, 45–90. Later on, Hitler played a similar game with Stanley Baldwin and Neville Chamberlain. See also E. Malcolm Carroll, *Germany and the Great Powers, 1866–1914* (New York: Prentice-Hall, 1938), pp. 337–341.

[51] "One of the most constant traditions of British diplomacy is that an alliance loses its validity as soon as common victory has been achieved." Harold Nicholson, *Curzon: The Last Phase 1919–1925* (London: Constable, 1934), p. 192.

[52] *The New Republic*, vol. X, no. 120 (Feb. 17, 1917), pp. 59–61, editorial, "The Defense of the Atlantic World." There is another important passage in the editorial: "The real danger to a decent peace has always been that the western nations would become so dependent on Russia and Japan that they must pay any price for their loyalty." The profound web of interest on the two shores of the Atlantic was foreseen by the Russian liberal Alexander Herzen in 1858 when the first transatlantic cable connected England and North America: "What can a country which feels the beat of an uninterrupted pulse with America not do, for the ocean will become an internal system! In truth, there are not two states but two different shores, belonging to the Anglo-Saxons."

[53] H. C. F. Bell, *Woodrow Wilson and the People* (New York: Doubleday, 1945).

[54] See Chapter Two, Note 44.

[55] David Lloyd George, *Memoirs of the Peace Conference* (New Haven: Yale University Press, 1939), vol. I, pp. 21 f.

[56] Allan Nevins, *Henry White: Thirty Years of American Diplomacy* (New York: Harper, 1930), pp. 353–355. Henry White (1850–1927) was the only Republican member of Wilson's peace delegation to Paris. He became a fervent adherent of the League idea. See also Ruhl Jacob Bartlett, *The League to Enforce Peace* (Chapel Hill: University of North Carolina Press, 1945); *Enforced Peace,* Proceedings of the 1st annual national assemblage of the League to Enforce Peace, Washington, May 26–27, 1916 (New York: League to Enforce Peace, 1916). A previous conference was held at Independence Hall, Philadelphia, on Bunker Hill Day (June 17), 1915. See also Charles Robert Ashbee, *The American League to Enforce Peace: An English Interpretation,* introduction by G. Lowes Dickinson (London: Allen & Unwin, 1917).

[57] Daniel J. Boorstin, "American Nationalism and the Image of Europe, 1914–1945," paper read before the Mississippi Valley Historical Association on April 22, 1954.

[58] William MacDonald, "Madness at Versailles," *The Nation,* vol. 108 (March 17, 1919), pp. 778–780.

[59] See about Keynes' book, Etienne Mantoux, *The Carthaginian Peace; or, the Economic Consequences of Mr. Keynes* (New York: Scribner's, 1952). See also Paul Birdsall, *Versailles Twenty Years After* (New York: Reynal & Hitchcock, 1941), and T. E. Jessup, *The Treaty of Versailles: Was It Just?* (London: Thomas Nelson, 1942). About the theories advanced by American historians and political scientists on American participation in World War I, see Richard W. Leopold, "The Problem of American Intervention, 1917: An Historical Retrospect," *World Politics,* vol. II (April, 1950), pp. 405–425; and Selig Adler, "The War-Guilt Question and American Disillusionment, 1918–1928," *Journal of Modern History,* vol. XXIII (1951), pp. 1–28; and about similar theories in England, R. B. McCallum, *Public Opinion and the Last Peace* (New York: Oxford University Press, 1944).

[60] In addition to Wilson's address at Columbus, Ohio, see his addresses delivered at Coeur d'Alene, Idaho, September 12, 1919, and at St. Louis, Mo., September 5, 1919. Keynes also foresaw Germany's expansion eastward, but he welcomed it as a reassurance for the West. "That [France] has anything to fear from Germany in the future which we can foresee, except what she may herself provoke, is a delusion," he wrote in his *A Revision of the Treaty* in 1922. "When Germany has recovered her strength and pride, as in due time she will, many years must pass before she again casts her eyes westward. Germany's future now lies to the East, and in that direction her hopes and ambitions, when they revive, will certainly turn" (p. 186).

[61] Lloyd George, *Memoirs of the Peace Conference, op. cit.,* vol. II, p. 545.

[62] See the quotations in Kohn, *The Twentieth Century: A Mid-Way Account of the Western World* (New York: Macmillan, 1949), pp. 201–204.

[63] Robert Lansing, *The Peace Negotiations: A Personal Narrative* (Boston: Houghton Mifflin, 1921), pp. 97 f. See also Kohn, "A New Look at Nationalism," *The Virginia Quarterly Review,* vol. XXXII (Summer, 1956), pp. 321–332,

and his "Some Reflections on Colonialism," *The Review of Politics,* vol. XVIII (July, 1956), pp. 259–268. In his article "On the National Pride of the Great Russians," Lenin emphasized: "We are not in any way champions of small nations; we are unconditionally, other things being equal, for centralization and against the Philistine ideal of federative relations," in F. C. Barghoorn, *Soviet Russian Nationalism* (New York: Oxford University Press, 1956), p. 86.

[64] As an example of isolationist arguments, see Jerome Frank, *Save America First* (New York: Harper, 1938). The history of the America First Committee was written by Wayne S. Cole, *America First: The Battle Against Intervention, 1940–1941* (Madison: University of Wisconsin Press, 1953). On Anglo-American relations in that period (as well as for the whole of American history), see H. C. Allen, *Great Britain and the United States* (London: Macmillan, 1955).

[65] After 1945 other Americans repeated the same argument: they pointed to the Greek "monarcho-fascists," to Syngman Rhee and Chiang Kai-shek as non-democrats who should therefore not be protected against totalitarian aggression. Yet the British rightly came to the help of semi-fascist Poland when it was invaded by Germany in 1939 and of fascist Greece at the time of the Italian-German aggression in 1940–41. Nor did Churchill hesitate in June, 1941, to proclaim his full-hearted support of totalitarian Russia when she was invaded by Germany.

[66] Kohn, *The Twentieth Century, op. cit.,* p. 205.

[67] *Dictionary of American History* (New York: Scribner, 1940), vol. V, p. 487.

[68] See Victor Raúl Haya de La Torre, *Treinta años de aprismo* (Mexico: Fondo de Cultura Económica, 1956). APRA regarded itself as a direct descendant of the two most successful movements in twentieth century Latin America, the University Reform Movement, "que en esencia fue el primer grito de emancipación de nuestro coloniaje mental, heraldo de una nueva conciencia de Indoamérica," and the Mexican revolution, the first popular anti-imperialist movement of the century.

[69] See Elliot Roosevelt, *As He Saw It* (New York: Duell, Sloane & Pierce, 1945), and Robert B. Looper, "Roosevelt and the British Empire," *Occidente,* vol. XII (Milan and Oxford, 1956), nos. 4 and 5.

[70] Walter Lippmann, "The Generation That Was Duped," *New York Herald Tribune,* June 16, 1940. Other American voices of that time demanding America's active participation in the war were the editorial "An End of Neutrality," *New York Herald Tribune,* June 4, 1940; Walter Millis, "A Statement of Conviction," *ibid.,* June 18, 1940; "It Is Time to Stop Wishing," and "Must Great Britain Carry on Alone?", editorials in the *Courier Journal,* Louisville, Ky., June 16 and June 19, 1940. See also, for American university circles, the discussion in the *Daily Maroon* (University of Chicago) of April 8, 1941, between Chancellor Robert M. Hutchins and some of the most distinguished members of his faculty; the article "We Have Waited Long Enough," by Charles G. Bolte, *The Dartmouth,* April 23, 1941; and the editorial in *The Williams Record* of April 26, 1941. See also Walter Johnson, *The Battle Against Isolation* (Chicago: University of Chicago Press, 1944), and Robert E. Osgood, *Ideals and Self-Interest in America's Foreign Relations* (Chicago: University of Chicago Press, 1953).

[71] See Oscar Handlin, "So the Voters Want Moderation? The Politics of Evasion," *Commentary,* vol. XXII (September, 1956), pp. 197–198. On previous periods see James Morton Smith, *Freedom's Fetters: The Alien and*

Sedition Laws and American Civil Liberties (Ithaca: Cornell University Press, 1956).

[72] Eric F. Goldman, *The Crucial Decade: America 1945–1955* (New York: Knopf, 1956). "The generation that began to read American history during the 1930's has since had to unlearn a good deal," Richard Hofstadter in *Commentary,* vol. XXII (September, 1956), p. 273.

[73] Robert Strausz-Hupé and Stefan T. Possony, *International Relations in the Age of the Conflict Between Democracy and Dictatorship,* 2nd. ed. (New York: McGraw-Hill, 1954), pp. 785 f. See also Strausz-Hupé, *The Zone of Indifference* (New York: Putnam, 1952). Already during the war Professor Ross Hoffman wrote: "The Western community . . . is an impressive historic, economic and political reality. . . . By the beginning of the nineteenth century, the Atlantic had been transformed into the Mediterranean of Western civilization. The spread of British, French, and American ideas of liberty and constitutional government has made the region of this vast inland sea the citadel of what today is rather loosely called Democracy." *Thought,* a quarterly published by Fordham University, vol. XX, no. 76, p. 25.

[74] See D. W. Brogan, "The Post-Imperial Age," *The New Republic,* December 17, 1956, and Woodrow Wyatt, "This British Vigour," *The New York Times Magazine,* December 16, 1956.

[75] Henry Steele Commager, *The American Mind: An Interpretation of American Thought and Character Since the 1880's* (New Haven: Yale University Press, 1950), pp. 409 ff., 441 ff.

[76] Amy Lowell, *Tendencies in Modern American Poetry* (Boston: Houghton Mifflin, 1917), p. v. She called Whittier, Bryant, Emerson, Longfellow, and Holmes "English provincial poets, in the sense that America was still a literary province of the Mother Country," p. 15. "The outstanding spiritual phenomenon of the times [1920–1928] was the remarkable intensification of nationalism," Preston William Slosson, *The Great Crusade and After, 1914–1928* (New York: Macmillan, 1930), p. 287.

[77] The same process happened at the same time in Switzerland. The Swiss spoke of the intellectual defense of their country, "geistige Landesverteidigung"; see Kohn, *Nationalism and Liberty: The Swiss Example, op. cit.,* p. 128. On the similar process in the United States, see Ralph Henry Gabriel, *The Course of American Democratic Thought,* 2nd ed. (New York: Ronald Press, 1956), pp. 450 ff.

[78] Ralph Henry Gabriel, *op. cit.,* p. 452.

[79] See Chapter Two, Notes 21–25, and on the reception of Mill's essay in England, J. C. Rees, *Mill and His Early Critics* (Leicester: University College, 1956).

[80] Adlai E. Stevenson, quoted by James Reston, *The New York Times,* September 17, 1956.

Index

265